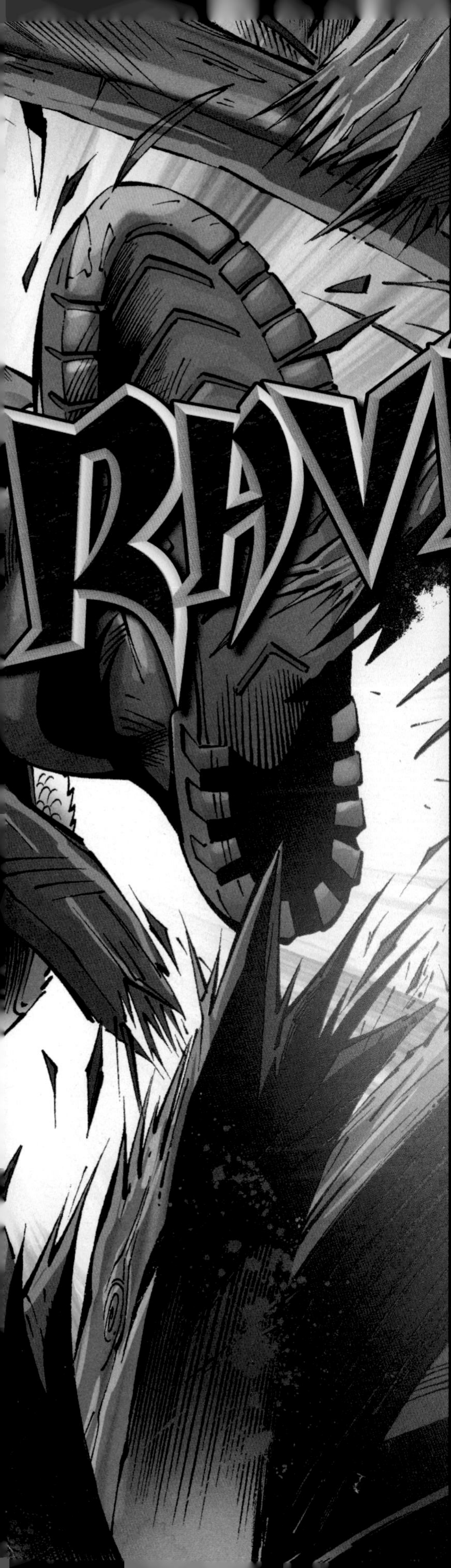

Teen Titans

RAVAGER
FRESH HELL

Sean McKeever
David Hine
Writers

Yildiray Cinar
Georges Jeanty
Pencillers

Julio Ferreira
Mark McKenna
Inkers

JD Smith
Rod Reis
Colorists

Sal Cipriano
Pat Brosseau
Letterers

Yildiray Cinar
Collection cover

Deathstroke & Ravager created by
Marv Wolfman & George Pérez

Michael Marts
Brian Cunningham
Rachel Gluckstern Editors-Original Series
Janelle Siegel
Rex Ogle Assistant Editors-Original Series
Bob Harras Group Editor-Collected Editions
Bob Joy Editor
Robbin Brosterman Design Director-Books
Curtis King Jr. Senior Art Director

DC COMICS
Diane Nelson President
Dan DiDio and **Jim Lee** Co-Publishers
Geoff Johns Chief Creative Officer
Patrick Caldon EVP-Finance & Administration
John Rood EVP-Sales, Marketing & Business Development
Amy Genkins SVP-Business & Legal Affairs
Steve Rotterdam SVP-Sales & Marketing
John Cunningham VP-Marketing
Terri Cunningham VP-Managing Editor
Alison Gill VP-Manufacturing
David Hyde VP-Publicity
Sue Pohja VP-Book Trade Sales
Alyssa Soll VP-Advertising and Custom Publishing
Bob Wayne VP-Sales
Mark Chiarello Art Director

TEEN TITANS: RAVAGER - FRESH HELL
Published by DC Comics. Cover, text and compilation Copyright © 2010 DC Comics.
All Rights Reserved.

Originally published in single magazine form in FACES OF EVIL: DEATHSTROKE 1,
TEEN TITANS 71-76, 79-82. Copyright © 2009, 2010 DC Comics. All Rights Reserved.
All characters, their distinctive likenesses and related elements featured in this publication
are trademarks of DC Comics. The stories, characters and incidents featured in this
publication are entirely fictional. DC Comics does not read or accept unsolicited submissions
of ideas, stories or artwork.

DC Comics, 1700 Broadway, New York, NY 10019
A Warner Bros. Entertainment Company
Printed by Quad/Graphics,
Dubuque, IA, USA. 11/24/10. First Printing.
ISBN: 978-1-4012-2919-1

SUSTAINABLE Certified Chain of Custody
FORESTRY Promoting Sustainable
INITIATIVE Forest Management
www.sfiprogram.org
Fiber used in this product line meets the sourcing requirements
of the SFI program. www.sfiprogram.org PWC-SFICOC-260

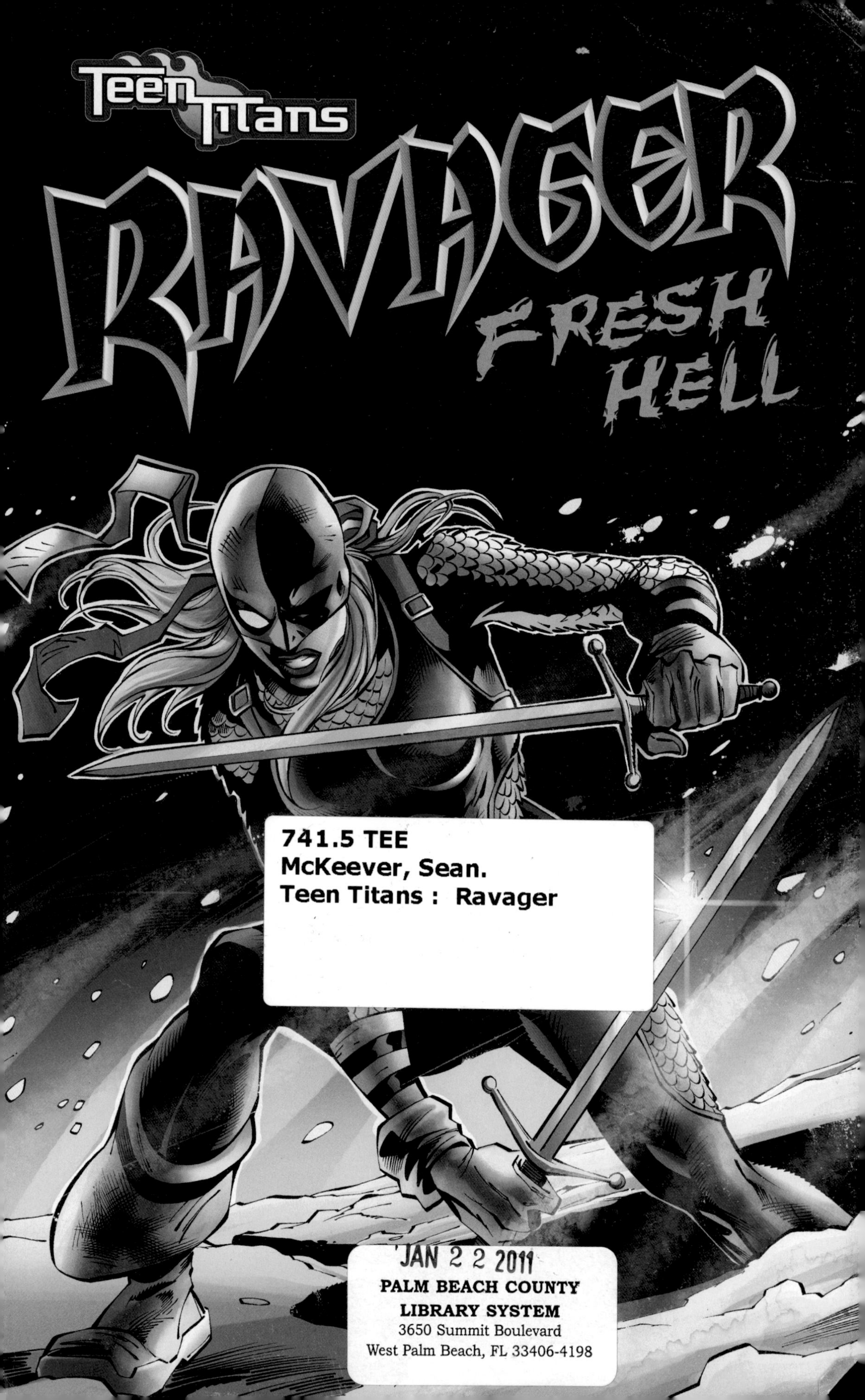
Teen Titans
RAVAGER
FRESH HELL

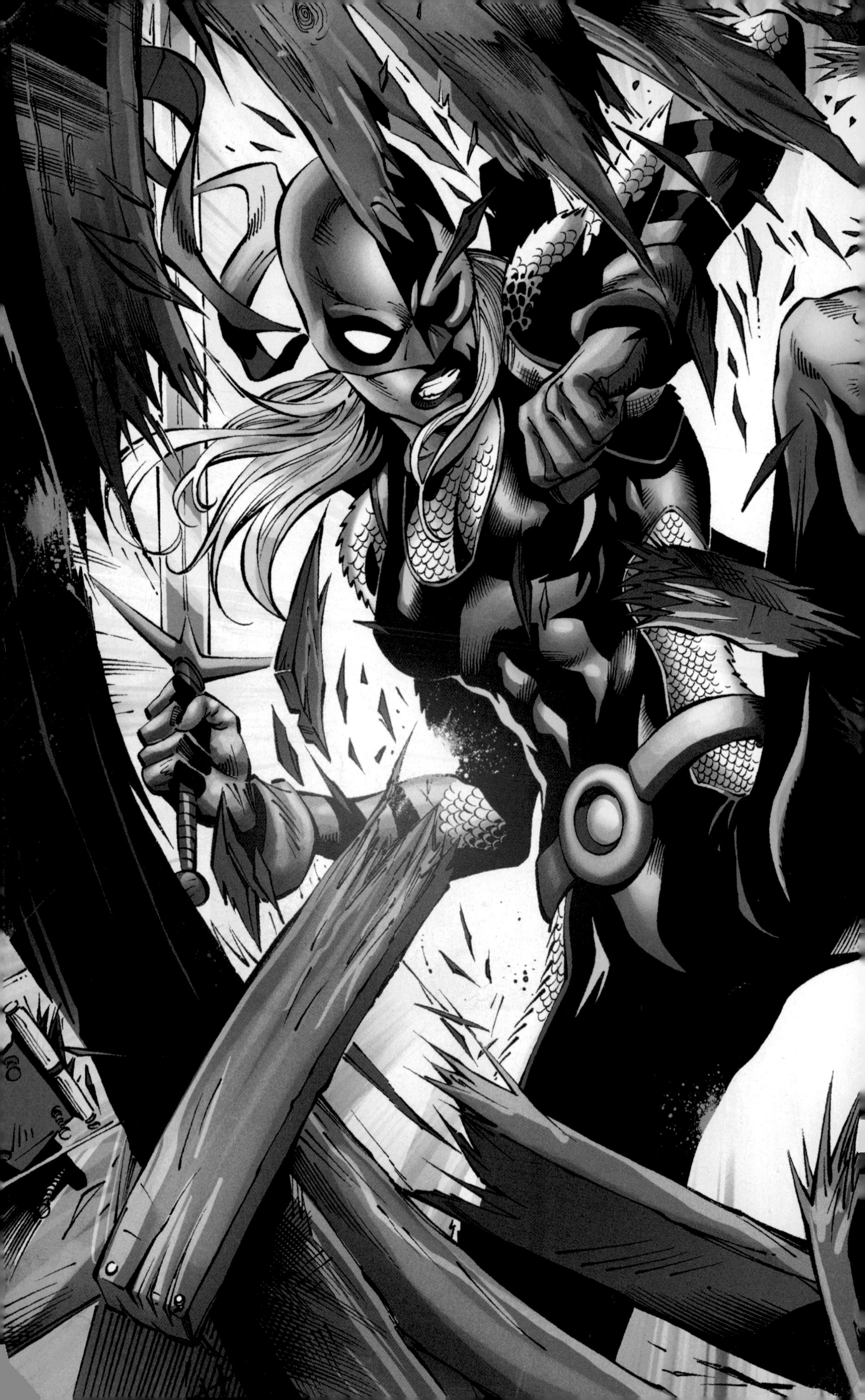

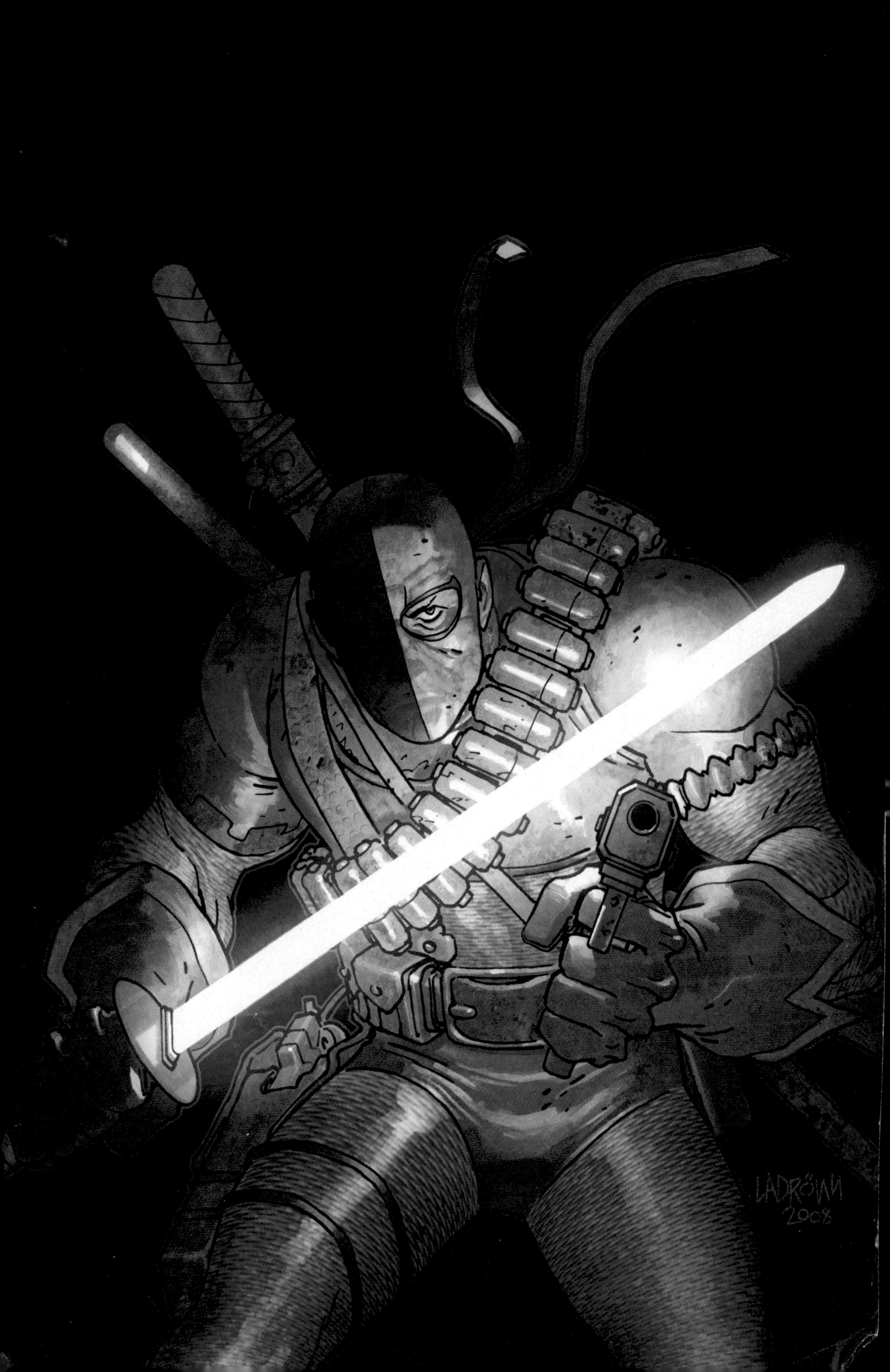
LADRÖNN
2008
Cover by Ladronn

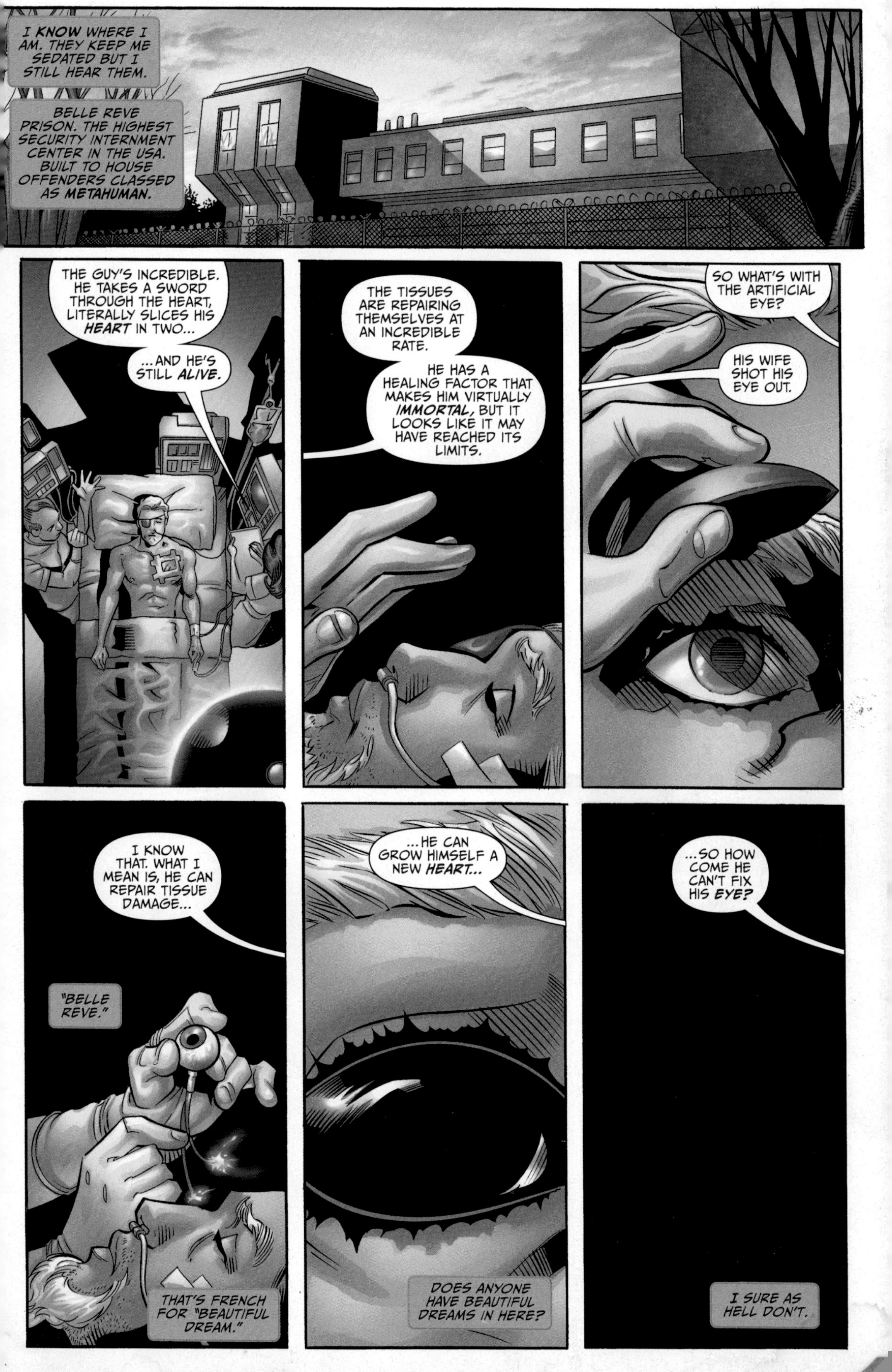
I KNOW WHERE I AM. THEY KEEP ME SEDATED BUT I STILL HEAR THEM.
BELLE REVE PRISON. THE HIGHEST SECURITY INTERNMENT CENTER IN THE USA. BUILT TO HOUSE OFFENDERS CLASSED AS METAHUMAN.
THE GUY'S INCREDIBLE. HE TAKES A SWORD THROUGH THE HEART, LITERALLY SLICES HIS HEART IN TWO...
...AND HE'S STILL ALIVE.
THE TISSUES ARE REPAIRING THEMSELVES AT AN INCREDIBLE RATE.
HE HAS A HEALING FACTOR THAT MAKES HIM VIRTUALLY IMMORTAL, BUT IT LOOKS LIKE IT MAY HAVE REACHED ITS LIMITS.
SO WHAT'S WITH THE ARTIFICIAL EYE?
HIS WIFE SHOT HIS EYE OUT.
I KNOW THAT. WHAT I MEAN IS, HE CAN REPAIR TISSUE DAMAGE...
"BELLE REVE."
THAT'S FRENCH FOR "BEAUTIFUL DREAM."
...HE CAN GROW HIMSELF A NEW HEART...
DOES ANYONE HAVE BEAUTIFUL DREAMS IN HERE?
...SO HOW COME HE CAN'T FIX HIS EYE?
I SURE AS HELL DON'T.

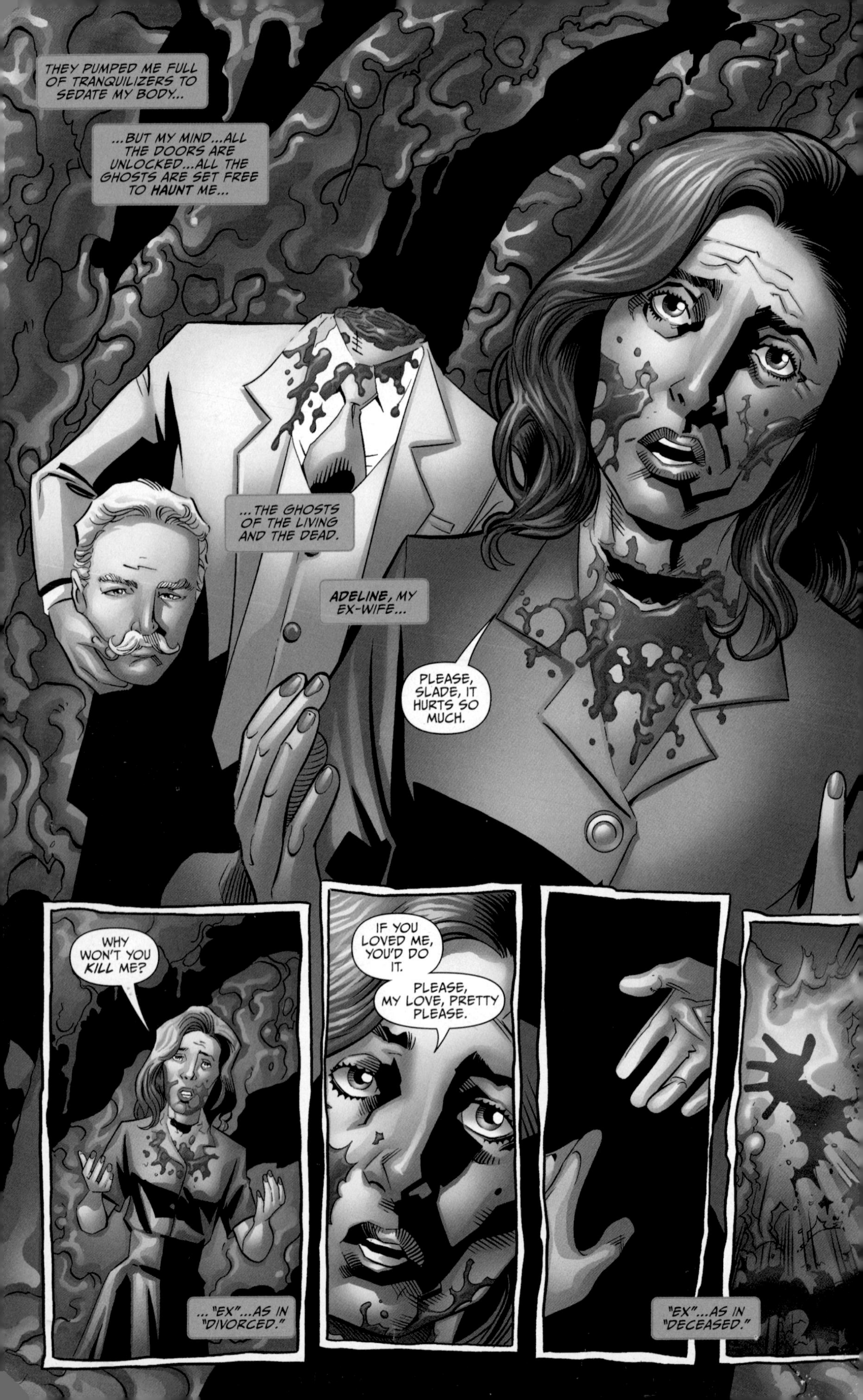
THEY PUMPED ME FULL OF TRANQUILIZERS TO SEDATE MY BODY...
...BUT MY MIND...ALL THE DOORS ARE UNLOCKED...ALL THE GHOSTS ARE SET FREE TO HAUNT ME...
...THE GHOSTS OF THE LIVING AND THE DEAD.
ADELINE, MY EX-WIFE...
PLEASE, SLADE, IT HURTS SO MUCH.
WHY WON'T YOU KILL ME?
..."EX"...AS IN "DIVORCED."
IF YOU LOVED ME, YOU'D DO IT.
PLEASE, MY LOVE, PRETTY PLEASE.
"EX"...AS IN "DECEASED."

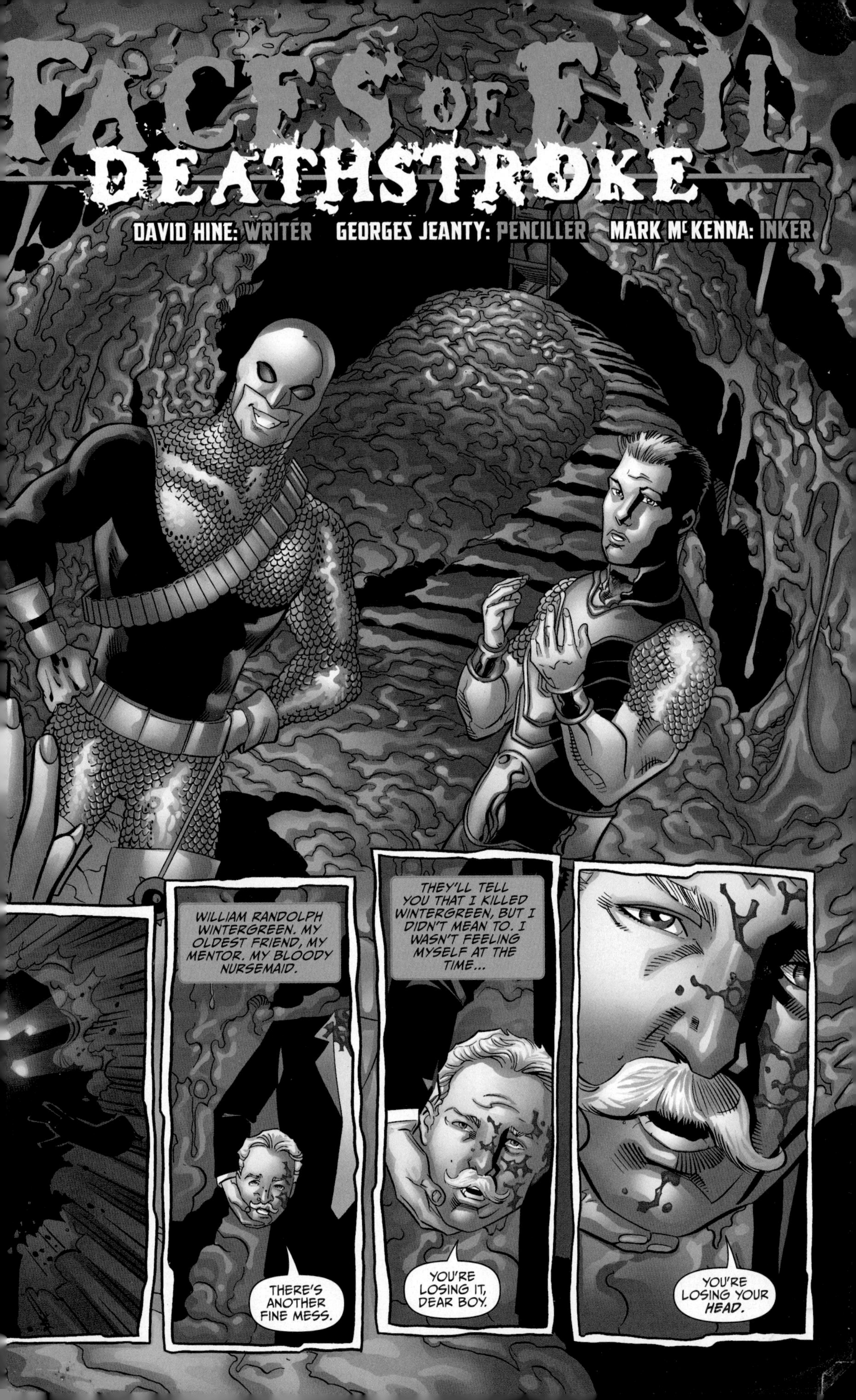
FACES OF EVIL
DEATHSTROKE
DAVID HINE: WRITER GEORGES JEANTY: PENCILLER MARK McKENNA: INKER
WILLIAM RANDOLPH WINTERGREEN. MY OLDEST FRIEND, MY MENTOR. MY BLOODY NURSEMAID.
THERE'S ANOTHER FINE MESS.
THEY'LL TELL YOU THAT I KILLED WINTERGREEN, BUT I DIDN'T MEAN TO. I WASN'T FEELING MYSELF AT THE TIME...
YOU'RE LOSING IT, DEAR BOY.
YOU'RE LOSING YOUR HEAD.

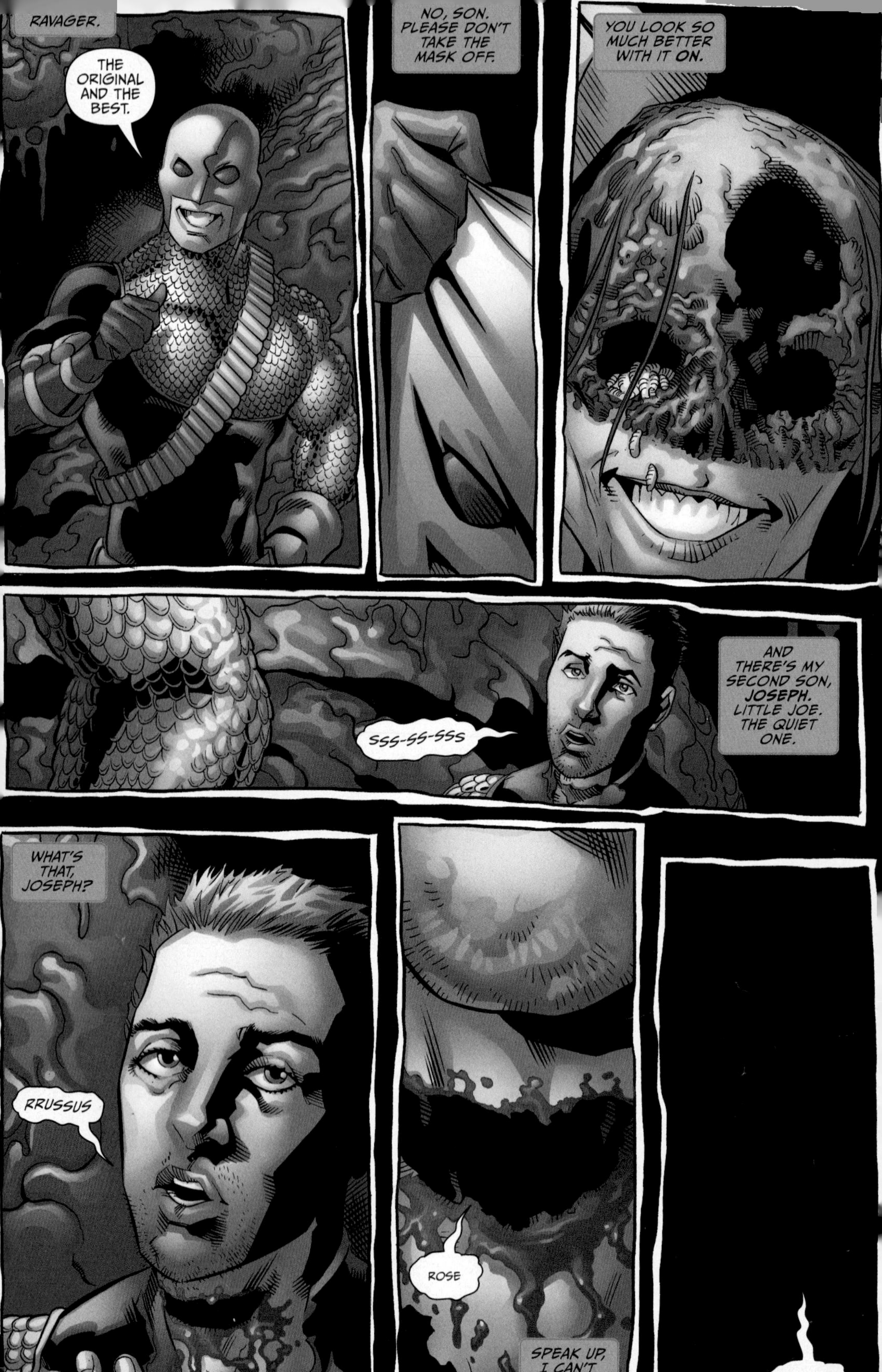
RAVAGER.
THE ORIGINAL AND THE BEST.
NO, SON. PLEASE DON'T TAKE THE MASK OFF.
YOU LOOK SO MUCH BETTER WITH IT ON.
SSS-SS-SSS
AND THERE'S MY SECOND SON, JOSEPH. LITTLE JOE. THE QUIET ONE.
WHAT'S THAT, JOSEPH?
RRUSSUS
ROSE
SPEAK UP, I CAN'T HEAR YOU.
ROSE.

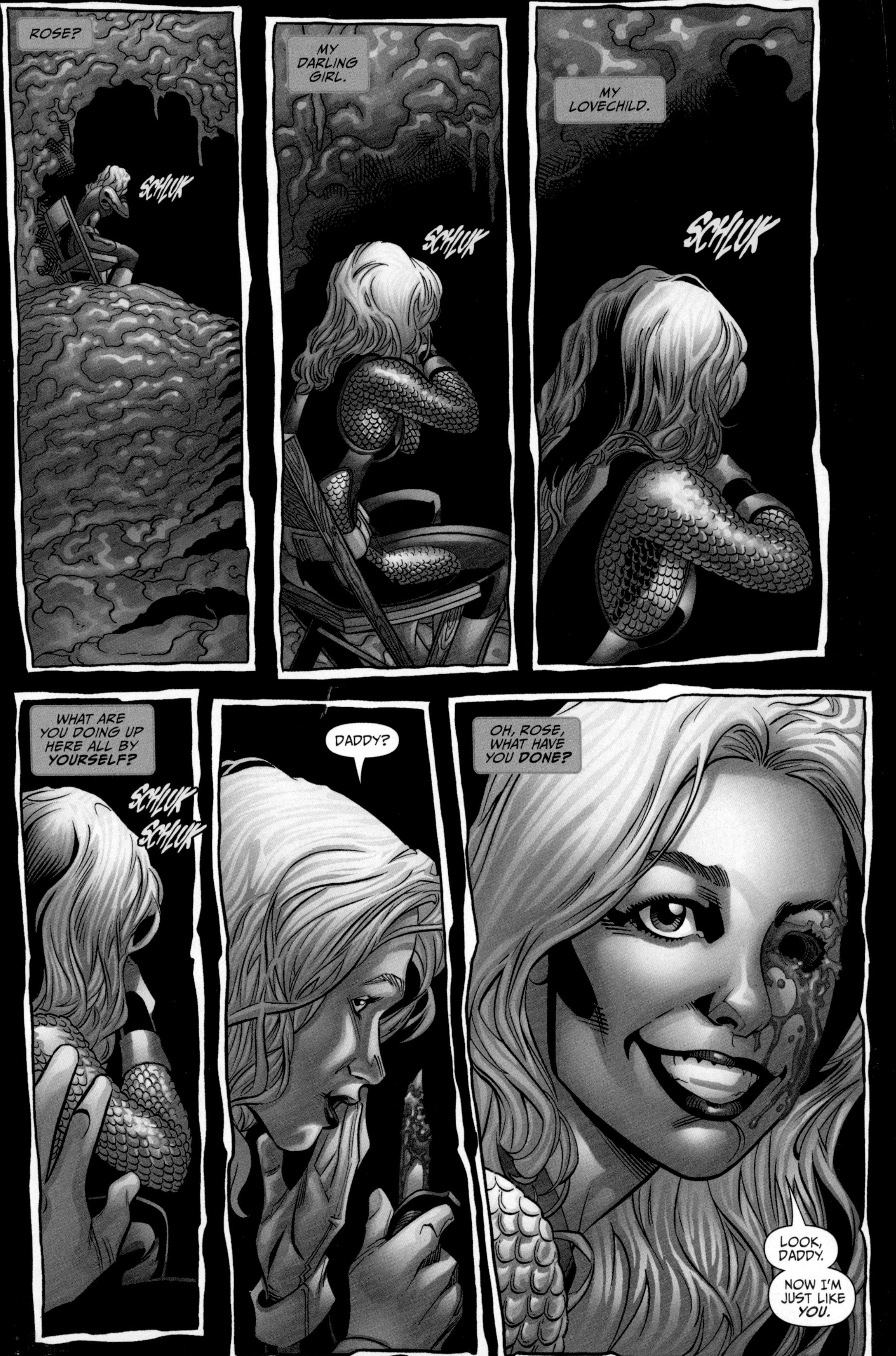
ROSE?
SCHLUK
MY DARLING GIRL.
SCHLUK
MY LOVECHILD.
SCHLUK
WHAT ARE YOU DOING UP HERE ALL BY YOURSELF?
SCHLUK SCHLUK
DADDY?
OH, ROSE, WHAT HAVE YOU DONE?
LOOK, DADDY.
NOW I'M JUST LIKE YOU.

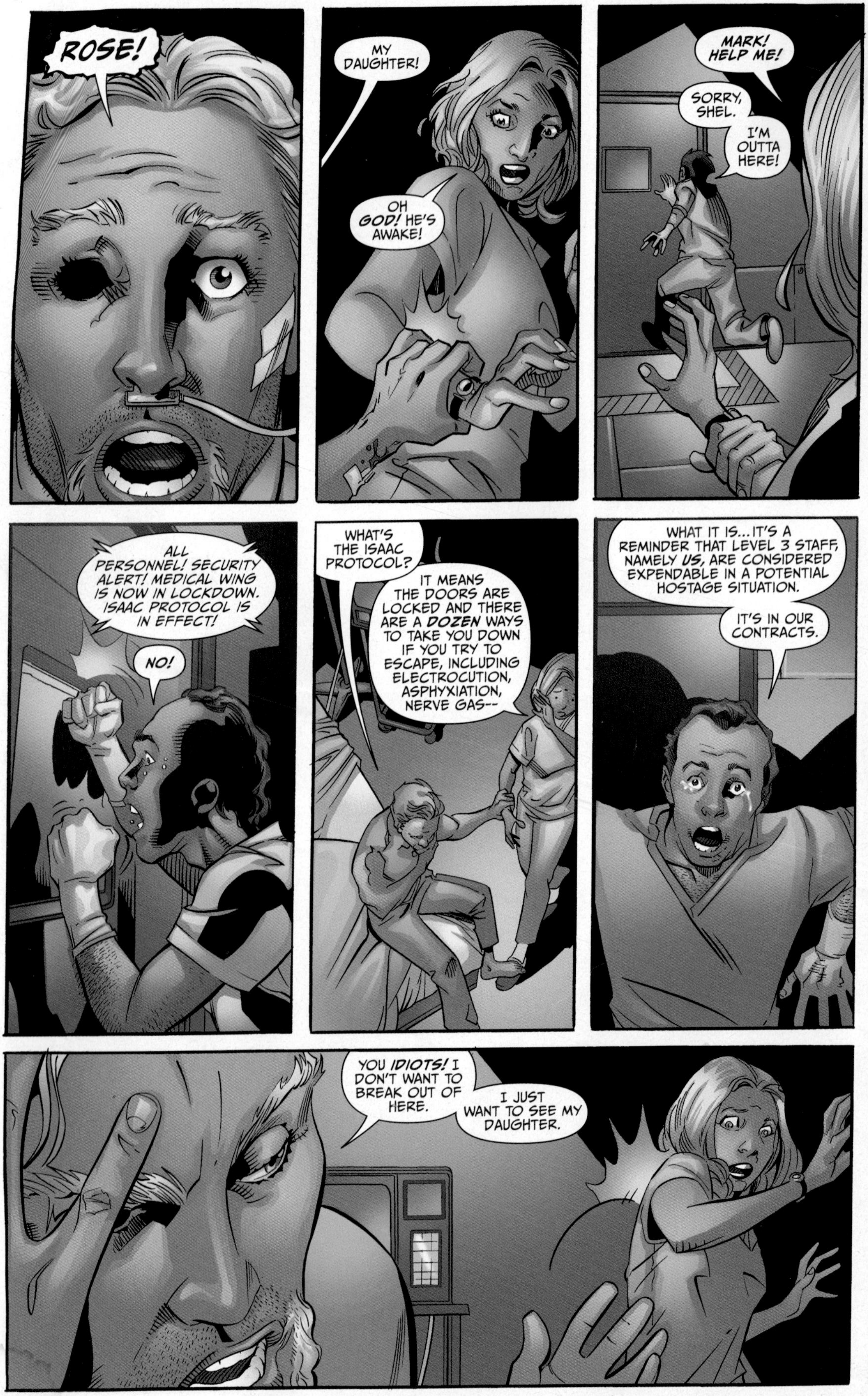
ROSE!
MY DAUGHTER!
OH GOD! HE'S AWAKE!
MARK! HELP ME!
SORRY, SHEL.
I'M OUTTA HERE!
ALL PERSONNEL! SECURITY ALERT! MEDICAL WING IS NOW IN LOCKDOWN. ISAAC PROTOCOL IS IN EFFECT!
NO!
WHAT'S THE ISAAC PROTOCOL?
IT MEANS THE DOORS ARE LOCKED AND THERE ARE A DOZEN WAYS TO TAKE YOU DOWN IF YOU TRY TO ESCAPE, INCLUDING ELECTROCUTION, ASPHYXIATION, NERVE GAS--
WHAT IT IS...IT'S A REMINDER THAT LEVEL 3 STAFF, NAMELY US, ARE CONSIDERED EXPENDABLE IN A POTENTIAL HOSTAGE SITUATION.
IT'S IN OUR CONTRACTS.
YOU IDIOTS! I DON'T WANT TO BREAK OUT OF HERE.
I JUST WANT TO SEE MY DAUGHTER.

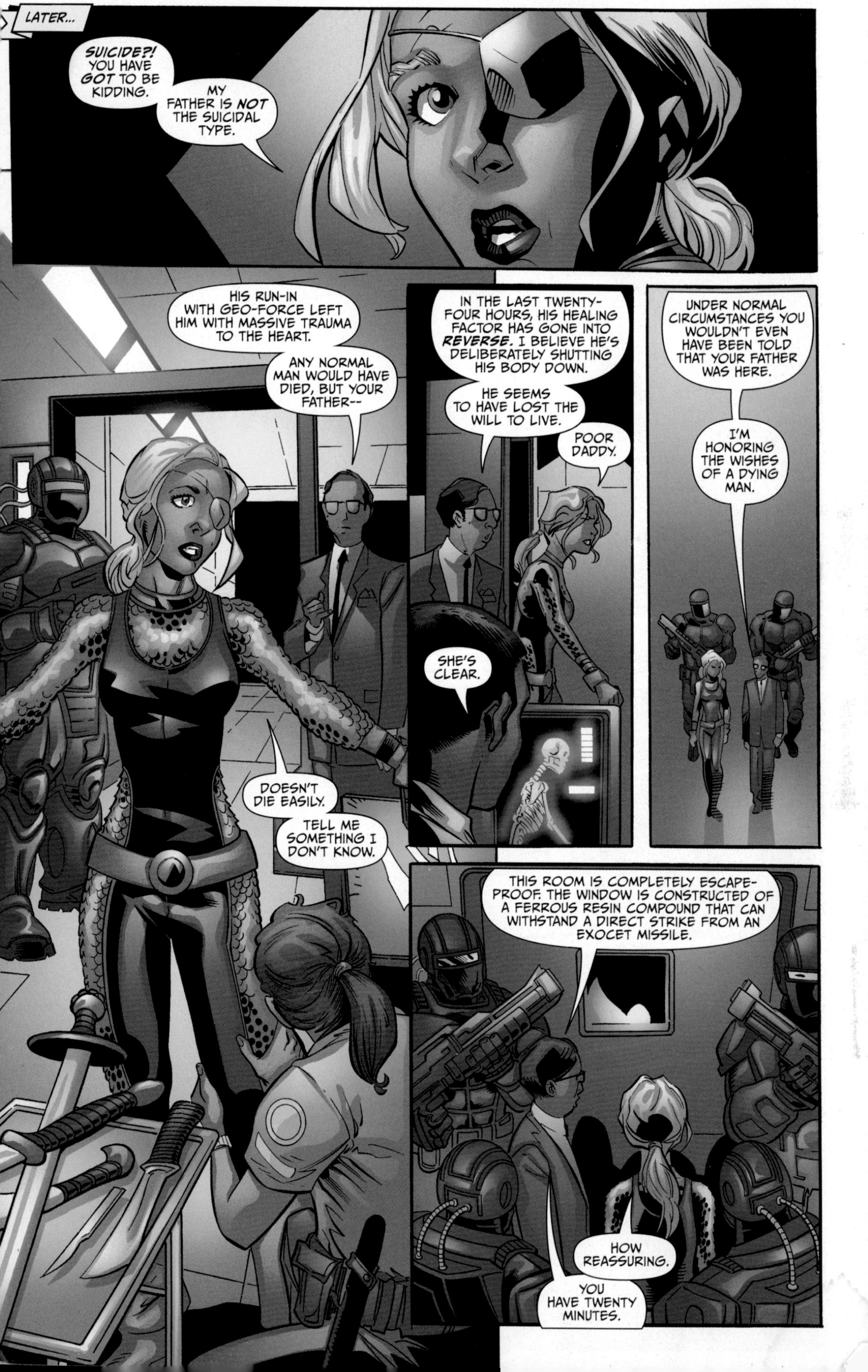
LATER...
SUICIDE?! YOU HAVE GOT TO BE KIDDING.
MY FATHER IS NOT THE SUICIDAL TYPE.
HIS RUN-IN WITH GEO-FORCE LEFT HIM WITH MASSIVE TRAUMA TO THE HEART.
ANY NORMAL MAN WOULD HAVE DIED, BUT YOUR FATHER--
DOESN'T DIE EASILY.
TELL ME SOMETHING I DON'T KNOW.
IN THE LAST TWENTY-FOUR HOURS, HIS HEALING FACTOR HAS GONE INTO REVERSE. I BELIEVE HE'S DELIBERATELY SHUTTING HIS BODY DOWN.
HE SEEMS TO HAVE LOST THE WILL TO LIVE.
POOR DADDY.
SHE'S CLEAR.
UNDER NORMAL CIRCUMSTANCES YOU WOULDN'T EVEN HAVE BEEN TOLD THAT YOUR FATHER WAS HERE.
I'M HONORING THE WISHES OF A DYING MAN.
THIS ROOM IS COMPLETELY ESCAPE-PROOF. THE WINDOW IS CONSTRUCTED OF A FERROUS RESIN COMPOUND THAT CAN WITHSTAND A DIRECT STRIKE FROM AN EXOCET MISSILE.
HOW REASSURING.
YOU HAVE TWENTY MINUTES.

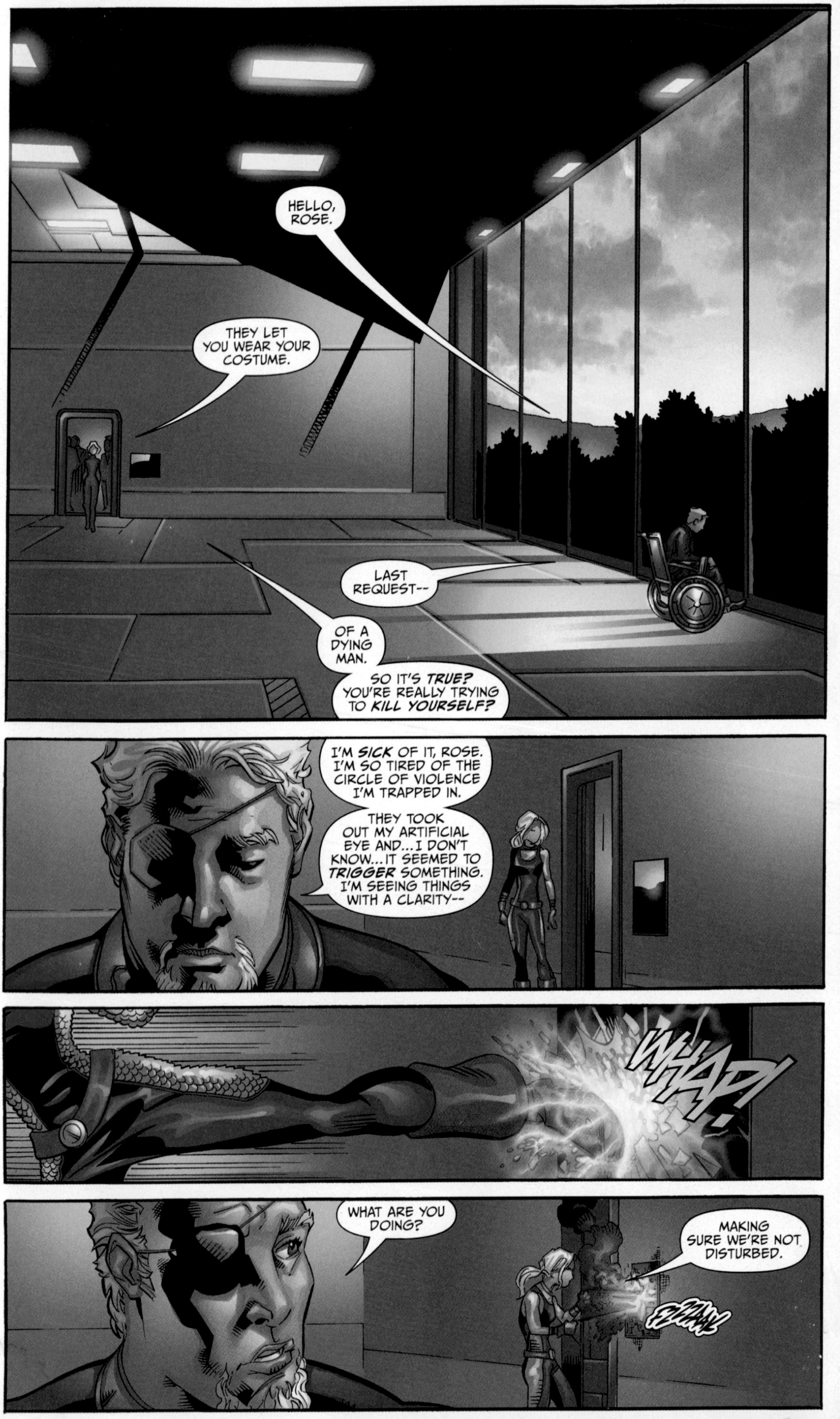
HELLO, ROSE.
THEY LET YOU WEAR YOUR COSTUME.
LAST REQUEST--
OF A DYING MAN.
SO IT'S *TRUE?* YOU'RE REALLY TRYING TO *KILL YOURSELF?*
I'M *SICK* OF IT, ROSE. I'M SO TIRED OF THE CIRCLE OF VIOLENCE I'M TRAPPED IN.
THEY TOOK OUT MY ARTIFICIAL EYE AND...I DON'T KNOW...IT SEEMED TO *TRIGGER* SOMETHING. I'M SEEING THINGS WITH A CLARITY--
WHAP!
WHAT ARE YOU DOING?
MAKING SURE WE'RE NOT DISTURBED.

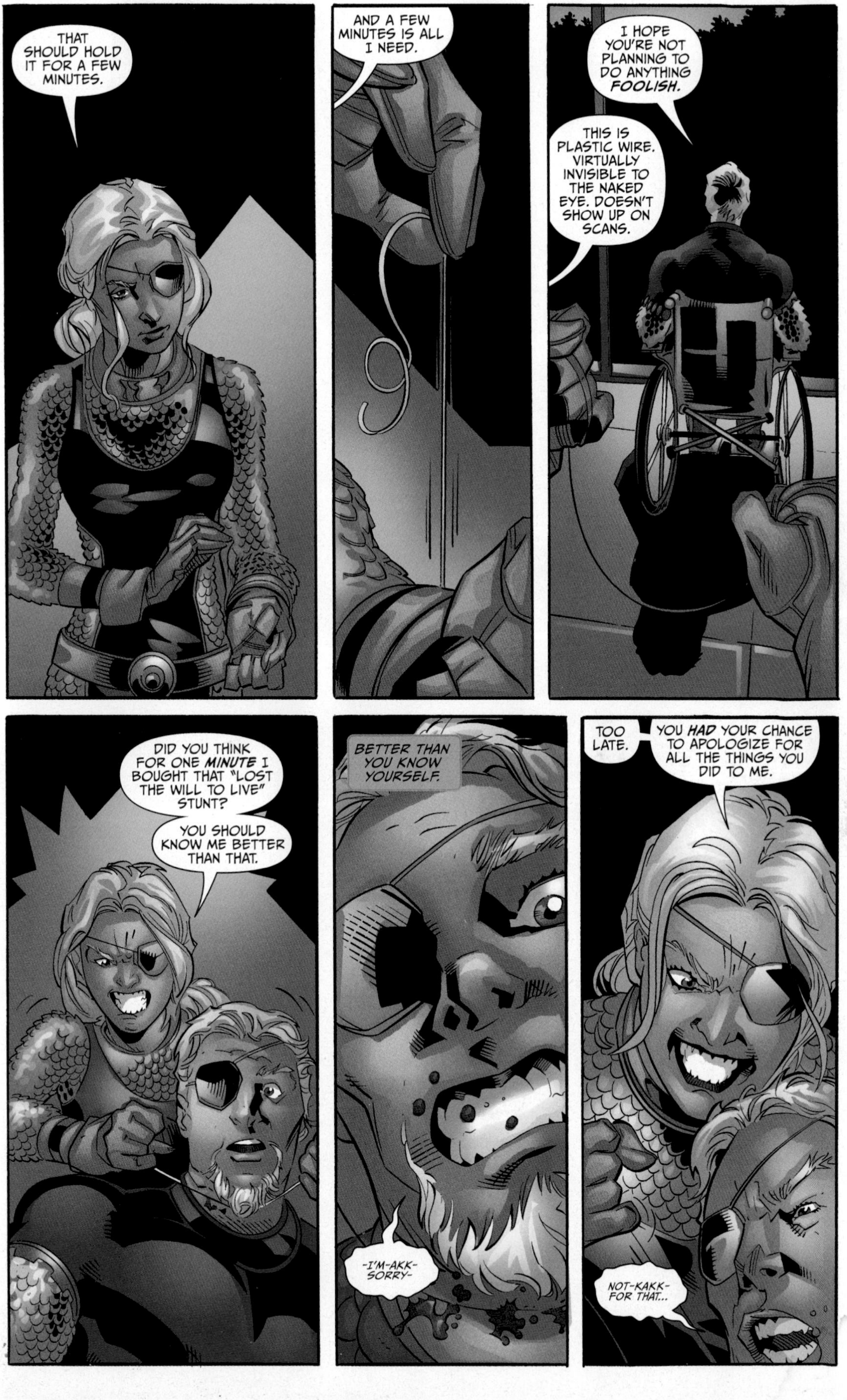
THAT SHOULD HOLD IT FOR A FEW MINUTES.
AND A FEW MINUTES IS ALL I NEED.
I HOPE YOU'RE NOT PLANNING TO DO ANYTHING FOOLISH.
THIS IS PLASTIC WIRE. VIRTUALLY INVISIBLE TO THE NAKED EYE. DOESN'T SHOW UP ON SCANS.
DID YOU THINK FOR ONE MINUTE I BOUGHT THAT "LOST THE WILL TO LIVE" STUNT?
YOU SHOULD KNOW ME BETTER THAN THAT.
BETTER THAN YOU KNOW YOURSELF.
-I'M-AKK-SORRY-
TOO LATE.
YOU HAD YOUR CHANCE TO APOLOGIZE FOR ALL THE THINGS YOU DID TO ME.
NOT-KAKK-FOR THAT...

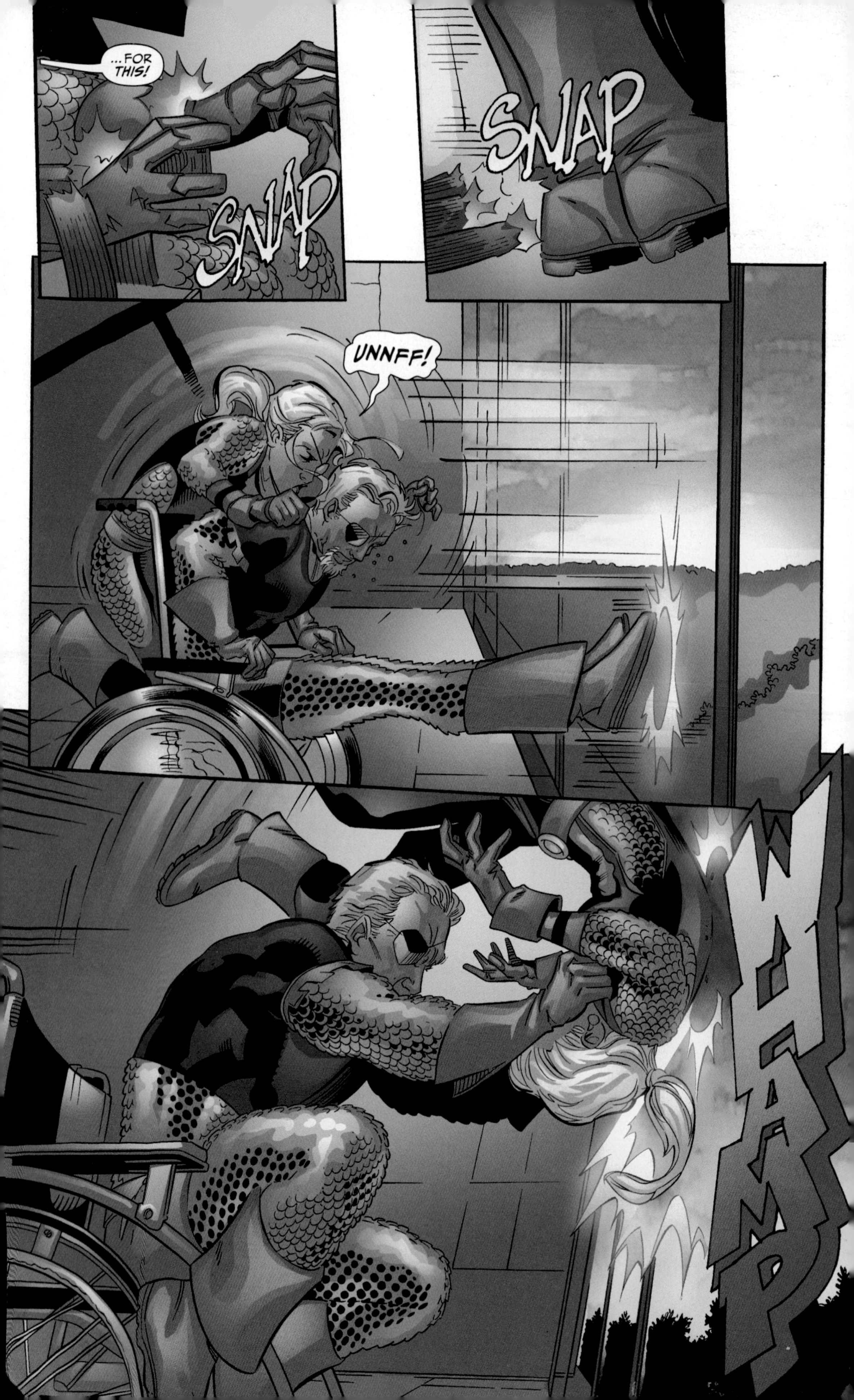
...FOR THIS!
SNAP
SNAP
UNNFF!
WHAMP

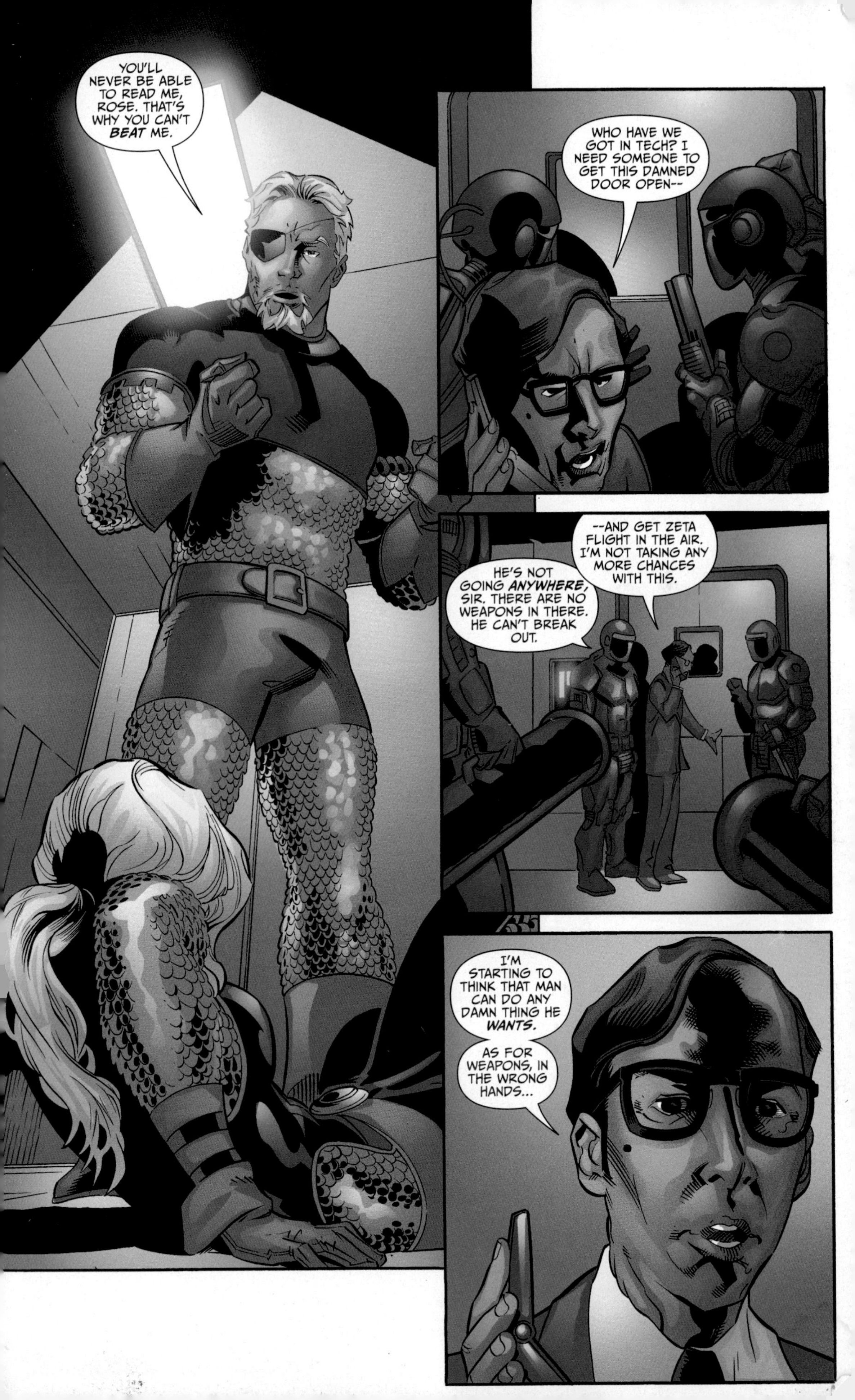
YOU'LL NEVER BE ABLE TO READ ME, ROSE. THAT'S WHY YOU CAN'T BEAT ME.
WHO HAVE WE GOT IN TECH? I NEED SOMEONE TO GET THIS DAMNED DOOR OPEN--
--AND GET ZETA FLIGHT IN THE AIR. I'M NOT TAKING ANY MORE CHANCES WITH THIS.
HE'S NOT GOING ANYWHERE, SIR. THERE ARE NO WEAPONS IN THERE. HE CAN'T BREAK OUT.
I'M STARTING TO THINK THAT MAN CAN DO ANY DAMN THING HE WANTS.
AS FOR WEAPONS, IN THE WRONG HANDS...

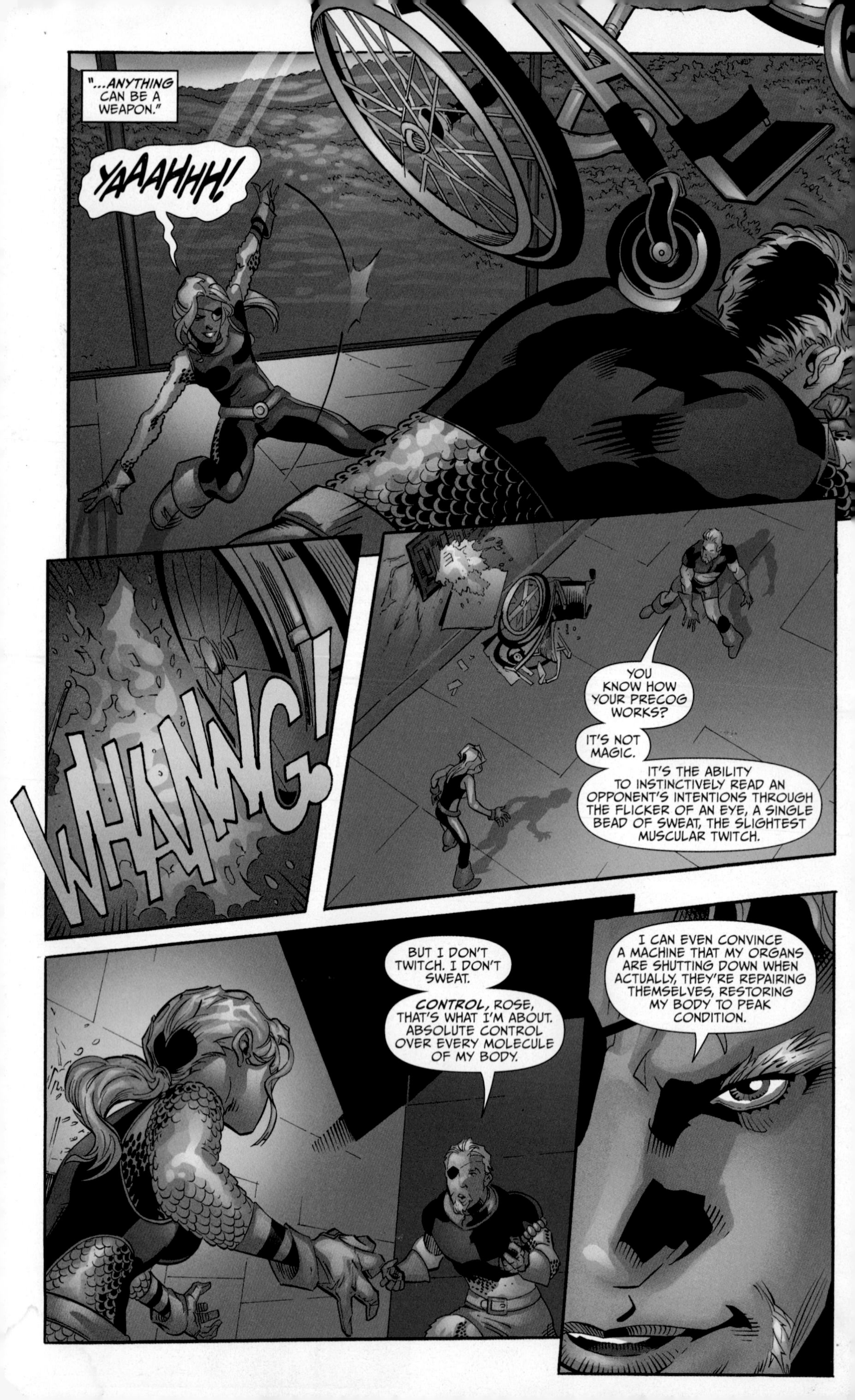
"...ANYTHING CAN BE A WEAPON."
YAAAHHH!
WHANNG!
YOU KNOW HOW YOUR PRECOG WORKS?
IT'S NOT MAGIC.
IT'S THE ABILITY TO INSTINCTIVELY READ AN OPPONENT'S INTENTIONS THROUGH THE FLICKER OF AN EYE, A SINGLE BEAD OF SWEAT, THE SLIGHTEST MUSCULAR TWITCH.
BUT I DON'T TWITCH. I DON'T SWEAT.
CONTROL, ROSE, THAT'S WHAT I'M ABOUT. ABSOLUTE CONTROL OVER EVERY MOLECULE OF MY BODY.
I CAN EVEN CONVINCE A MACHINE THAT MY ORGANS ARE SHUTTING DOWN WHEN ACTUALLY, THEY'RE REPAIRING THEMSELVES, RESTORING MY BODY TO PEAK CONDITION.

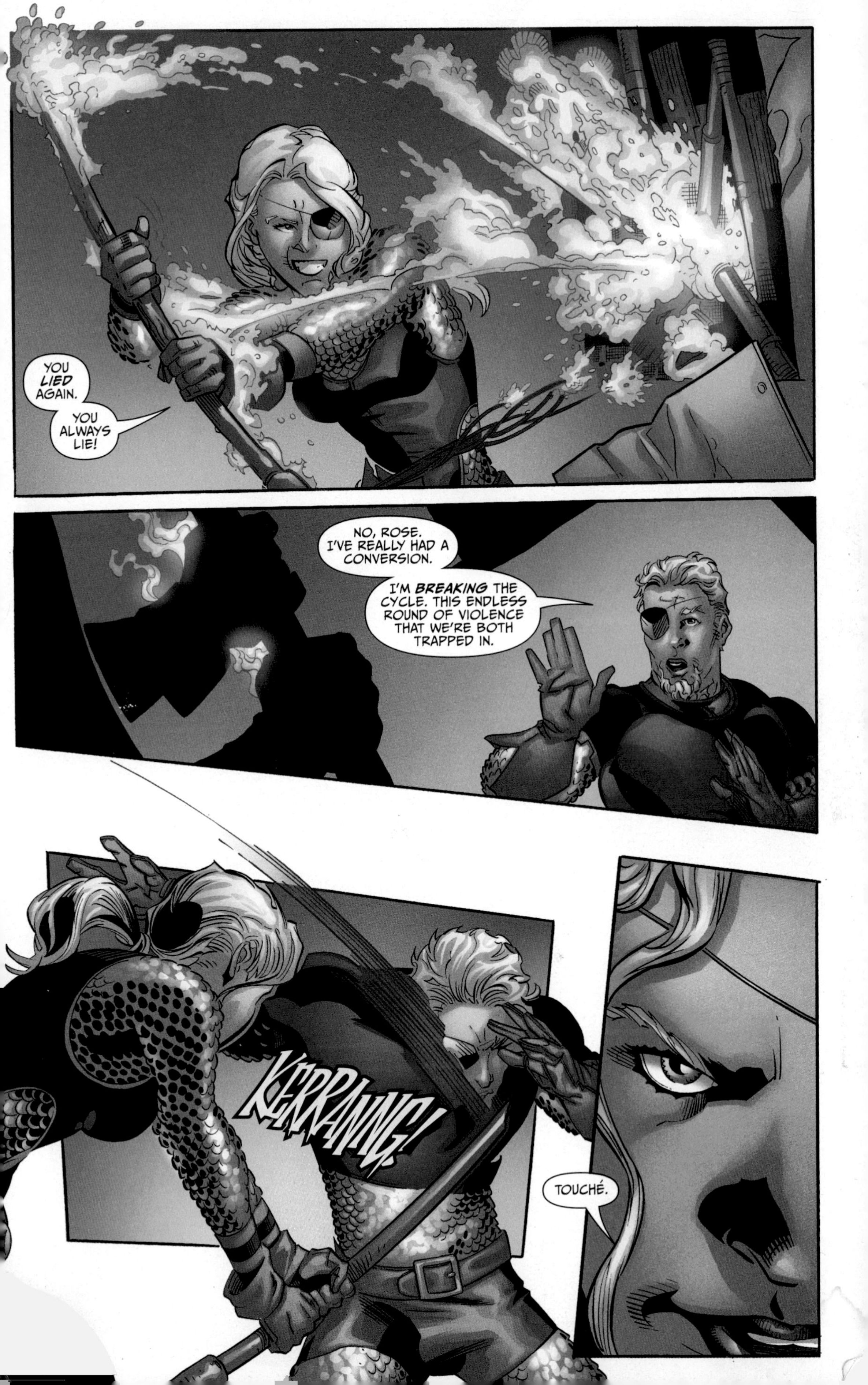
YOU *LIED* AGAIN.
YOU ALWAYS LIE!
NO, ROSE. I'VE REALLY HAD A CONVERSION.
I'M *BREAKING* THE CYCLE. THIS ENDLESS ROUND OF VIOLENCE THAT WE'RE BOTH TRAPPED IN.
KERRANNG!
TOUCHÉ.

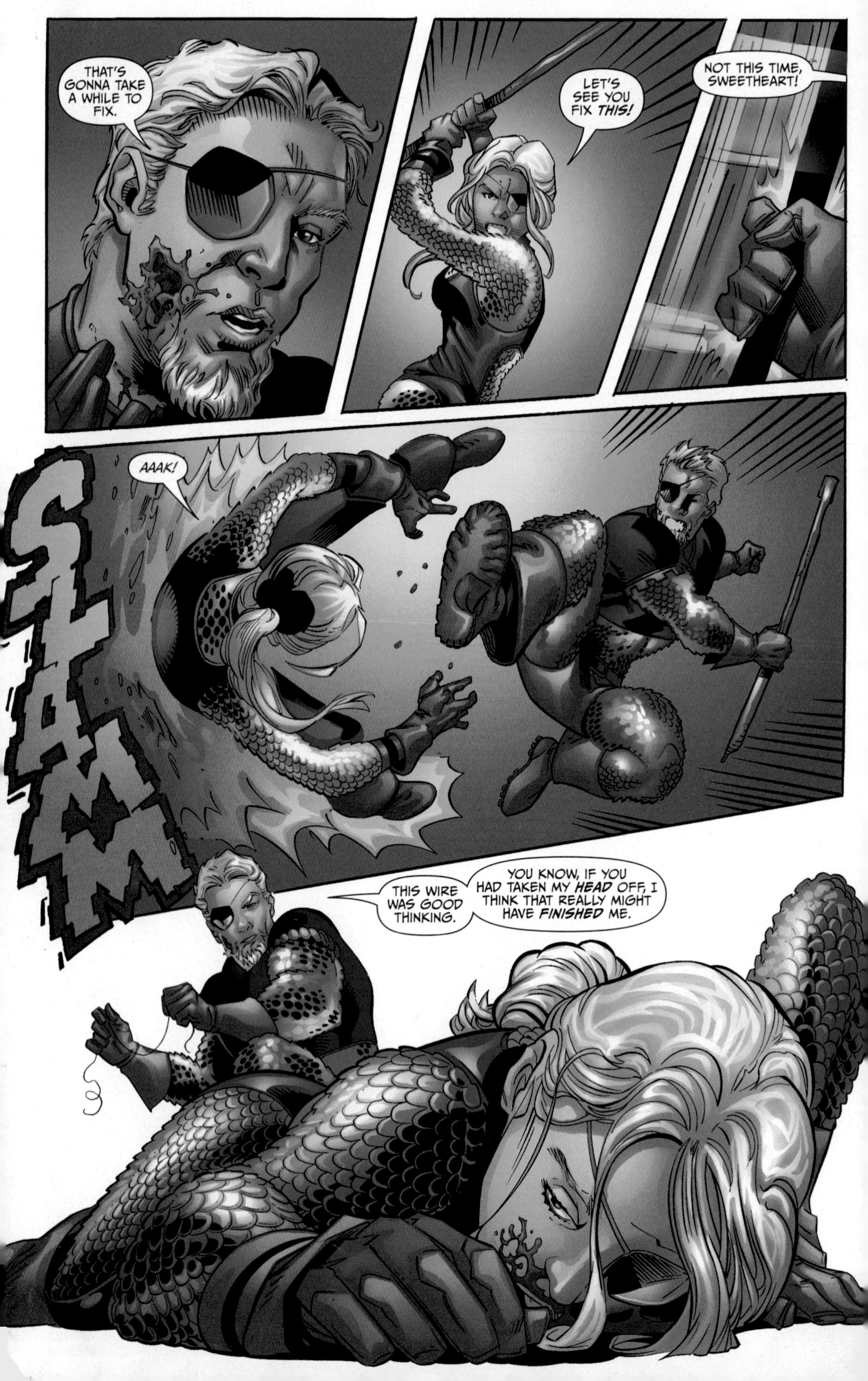

THAT'S GONNA TAKE A WHILE TO FIX.
LET'S SEE YOU FIX *THIS!*
NOT THIS TIME, SWEETHEART!
AAAK!
SLAM
THIS WIRE WAS GOOD THINKING.
YOU KNOW, IF YOU HAD TAKEN MY *HEAD* OFF, I THINK THAT REALLY MIGHT HAVE *FINISHED* ME.

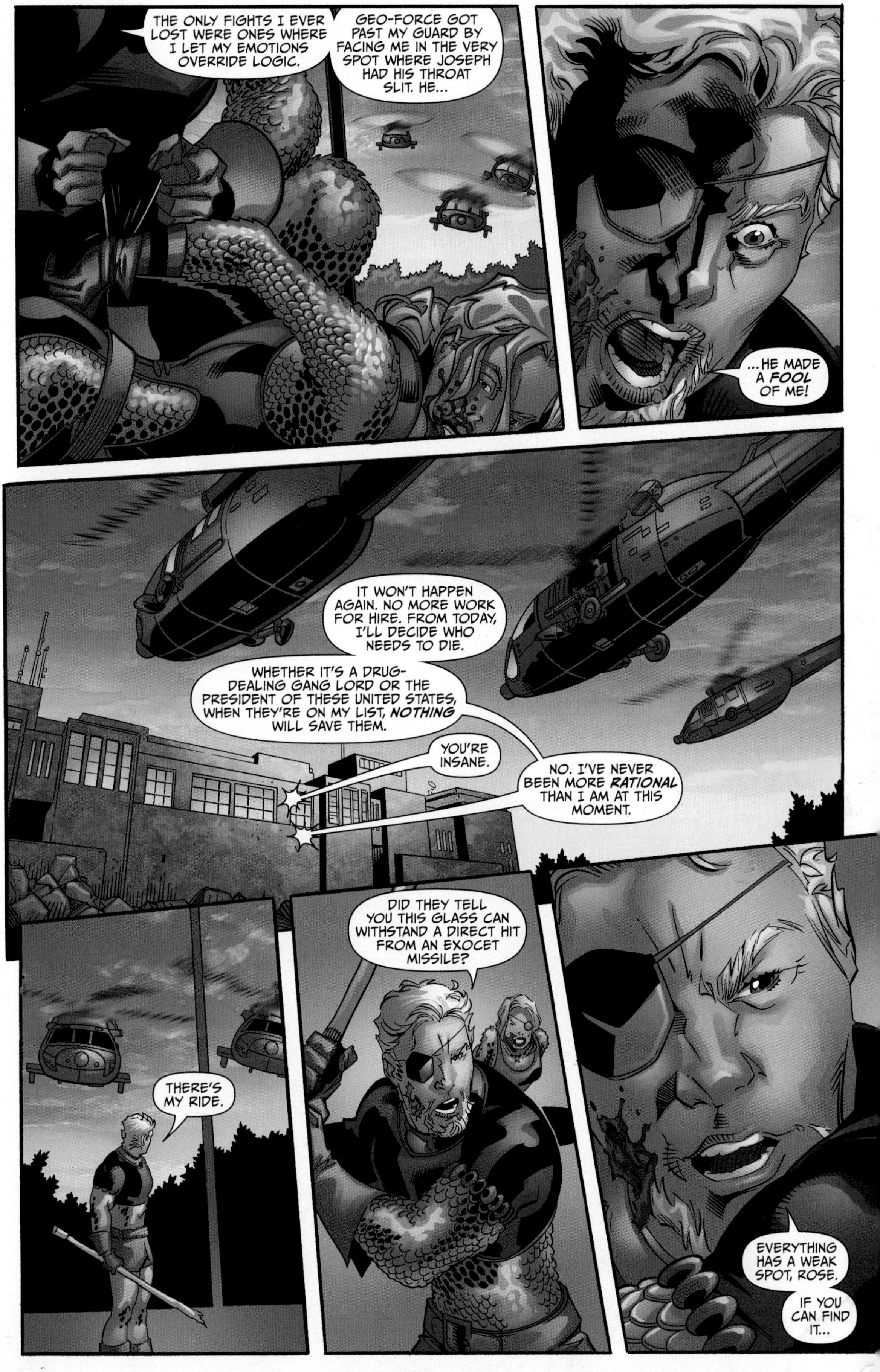

THE ONLY FIGHTS I EVER LOST WERE ONES WHERE I LET MY EMOTIONS OVERRIDE LOGIC.
GEO-FORCE GOT PAST MY GUARD BY FACING ME IN THE VERY SPOT WHERE JOSEPH HAD HIS THROAT SLIT. HE...
...HE MADE A FOOL OF ME!
IT WON'T HAPPEN AGAIN. NO MORE WORK FOR HIRE. FROM TODAY, I'LL DECIDE WHO NEEDS TO DIE.
WHETHER IT'S A DRUG-DEALING GANG LORD OR THE PRESIDENT OF THESE UNITED STATES, WHEN THEY'RE ON MY LIST, NOTHING WILL SAVE THEM.
YOU'RE INSANE.
NO. I'VE NEVER BEEN MORE RATIONAL THAN I AM AT THIS MOMENT.
THERE'S MY RIDE.
DID THEY TELL YOU THIS GLASS CAN WITHSTAND A DIRECT HIT FROM AN EXOCET MISSILE?
EVERYTHING HAS A WEAK SPOT, ROSE.
IF YOU CAN FIND IT...

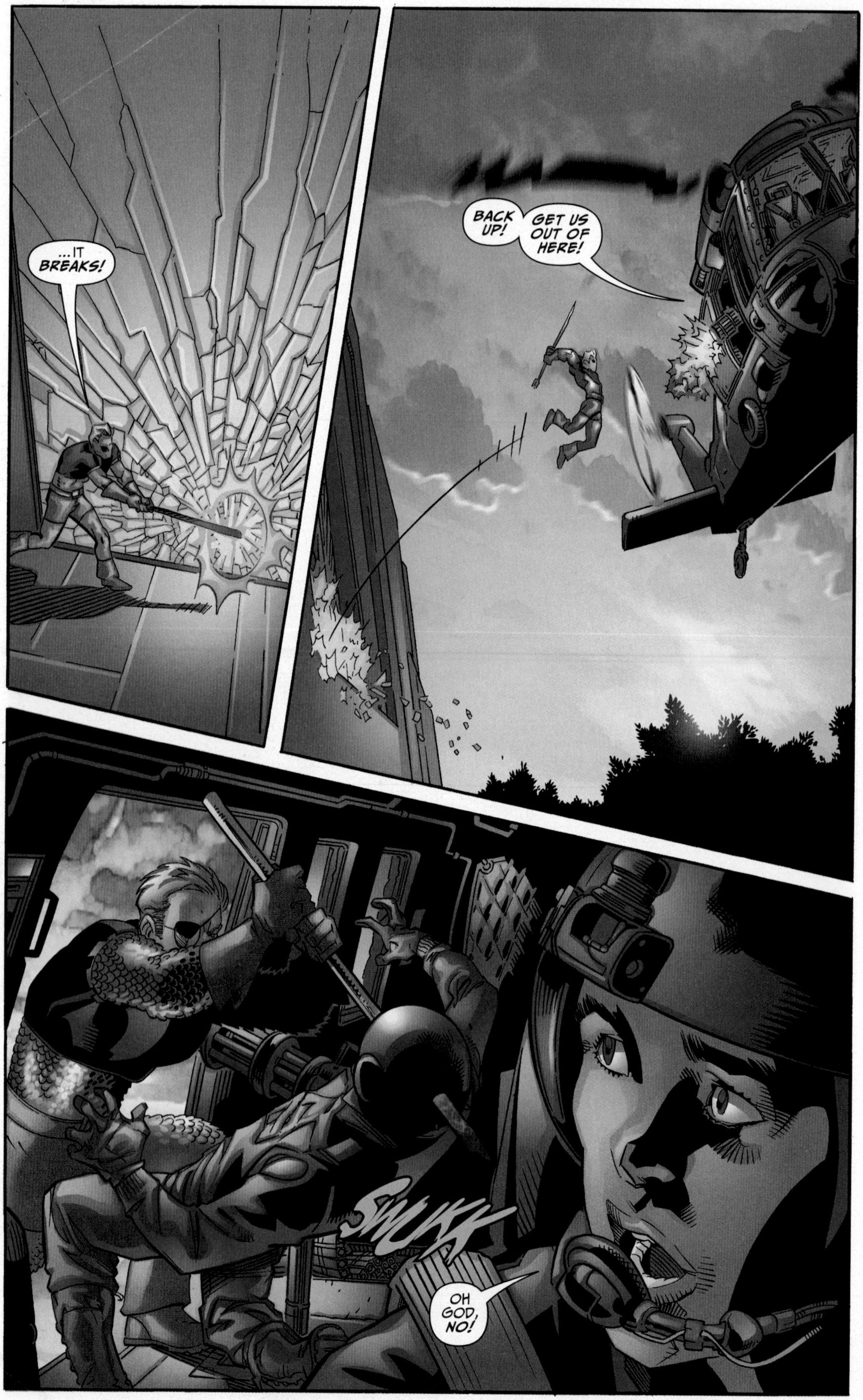
...IT BREAKS!
BACK UP!
GET US OUT OF HERE!
SNIKK
OH GOD, NO!

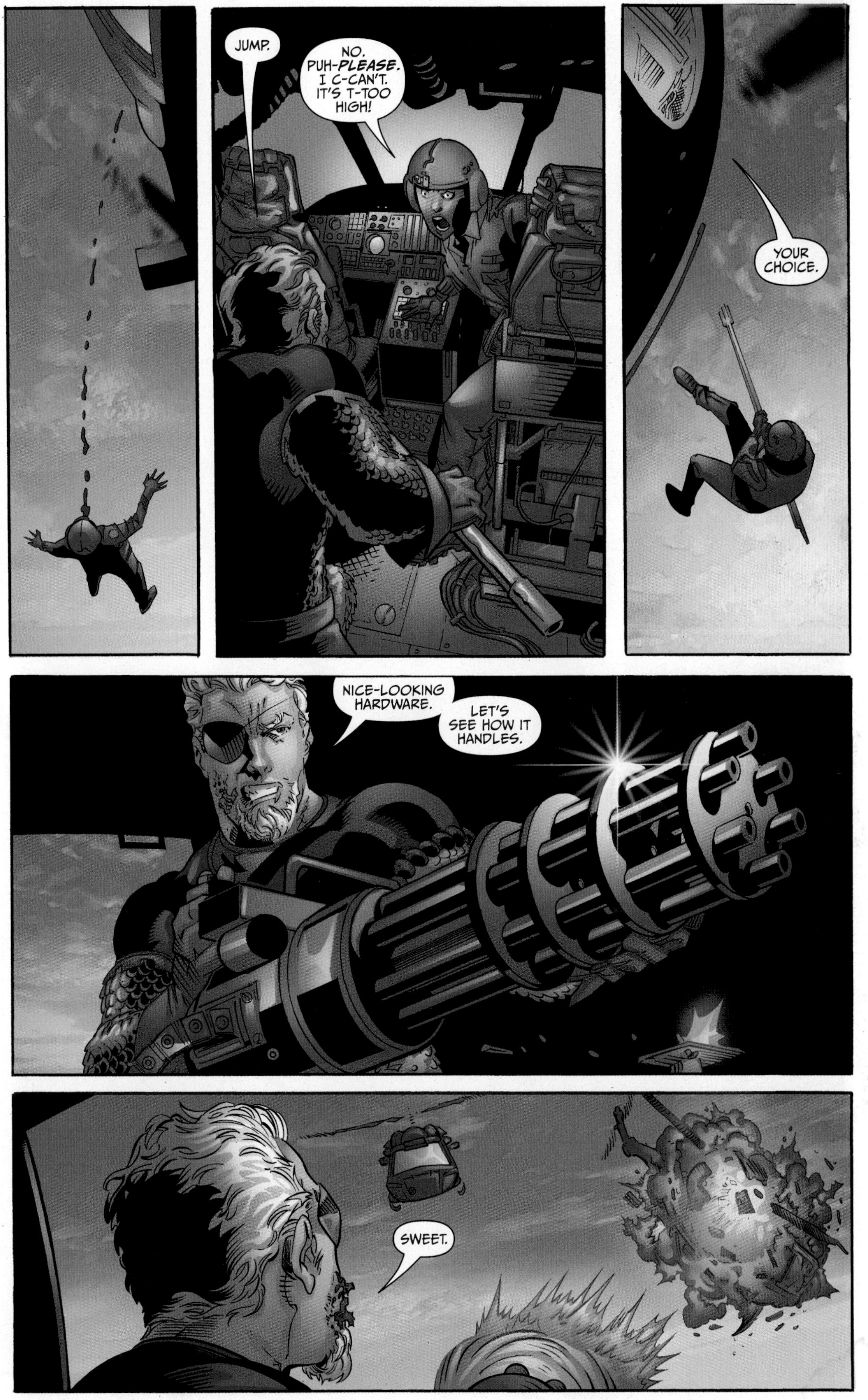
JUMP.
NO. PUH-*PLEASE.* I C-CAN'T. IT'S T-TOO HIGH!
YOUR CHOICE.
NICE-LOOKING HARDWARE.
LET'S SEE HOW IT HANDLES.
SWEET.

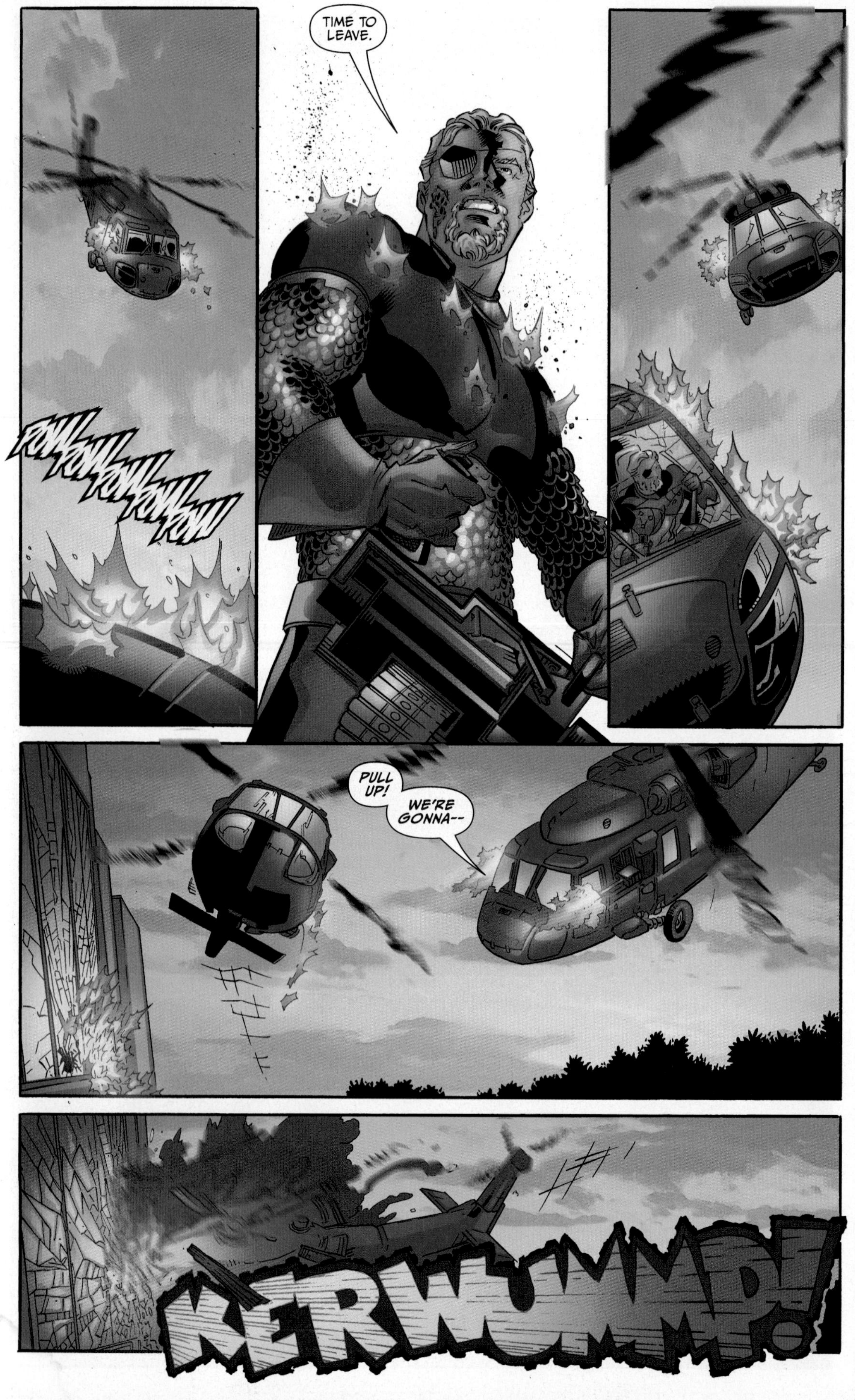
TIME TO LEAVE.
POW POW POW POW POW POW POW
PULL UP!
WE'RE GONNA--
KERWUMMP!

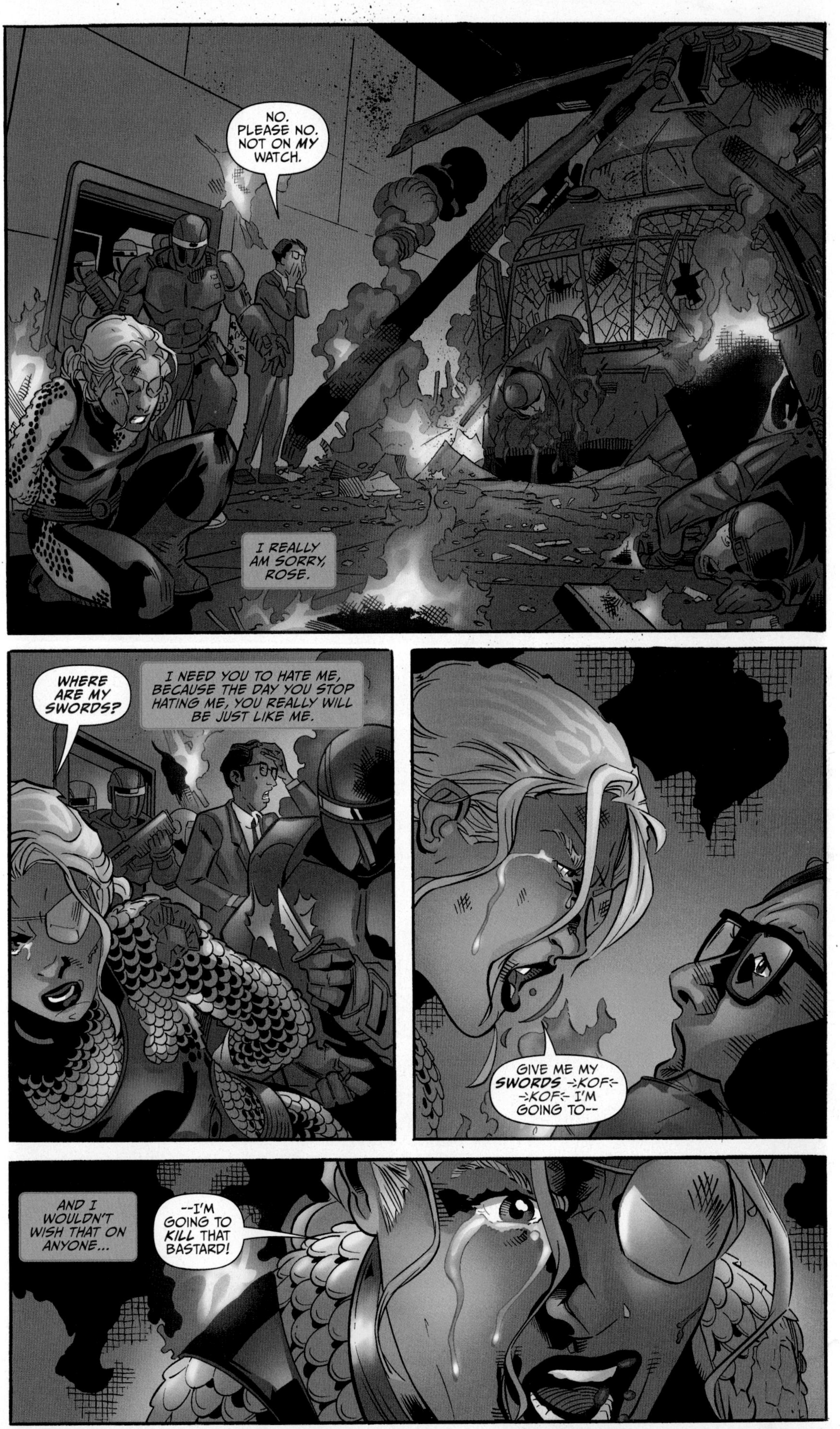
NO. PLEASE NO. NOT ON MY WATCH.
I REALLY AM SORRY, ROSE.
WHERE ARE MY SWORDS?
I NEED YOU TO HATE ME, BECAUSE THE DAY YOU STOP HATING ME, YOU REALLY WILL BE JUST LIKE ME.
GIVE ME MY SWORDS -KOF- -KOF- I'M GOING TO--
AND I WOULDN'T WISH THAT ON ANYONE...
--I'M GOING TO KILL THAT BASTARD!

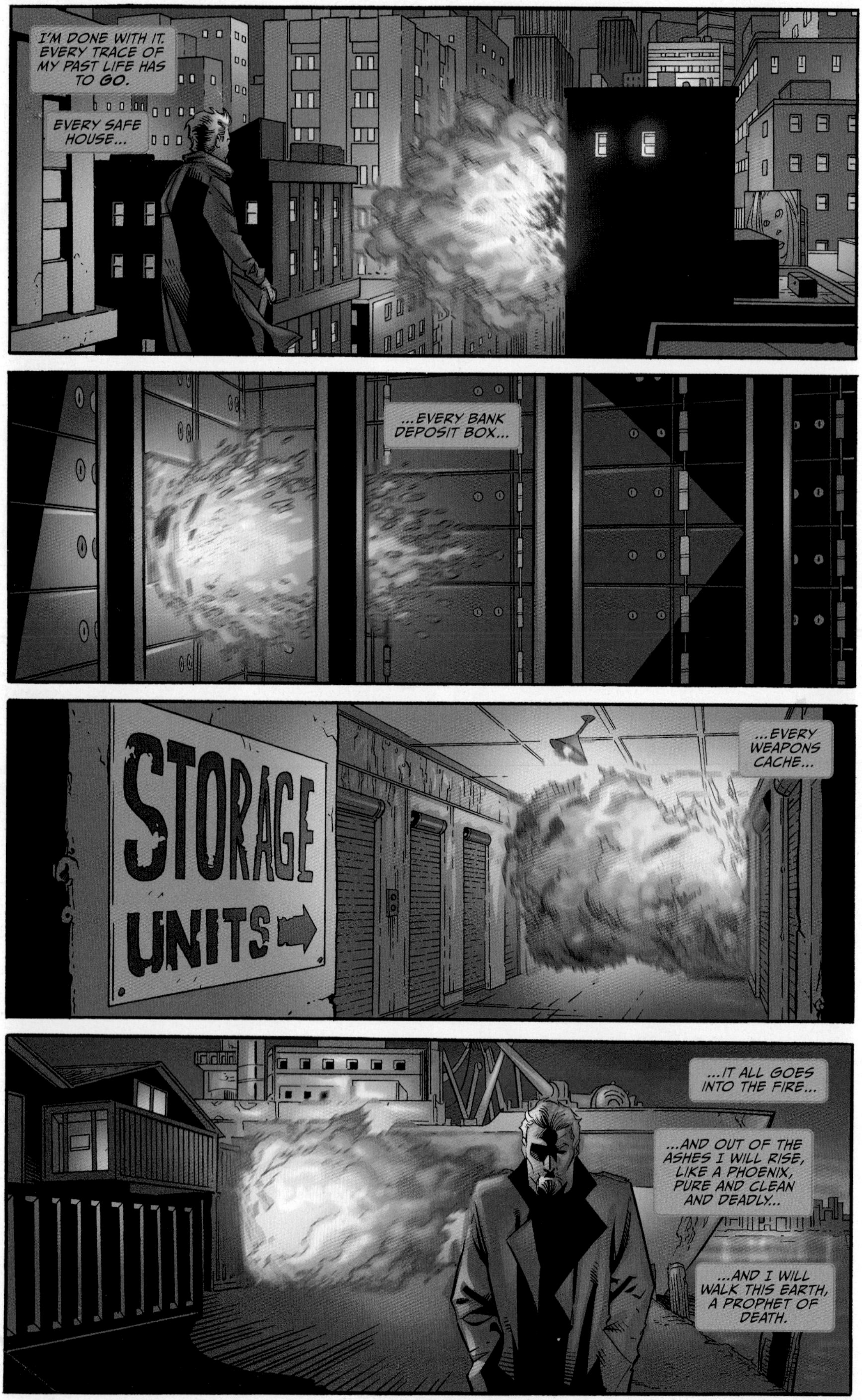
I'M DONE WITH IT. EVERY TRACE OF MY PAST LIFE HAS TO GO.
EVERY SAFE HOUSE...
...EVERY BANK DEPOSIT BOX...
STORAGE UNITS
...EVERY WEAPONS CACHE...
...IT ALL GOES INTO THE FIRE...
...AND OUT OF THE ASHES I WILL RISE, LIKE A PHOENIX, PURE AND CLEAN AND DEADLY...
...AND I WILL WALK THIS EARTH, A PROPHET OF DEATH.

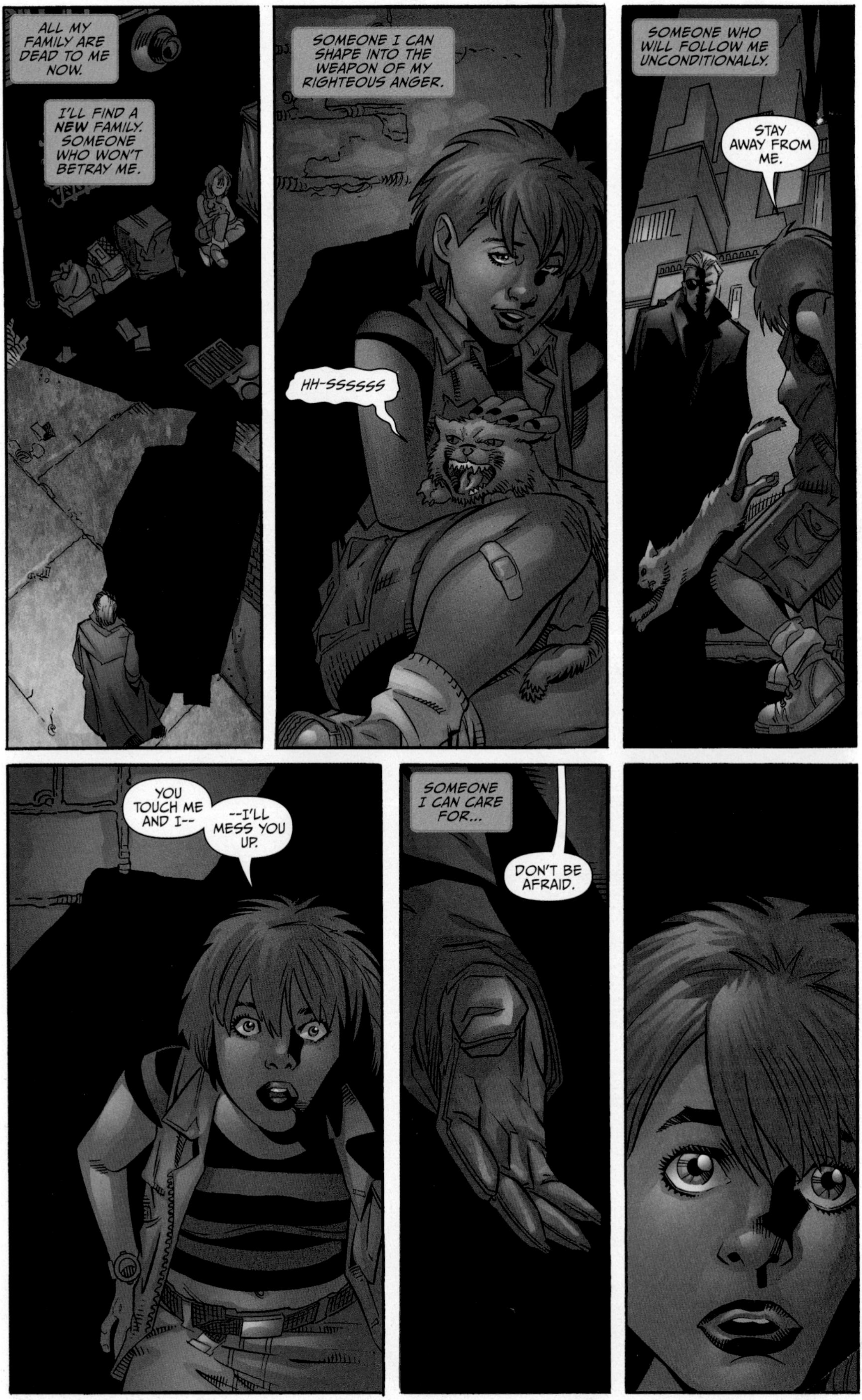

ALL MY FAMILY ARE DEAD TO ME NOW.
I'LL FIND A **NEW** FAMILY. SOMEONE WHO WON'T BETRAY ME.
SOMEONE I CAN SHAPE INTO THE WEAPON OF MY RIGHTEOUS ANGER.
HH-SSSSSS
SOMEONE WHO WILL FOLLOW ME UNCONDITIONALLY.
STAY AWAY FROM ME.
YOU TOUCH ME AND I--
--I'LL MESS YOU UP.
SOMEONE I CAN CARE FOR...
DON'T BE AFRAID.

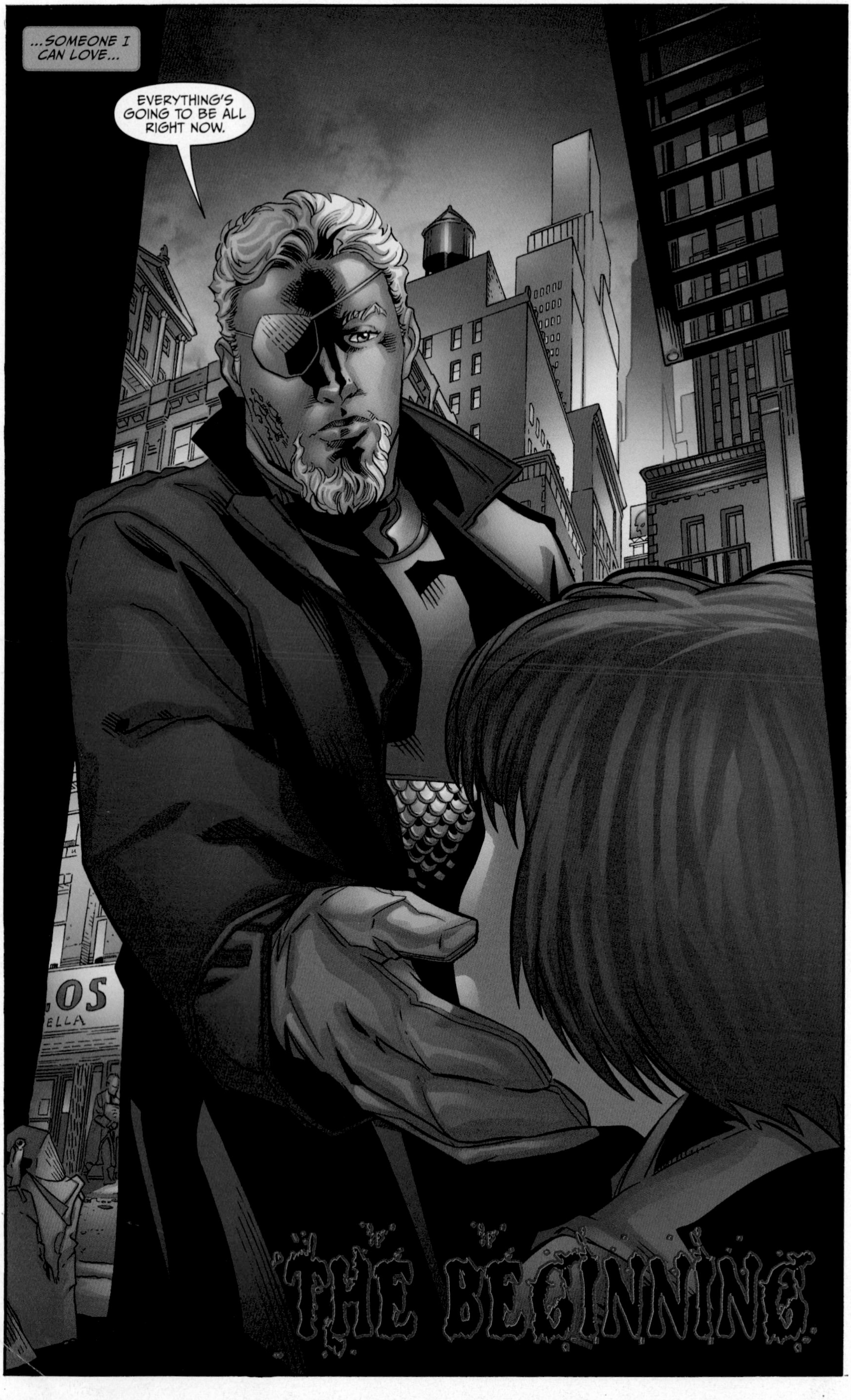
...SOMEONE I CAN LOVE...
EVERYTHING'S GOING TO BE ALL RIGHT NOW.
THE BEGINNING.

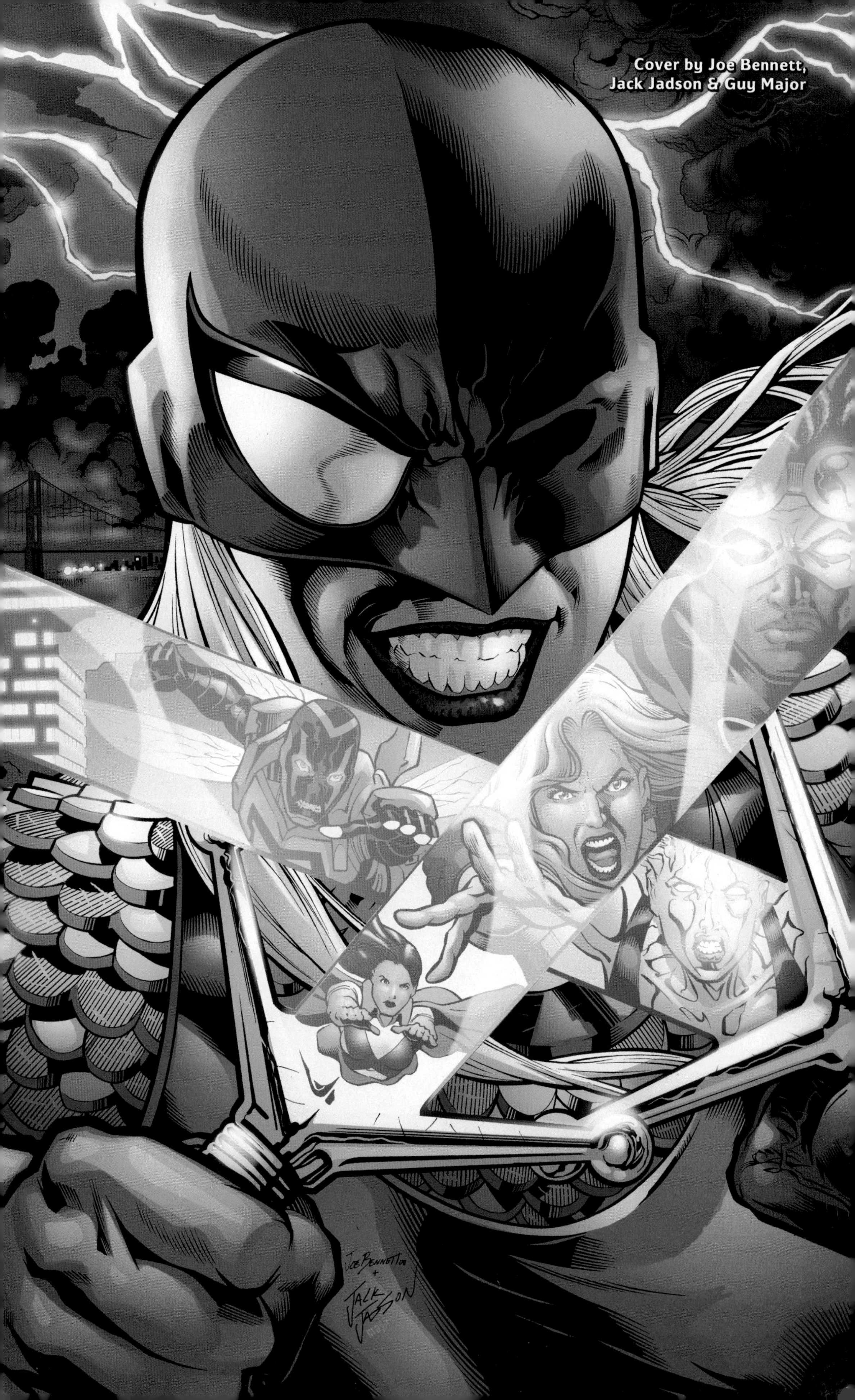

Cover by Joe Bennett,
Jack Jadson & Guy Major

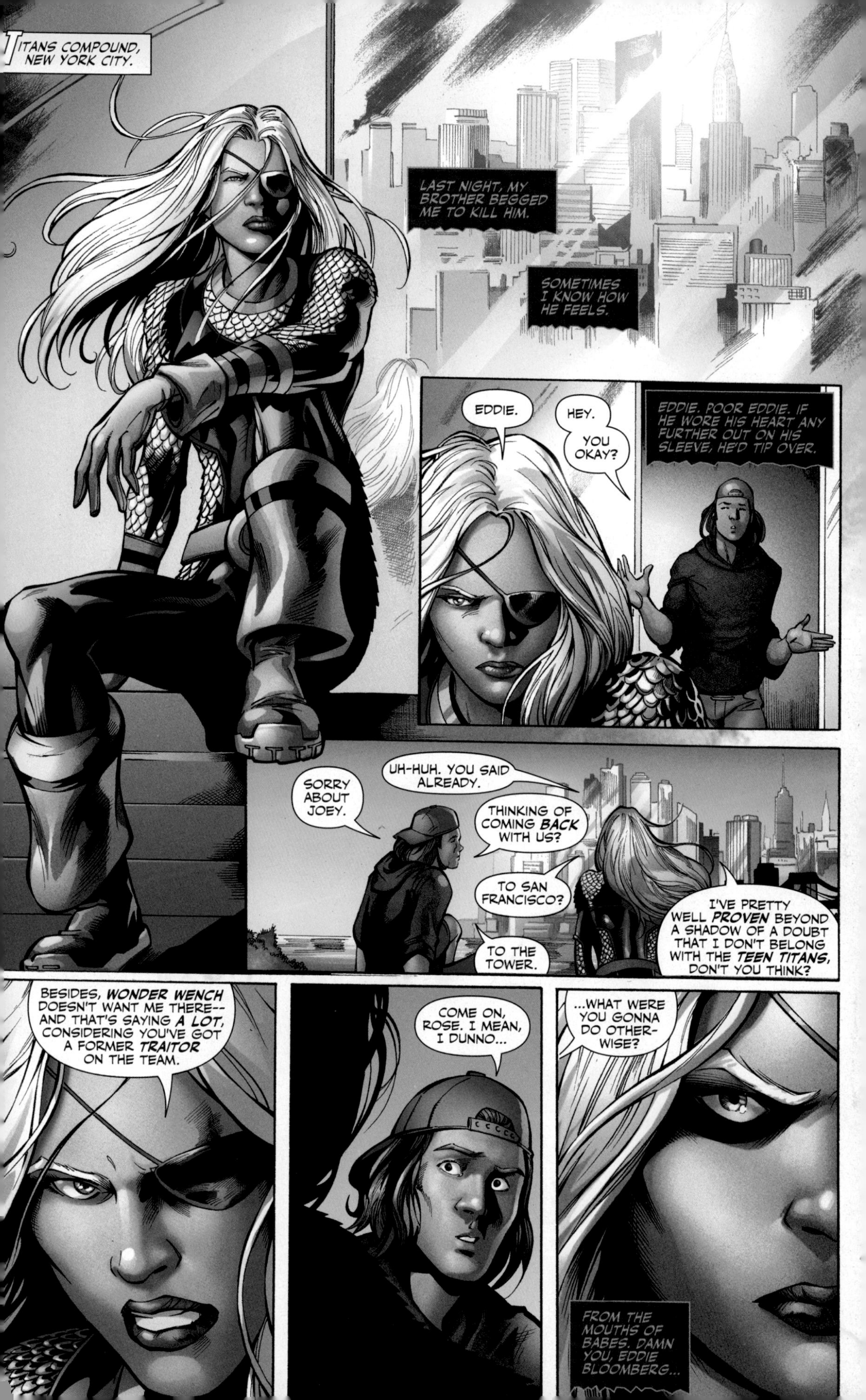
TITANS COMPOUND, NEW YORK CITY.
LAST NIGHT, MY BROTHER BEGGED ME TO KILL HIM.
SOMETIMES I KNOW HOW HE FEELS.
EDDIE.
HEY.
YOU OKAY?
EDDIE. POOR EDDIE. IF HE WORE HIS HEART ANY FURTHER OUT ON HIS SLEEVE, HE'D TIP OVER.
SORRY ABOUT JOEY.
UH-HUH. YOU SAID ALREADY.
THINKING OF COMING BACK WITH US?
TO SAN FRANCISCO?
TO THE TOWER.
I'VE PRETTY WELL PROVEN BEYOND A SHADOW OF A DOUBT THAT I DON'T BELONG WITH THE TEEN TITANS, DON'T YOU THINK?
BESIDES, WONDER WENCH DOESN'T WANT ME THERE-- AND THAT'S SAYING A LOT, CONSIDERING YOU'VE GOT A FORMER TRAITOR ON THE TEAM.
COME ON, ROSE. I MEAN, I DUNNO...
...WHAT WERE YOU GONNA DO OTHER-WISE?
FROM THE MOUTHS OF BABES. DAMN YOU, EDDIE BLOOMBERG...

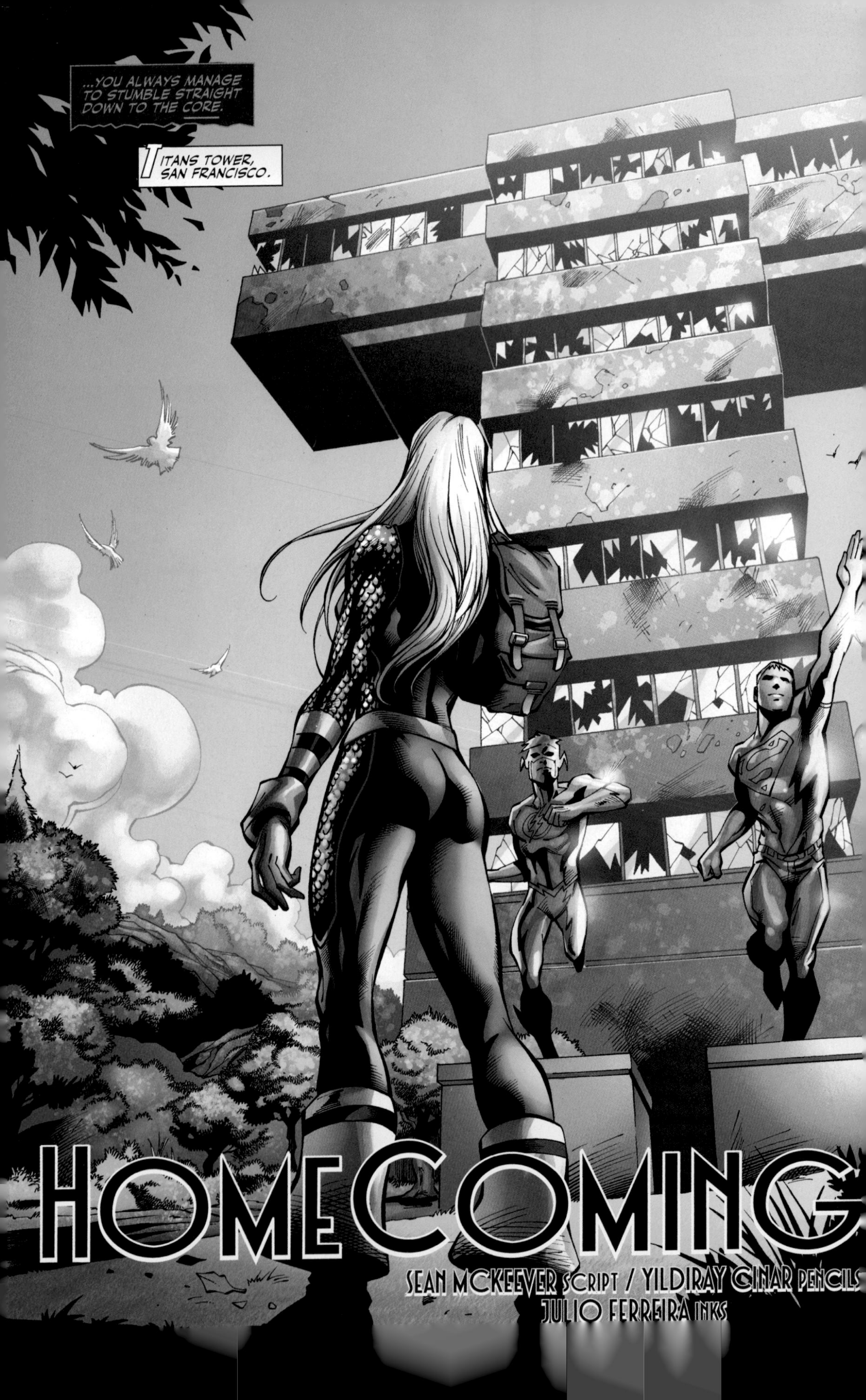
...YOU ALWAYS MANAGE TO STUMBLE STRAIGHT DOWN TO THE CORE.
TITANS TOWER, SAN FRANCISCO.
HOMECOMING
SEAN MCKEEVER SCRIPT / YILDIRAY CINAR PENCILS
JULIO FERREIRA INKS

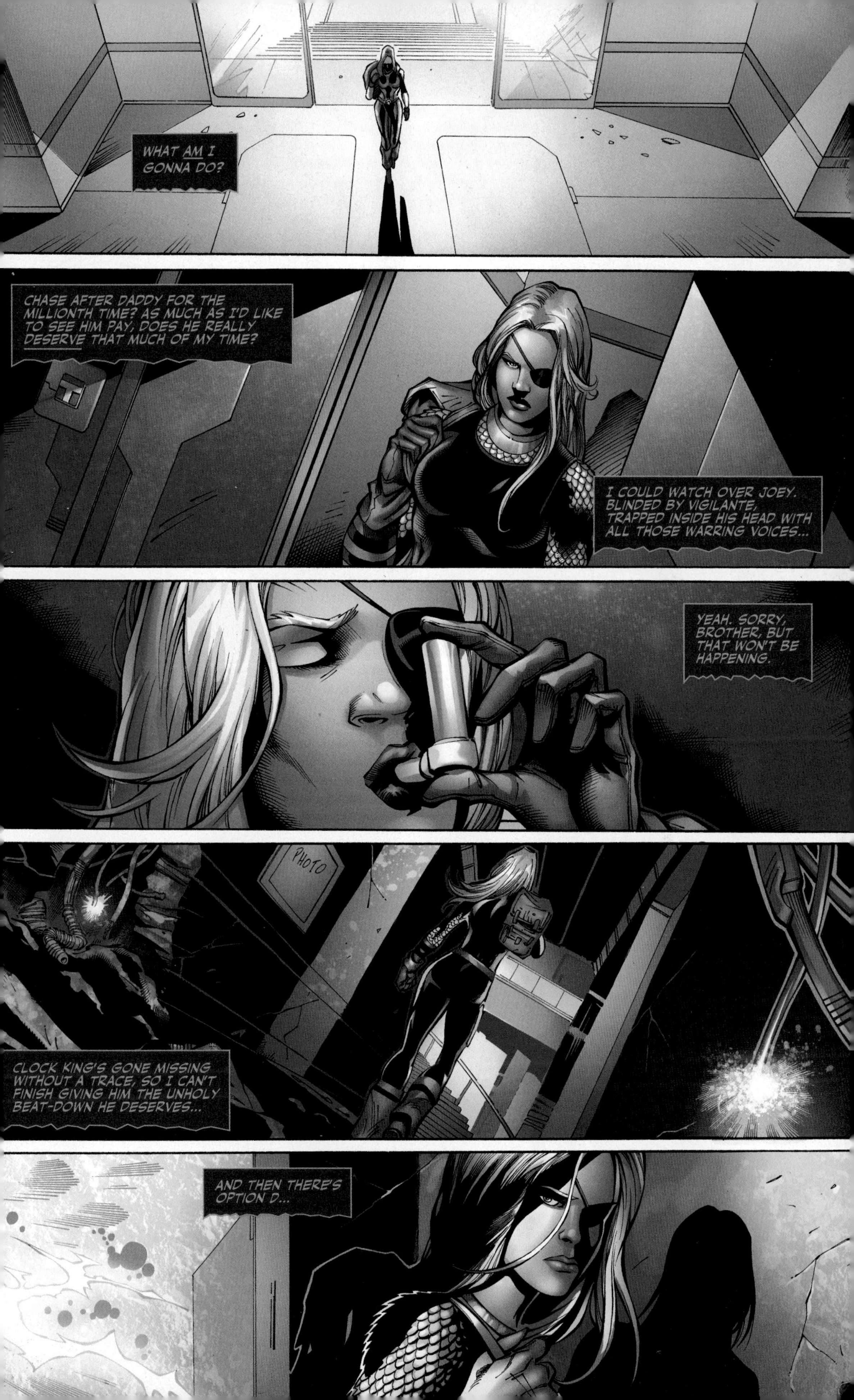
WHAT AM I GONNA DO?
CHASE AFTER DADDY FOR THE MILLIONTH TIME? AS MUCH AS I'D LIKE TO SEE HIM PAY, DOES HE REALLY DESERVE THAT MUCH OF MY TIME?
I COULD WATCH OVER JOEY. BLINDED BY VIGILANTE, TRAPPED INSIDE HIS HEAD WITH ALL THOSE WARRING VOICES...
YEAH. SORRY, BROTHER, BUT THAT WON'T BE HAPPENING.
PHOTO
CLOCK KING'S GONE MISSING WITHOUT A TRACE, SO I CAN'T FINISH GIVING HIM THE UNHOLY BEAT-DOWN HE DESERVES...
AND THEN THERE'S OPTION D...

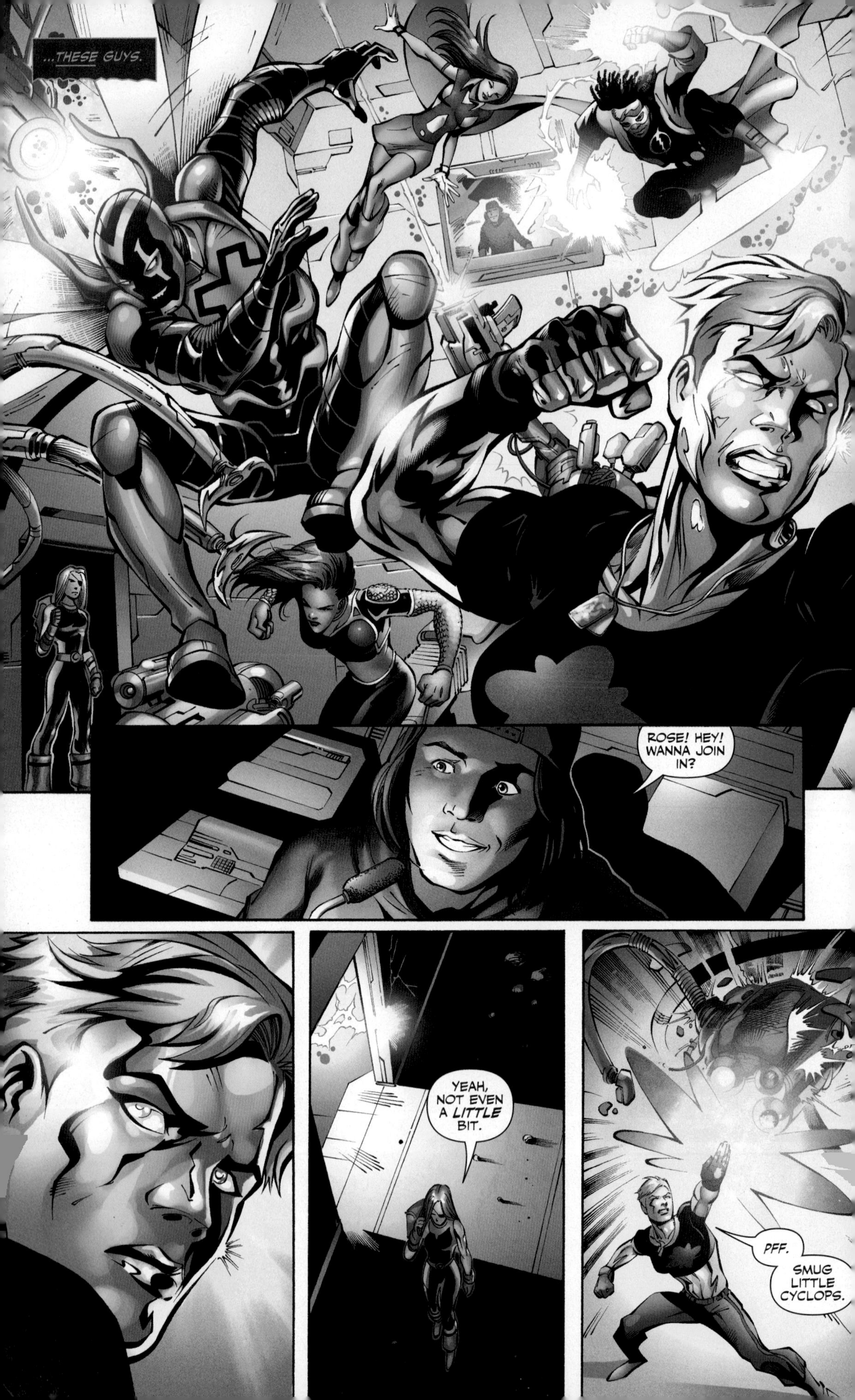
...THESE GUYS.
ROSE! HEY! WANNA JOIN IN?
YEAH, NOT EVEN A LITTLE BIT.
PFF.
SMUG LITTLE CYCLOPS.

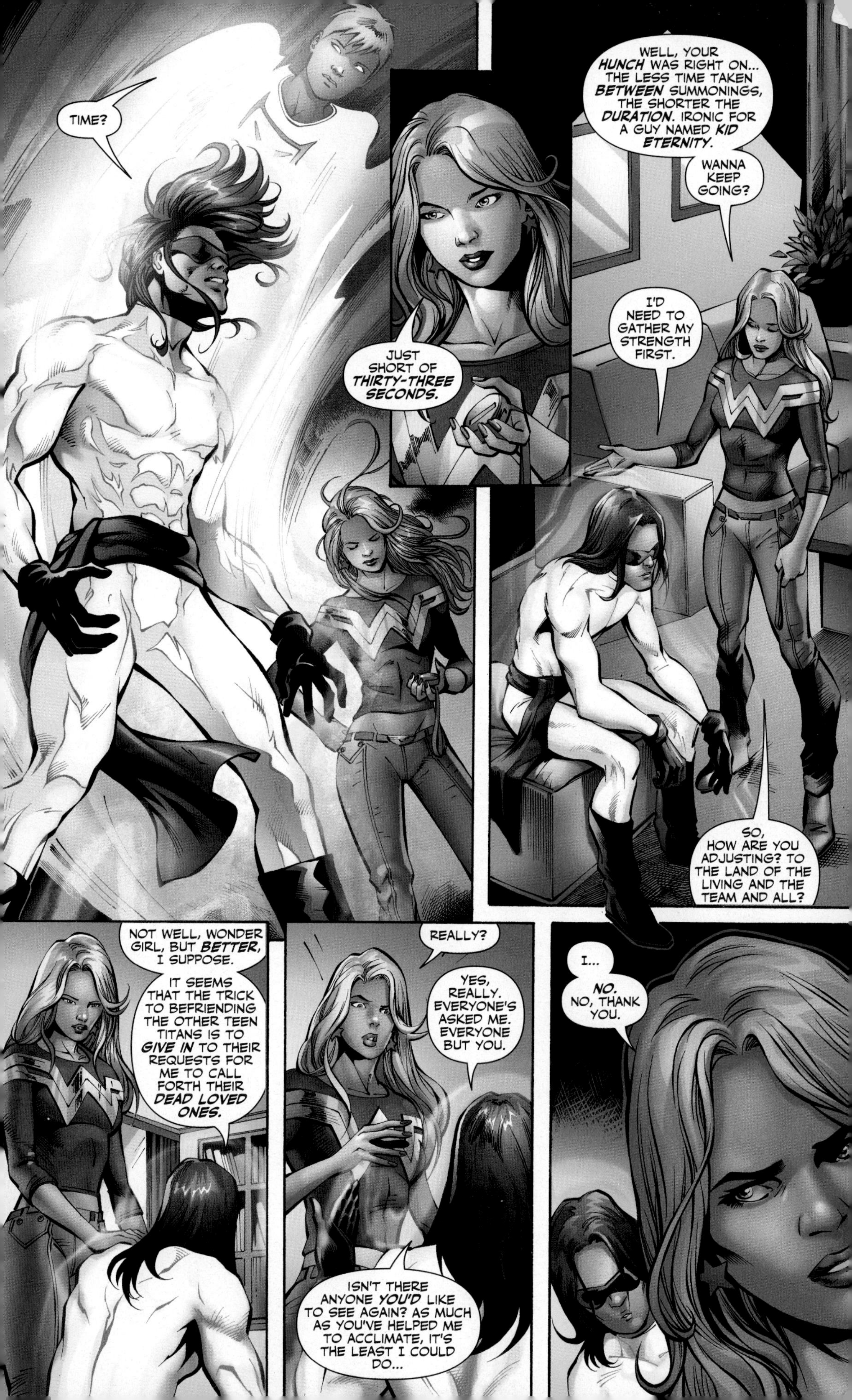
TIME?
JUST SHORT OF THIRTY-THREE SECONDS.
WELL, YOUR HUNCH WAS RIGHT ON... THE LESS TIME TAKEN BETWEEN SUMMONINGS, THE SHORTER THE DURATION. IRONIC FOR A GUY NAMED KID ETERNITY.
WANNA KEEP GOING?
I'D NEED TO GATHER MY STRENGTH FIRST.
SO, HOW ARE YOU ADJUSTING? TO THE LAND OF THE LIVING AND THE TEAM AND ALL?
NOT WELL, WONDER GIRL, BUT BETTER, I SUPPOSE.
IT SEEMS THAT THE TRICK TO BEFRIENDING THE OTHER TEEN TITANS IS TO GIVE IN TO THEIR REQUESTS FOR ME TO CALL FORTH THEIR DEAD LOVED ONES.
REALLY?
YES, REALLY. EVERYONE'S ASKED ME. EVERYONE BUT YOU.
ISN'T THERE ANYONE YOU'D LIKE TO SEE AGAIN? AS MUCH AS YOU'VE HELPED ME TO ACCLIMATE, IT'S THE LEAST I COULD DO...
I...
NO. NO, THANK YOU.

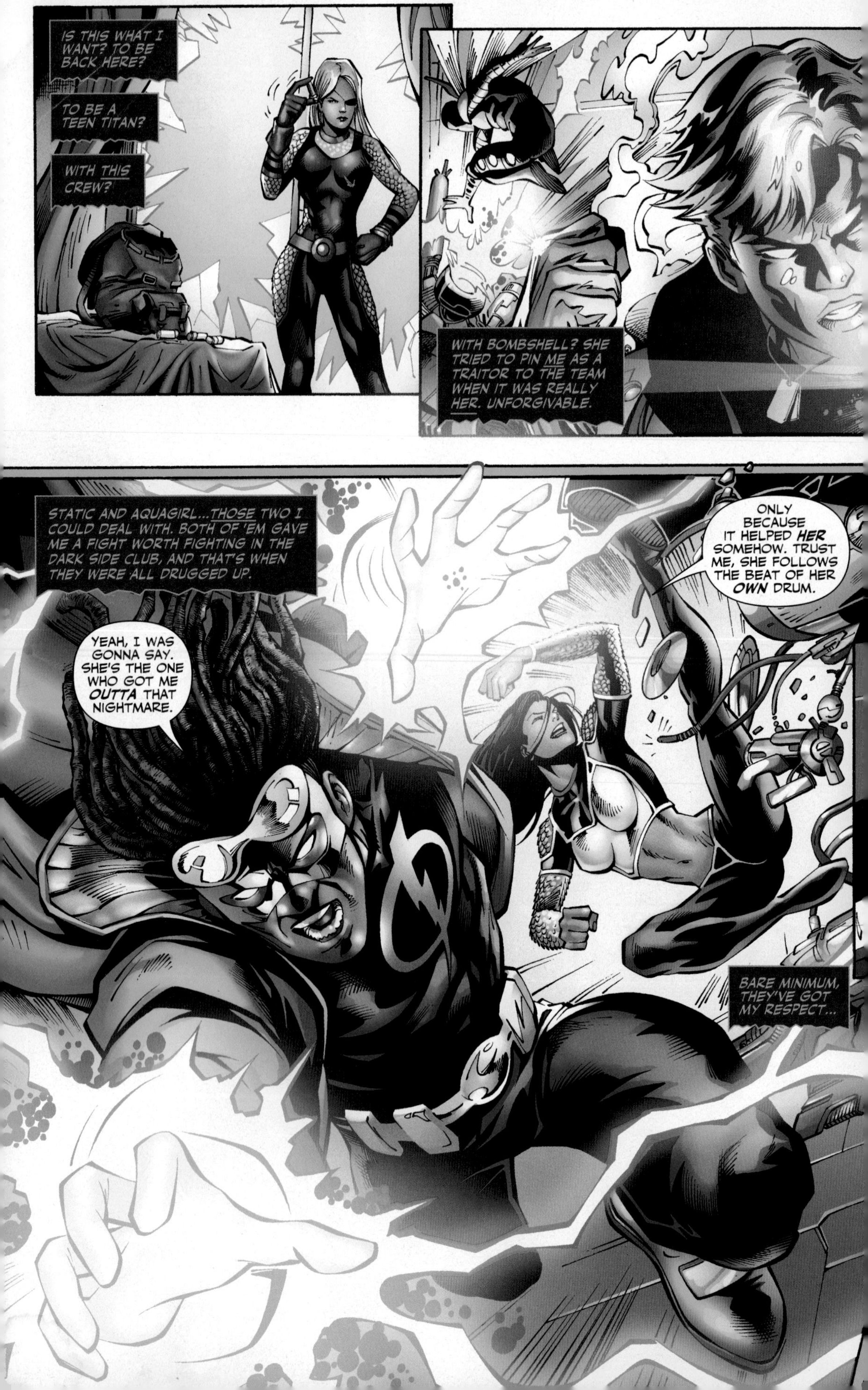

IS THIS WHAT I WANT? TO BE BACK HERE?
TO BE A TEEN TITAN?
WITH THIS CREW?
WITH BOMBSHELL? SHE TRIED TO PIN ME AS A TRAITOR TO THE TEAM WHEN IT WAS REALLY HER. UNFORGIVABLE.
STATIC AND AQUAGIRL...THOSE TWO I COULD DEAL WITH. BOTH OF 'EM GAVE ME A FIGHT WORTH FIGHTING IN THE DARK SIDE CLUB, AND THAT'S WHEN THEY WERE ALL DRUGGED UP.
ONLY BECAUSE IT HELPED HER SOMEHOW. TRUST ME, SHE FOLLOWS THE BEAT OF HER OWN DRUM.
YEAH, I WAS GONNA SAY. SHE'S THE ONE WHO GOT ME OUTTA THAT NIGHTMARE.
BARE MINIMUM, THEY'VE GOT MY RESPECT...

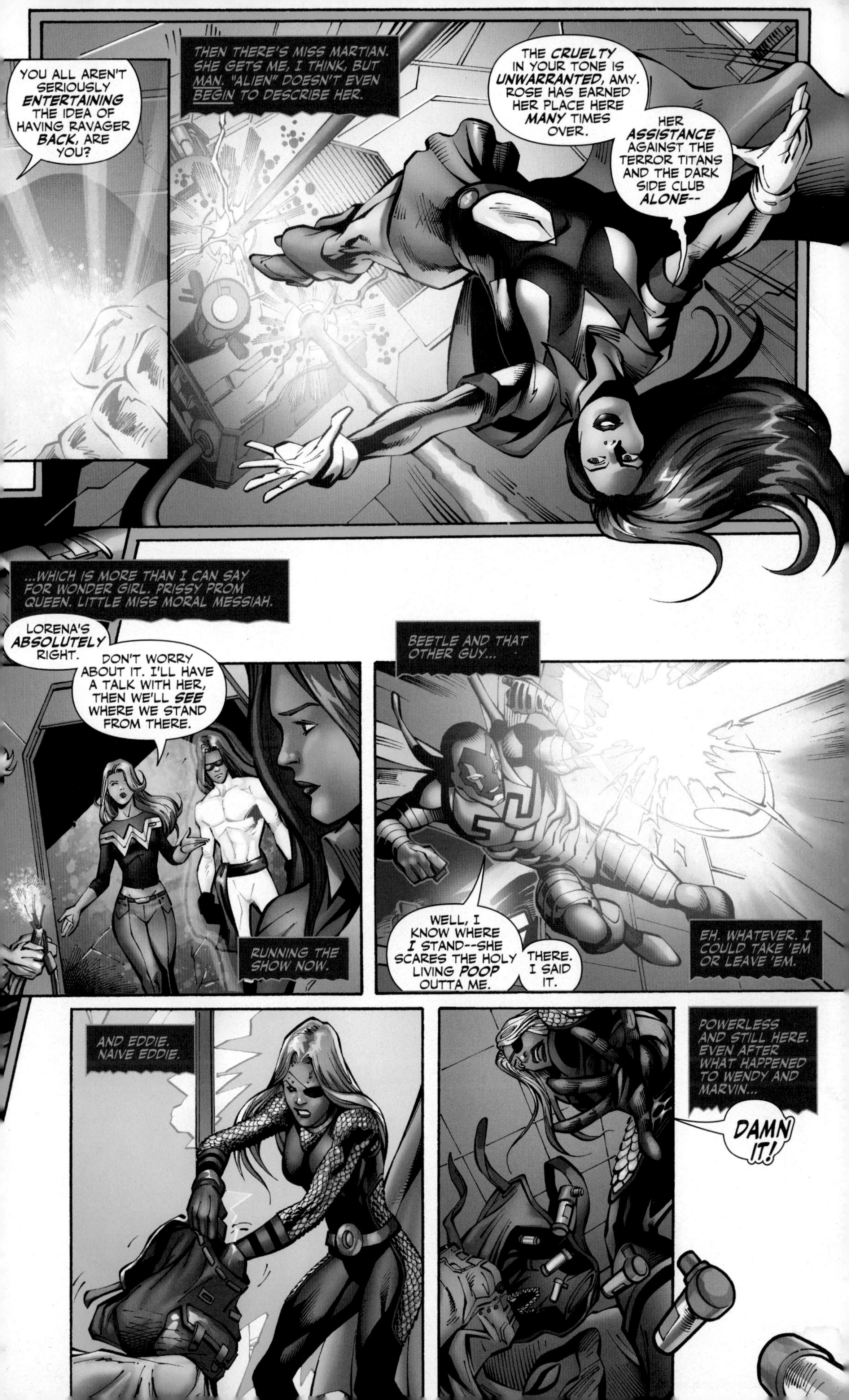

YOU ALL AREN'T SERIOUSLY ENTERTAINING THE IDEA OF HAVING RAVAGER BACK, ARE YOU?
THEN THERE'S MISS MARTIAN. SHE GETS ME, I THINK, BUT MAN. "ALIEN" DOESN'T EVEN BEGIN TO DESCRIBE HER.
THE CRUELTY IN YOUR TONE IS UNWARRANTED, AMY. ROSE HAS EARNED HER PLACE HERE MANY TIMES OVER.
HER ASSISTANCE AGAINST THE TERROR TITANS AND THE DARK SIDE CLUB ALONE--
...WHICH IS MORE THAN I CAN SAY FOR WONDER GIRL. PRISSY PROM QUEEN. LITTLE MISS MORAL MESSIAH.
LORENA'S ABSOLUTELY RIGHT.
DON'T WORRY ABOUT IT. I'LL HAVE A TALK WITH HER, THEN WE'LL SEE WHERE WE STAND FROM THERE.
RUNNING THE SHOW NOW.
BEETLE AND THAT OTHER GUY...
WELL, I KNOW WHERE I STAND--SHE SCARES THE HOLY LIVING POOP OUTTA ME.
THERE. I SAID IT.
EH. WHATEVER. I COULD TAKE 'EM OR LEAVE 'EM.
AND EDDIE. NAIVE EDDIE.
POWERLESS AND STILL HERE. EVEN AFTER WHAT HAPPENED TO WENDY AND MARVIN...
DAMN IT!

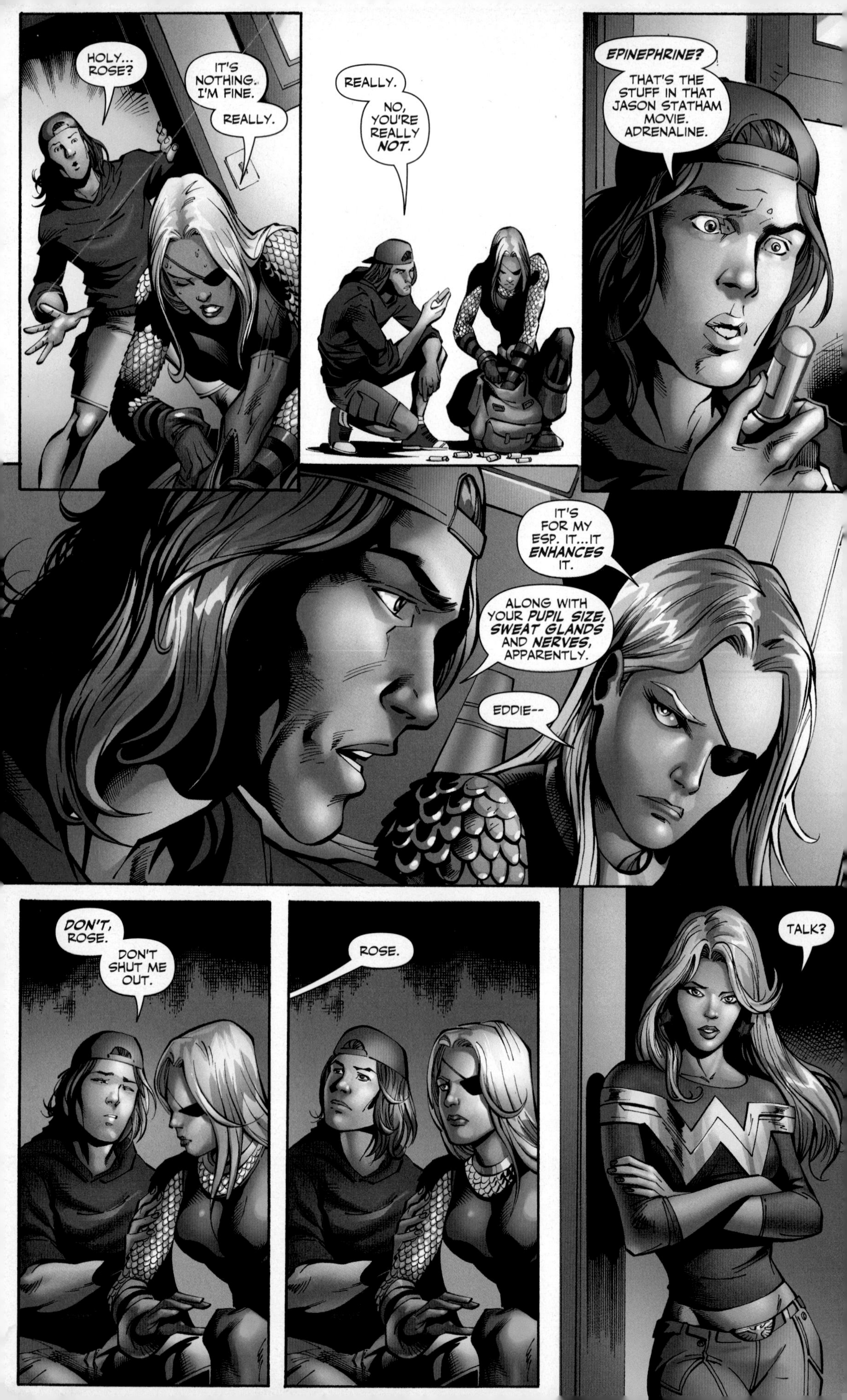

HOLY... ROSE?
IT'S NOTHING. I'M FINE.
REALLY.
REALLY.
NO, YOU'RE REALLY NOT.
EPINEPHRINE?
THAT'S THE STUFF IN THAT JASON STATHAM MOVIE. ADRENALINE.
IT'S FOR MY ESP. IT...IT ENHANCES IT.
ALONG WITH YOUR PUPIL SIZE, SWEAT GLANDS AND NERVES, APPARENTLY.
EDDIE--
DON'T, ROSE.
DON'T SHUT ME OUT.
ROSE.
TALK?

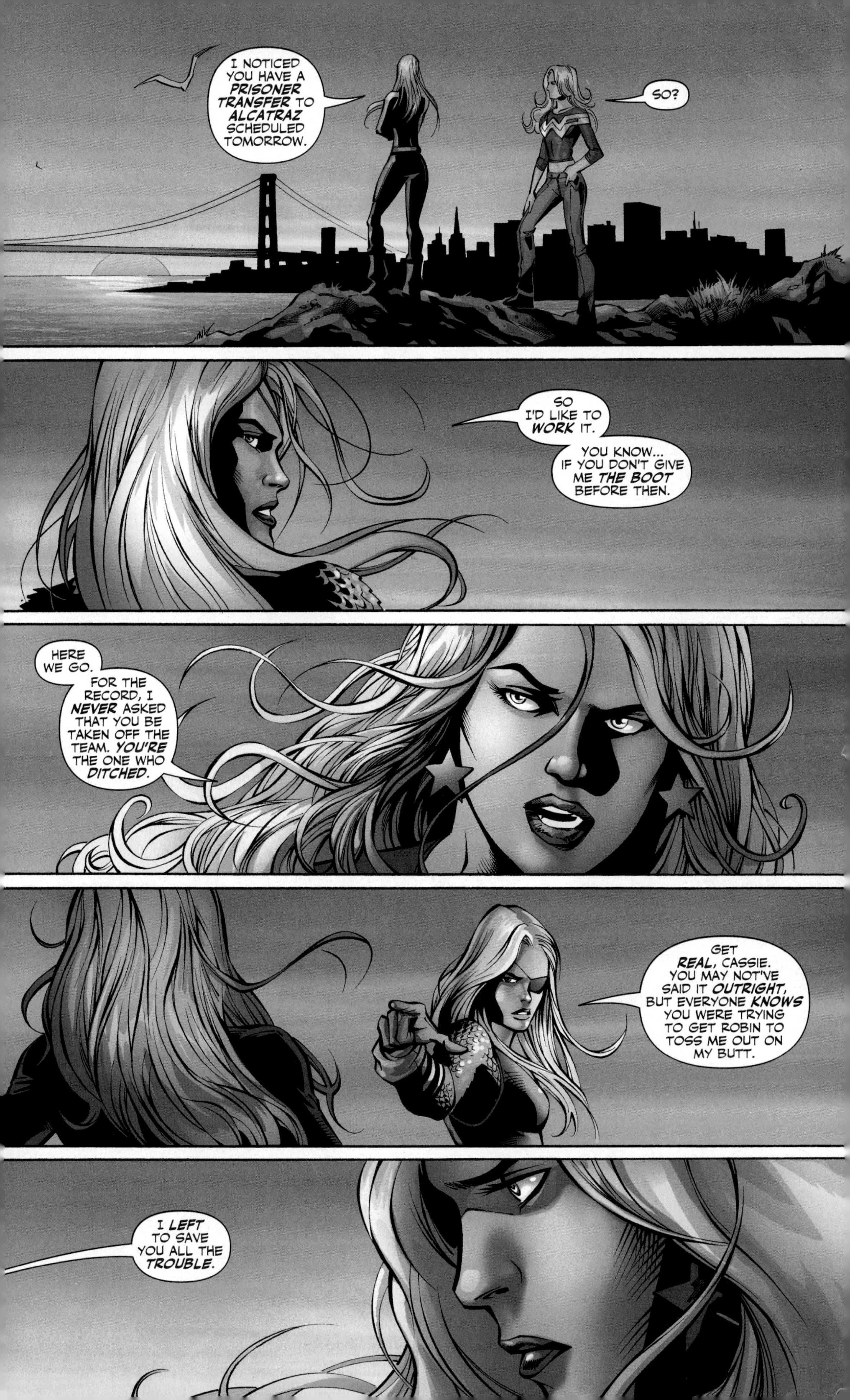
I NOTICED YOU HAVE A PRISONER TRANSFER TO ALCATRAZ SCHEDULED TOMORROW.
SO?
SO I'D LIKE TO WORK IT.
YOU KNOW... IF YOU DON'T GIVE ME THE BOOT BEFORE THEN.
HERE WE GO.
FOR THE RECORD, I NEVER ASKED THAT YOU BE TAKEN OFF THE TEAM. YOU'RE THE ONE WHO DITCHED.
GET REAL, CASSIE. YOU MAY NOT'VE SAID IT OUTRIGHT, BUT EVERYONE KNOWS YOU WERE TRYING TO GET ROBIN TO TOSS ME OUT ON MY BUTT.
I LEFT TO SAVE YOU ALL THE TROUBLE.

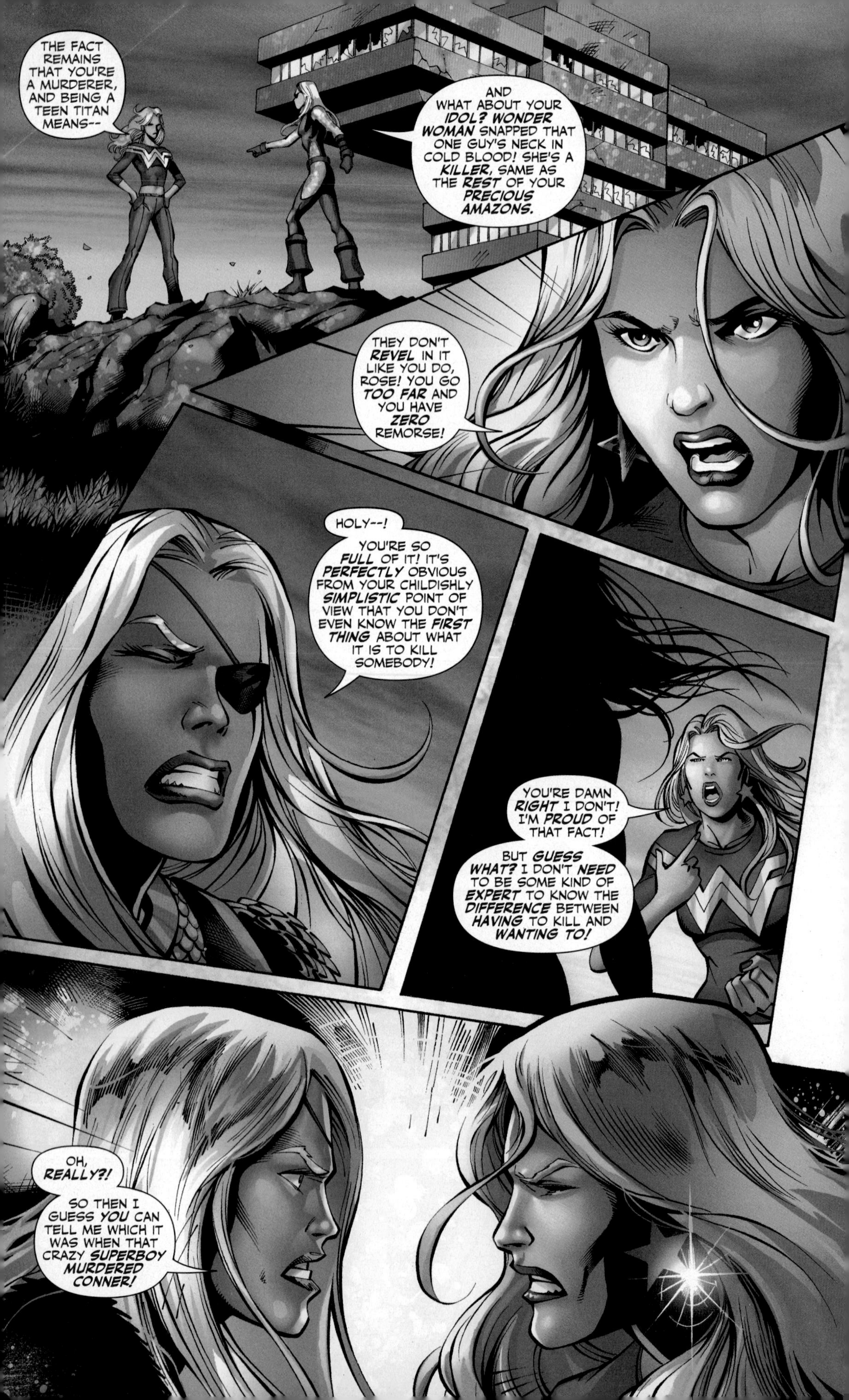
THE FACT REMAINS THAT YOU'RE A MURDERER, AND BEING A TEEN TITAN MEANS--
AND WHAT ABOUT YOUR IDOL? WONDER WOMAN SNAPPED THAT ONE GUY'S NECK IN COLD BLOOD! SHE'S A KILLER, SAME AS THE REST OF YOUR PRECIOUS AMAZONS.
THEY DON'T REVEL IN IT LIKE YOU DO, ROSE! YOU GO TOO FAR AND YOU HAVE ZERO REMORSE!
HOLY--!
YOU'RE SO FULL OF IT! IT'S PERFECTLY OBVIOUS FROM YOUR CHILDISHLY SIMPLISTIC POINT OF VIEW THAT YOU DON'T EVEN KNOW THE FIRST THING ABOUT WHAT IT IS TO KILL SOMEBODY!
YOU'RE DAMN RIGHT I DON'T! I'M PROUD OF THAT FACT!
BUT GUESS WHAT? I DON'T NEED TO BE SOME KIND OF EXPERT TO KNOW THE DIFFERENCE BETWEEN HAVING TO KILL AND WANTING TO!
OH, REALLY?!
SO THEN I GUESS YOU CAN TELL ME WHICH IT WAS WHEN THAT CRAZY SUPERBOY MURDERED CONNER!

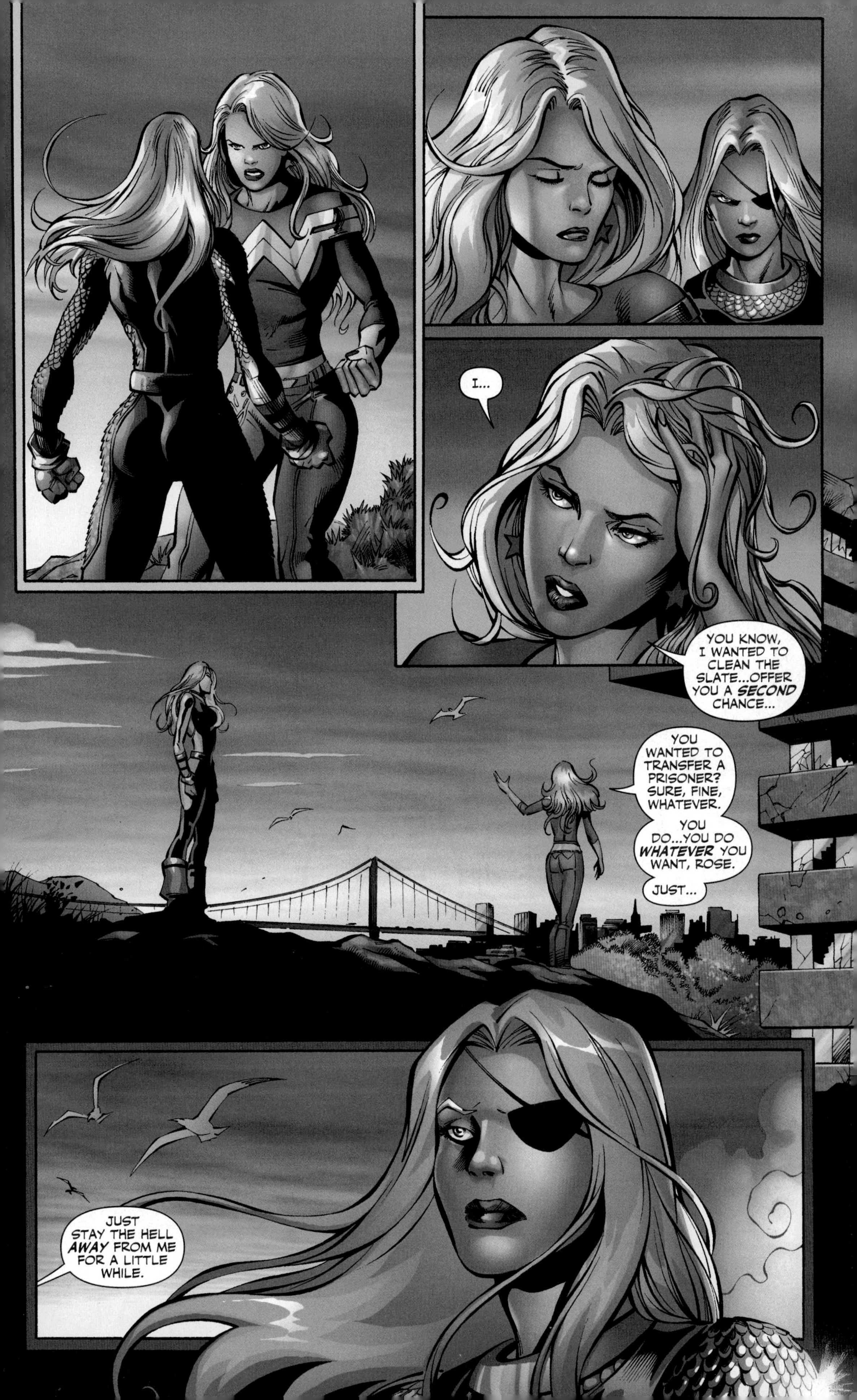

I...
YOU KNOW, I WANTED TO CLEAN THE SLATE...OFFER YOU A **SECOND** CHANCE...
YOU WANTED TO TRANSFER A PRISONER? SURE, FINE, WHATEVER.
YOU DO...YOU DO **WHATEVER** YOU WANT, ROSE.
JUST...
JUST STAY THE HELL **AWAY** FROM ME FOR A LITTLE WHILE.

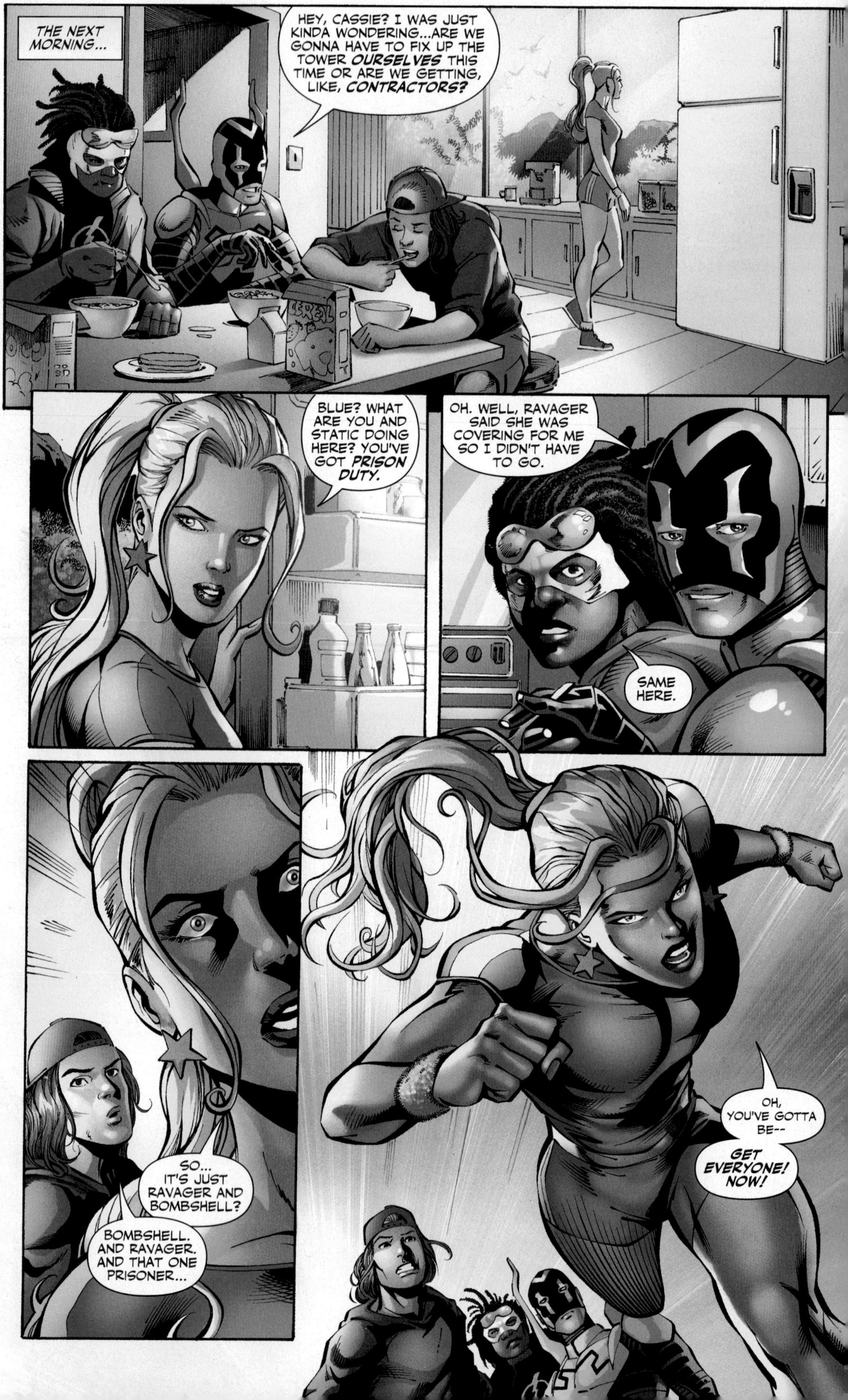
THE NEXT MORNING...
HEY, CASSIE? I WAS JUST KINDA WONDERING...ARE WE GONNA HAVE TO FIX UP THE TOWER OURSELVES THIS TIME OR ARE WE GETTING, LIKE, CONTRACTORS?
BLUE? WHAT ARE YOU AND STATIC DOING HERE? YOU'VE GOT PRISON DUTY.
OH. WELL, RAVAGER SAID SHE WAS COVERING FOR ME SO I DIDN'T HAVE TO GO.
SAME HERE.
SO... IT'S JUST RAVAGER AND BOMBSHELL?
BOMBSHELL. AND RAVAGER. AND THAT ONE PRISONER...
OH, YOU'VE GOTTA BE--
GET EVERYONE! NOW!

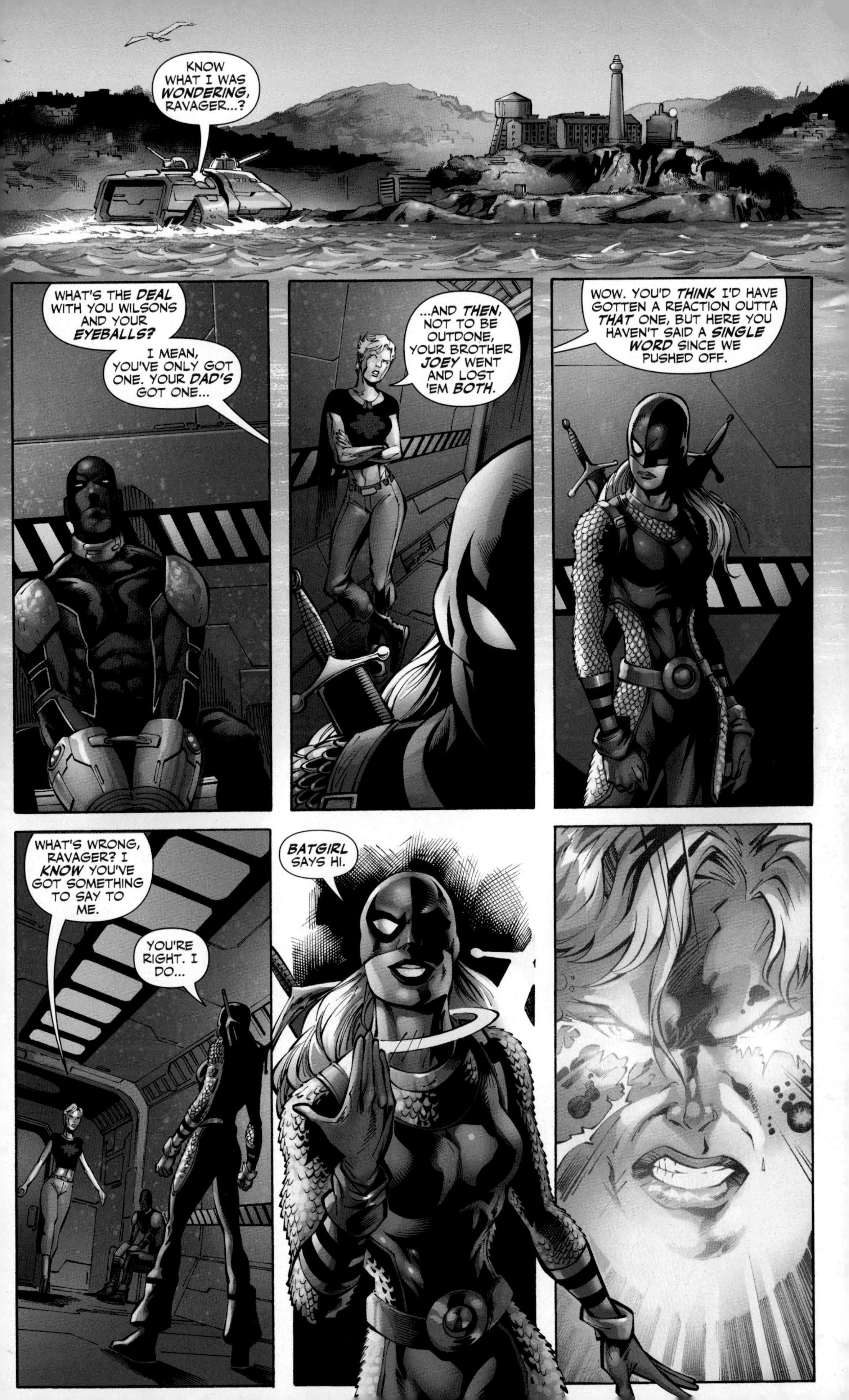
KNOW WHAT I WAS *WONDERING*, RAVAGER...?
WHAT'S THE *DEAL* WITH YOU WILSONS AND YOUR *EYEBALLS?*
I MEAN, YOU'VE ONLY GOT ONE. YOUR *DAD'S* GOT ONE...
...AND *THEN*, NOT TO BE OUTDONE, YOUR BROTHER *JOEY* WENT AND LOST 'EM *BOTH*.
WOW. YOU'D *THINK* I'D HAVE GOTTEN A REACTION OUTTA *THAT* ONE, BUT HERE YOU HAVEN'T SAID A *SINGLE WORD* SINCE WE PUSHED OFF.
WHAT'S WRONG, RAVAGER? I *KNOW* YOU'VE GOT SOMETHING TO SAY TO ME.
YOU'RE RIGHT. I DO...
BATGIRL SAYS HI.

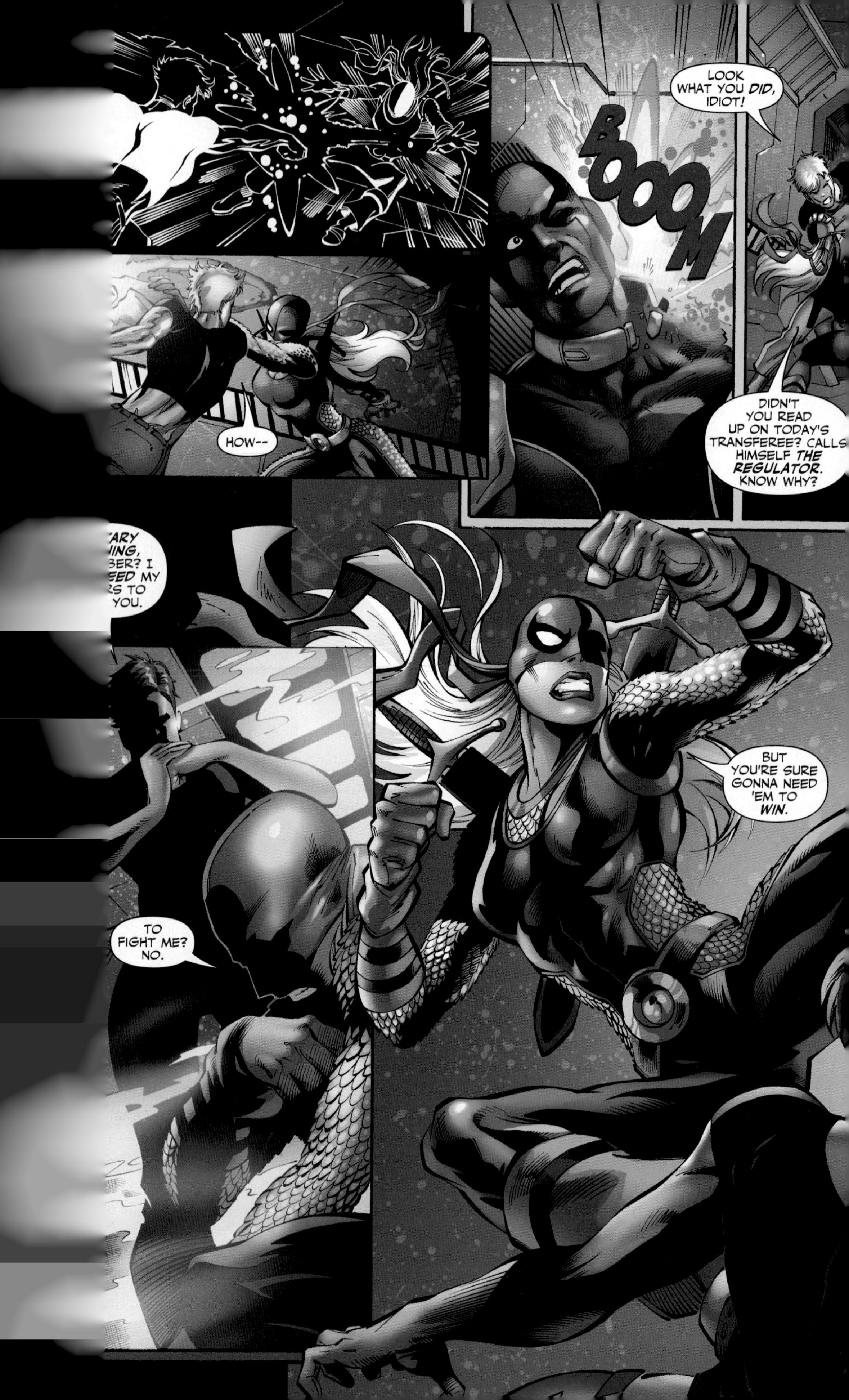
HOW--
LOOK WHAT YOU DID, IDIOT!
BOOOM
DIDN'T YOU READ UP ON TODAY'S TRANSFEREE? CALLS HIMSELF THE REGULATOR. KNOW WHY?
TARY
ING,
BER? I
EED MY
S TO
YOU.
BUT YOU'RE SURE GONNA NEED 'EM TO WIN.
TO FIGHT ME? NO.

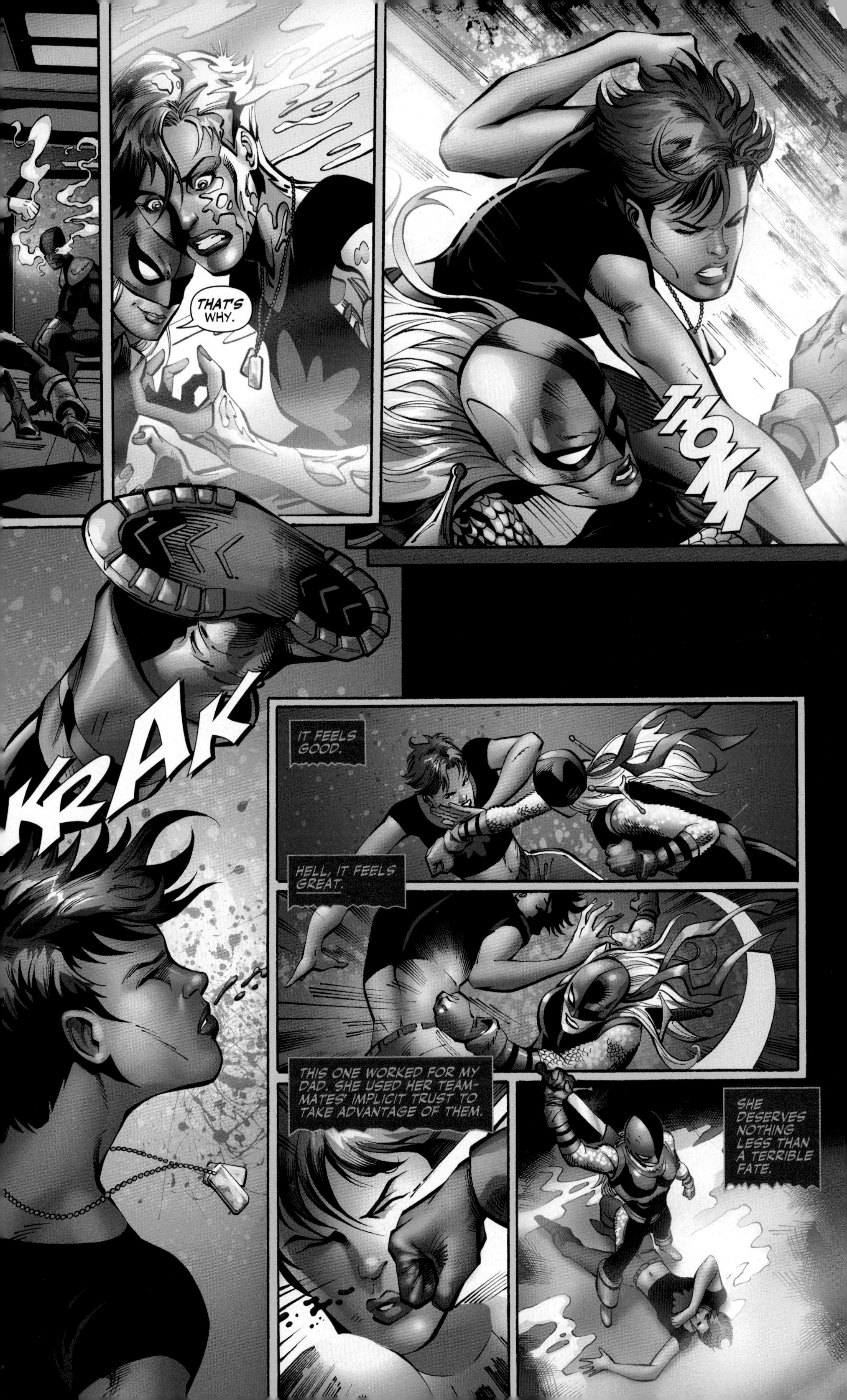
THAT'S WHY.
THONK
KRAK
IT FEELS GOOD.
HELL, IT FEELS GREAT.
THIS ONE WORKED FOR MY DAD. SHE USED HER TEAM-MATES' IMPLICIT TRUST TO TAKE ADVANTAGE OF THEM.
SHE DESERVES NOTHING LESS THAN A TERRIBLE FATE.

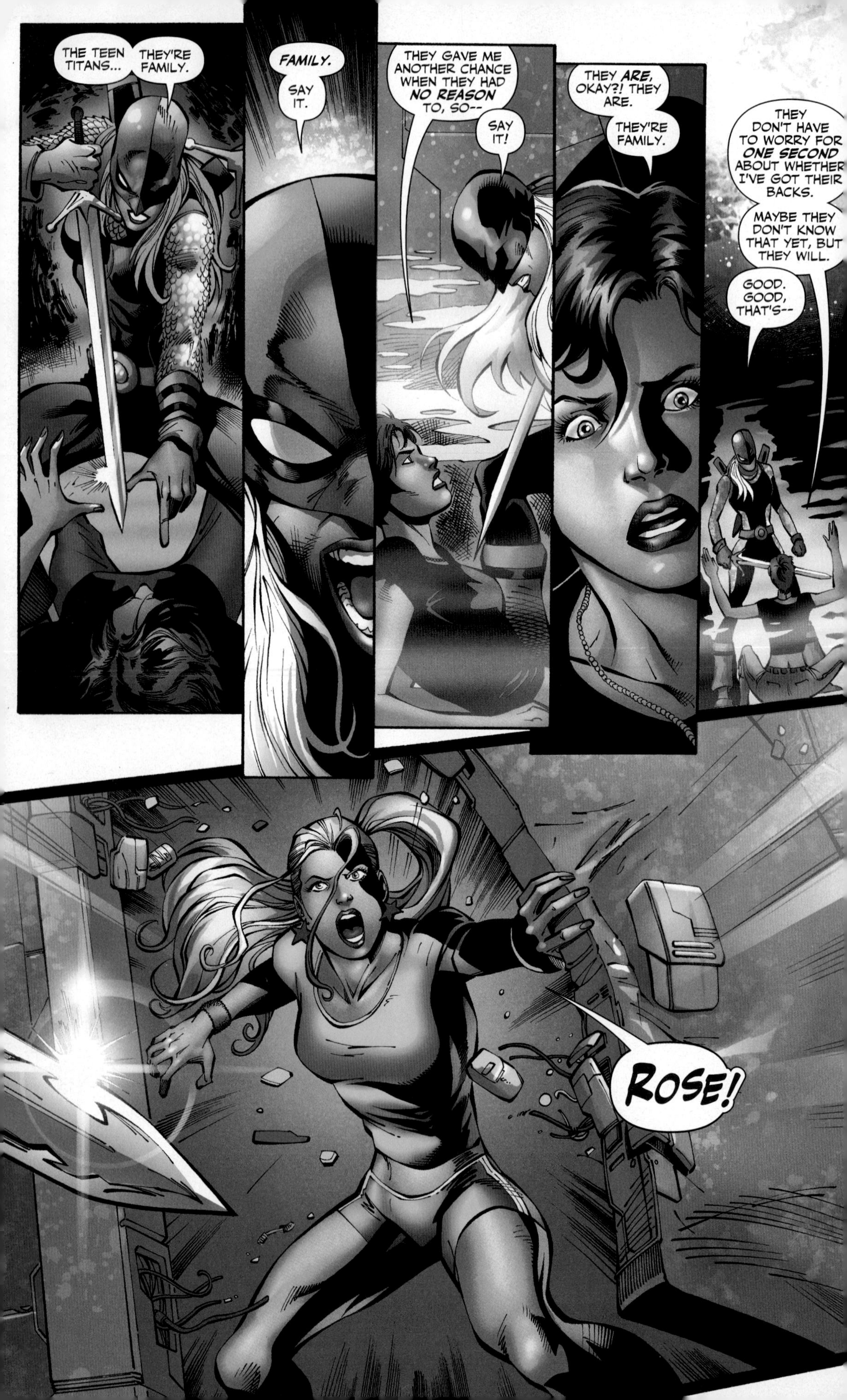

THE TEEN TITANS...
THEY'RE FAMILY.
FAMILY.
SAY IT.
THEY GAVE ME ANOTHER CHANCE WHEN THEY HAD NO REASON TO, SO--
SAY IT!
THEY ARE, OKAY?! THEY ARE.
THEY'RE FAMILY.
THEY DON'T HAVE TO WORRY FOR ONE SECOND ABOUT WHETHER I'VE GOT THEIR BACKS.
MAYBE THEY DON'T KNOW THAT YET, BUT THEY WILL.
GOOD. GOOD, THAT'S--
ROSE!

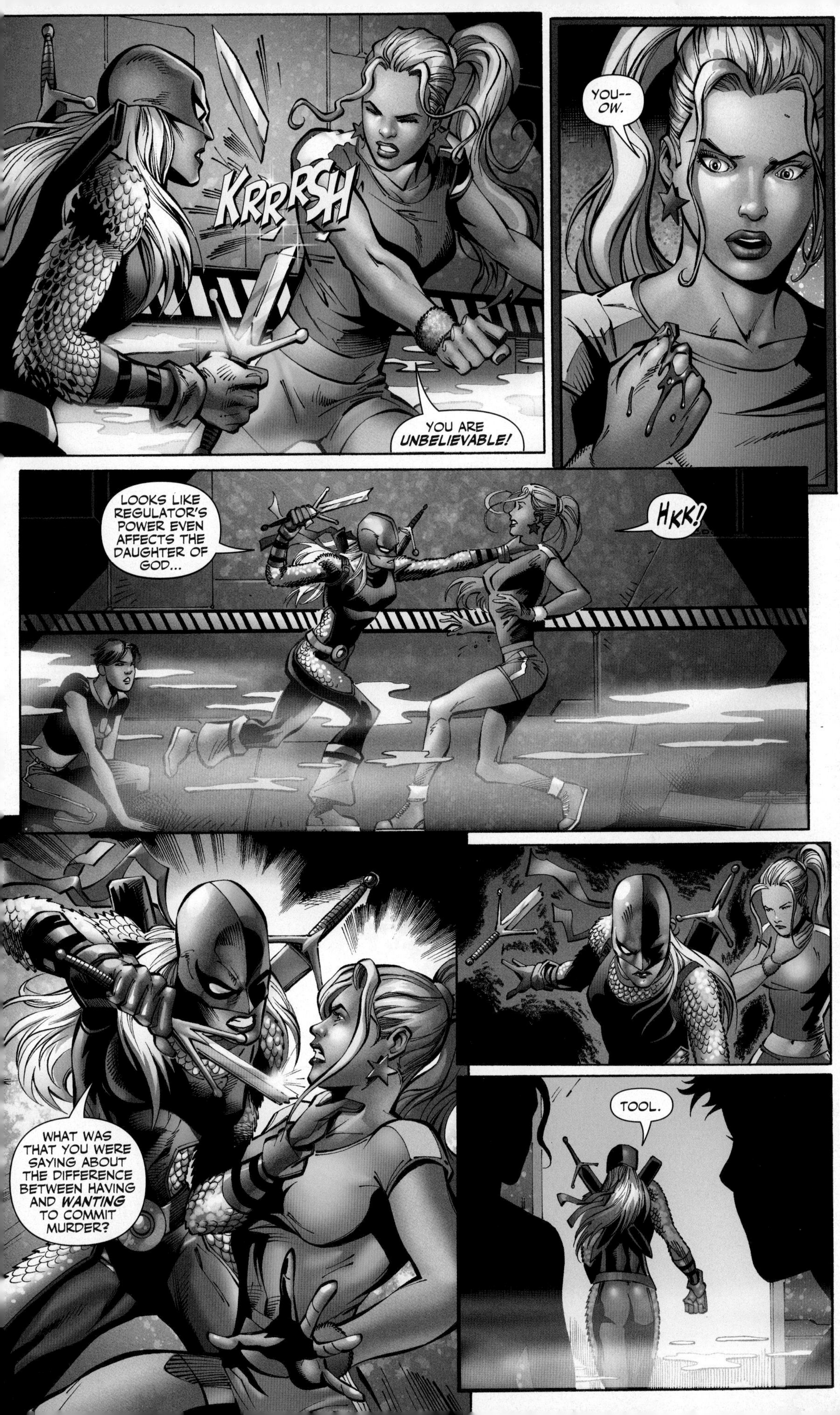
KRRRSH
YOU ARE UNBELIEVABLE!
YOU-- OW.
LOOKS LIKE REGULATOR'S POWER EVEN AFFECTS THE DAUGHTER OF GOD...
HKK!
WHAT WAS THAT YOU WERE SAYING ABOUT THE DIFFERENCE BETWEEN HAVING AND WANTING TO COMMIT MURDER?
TOOL.

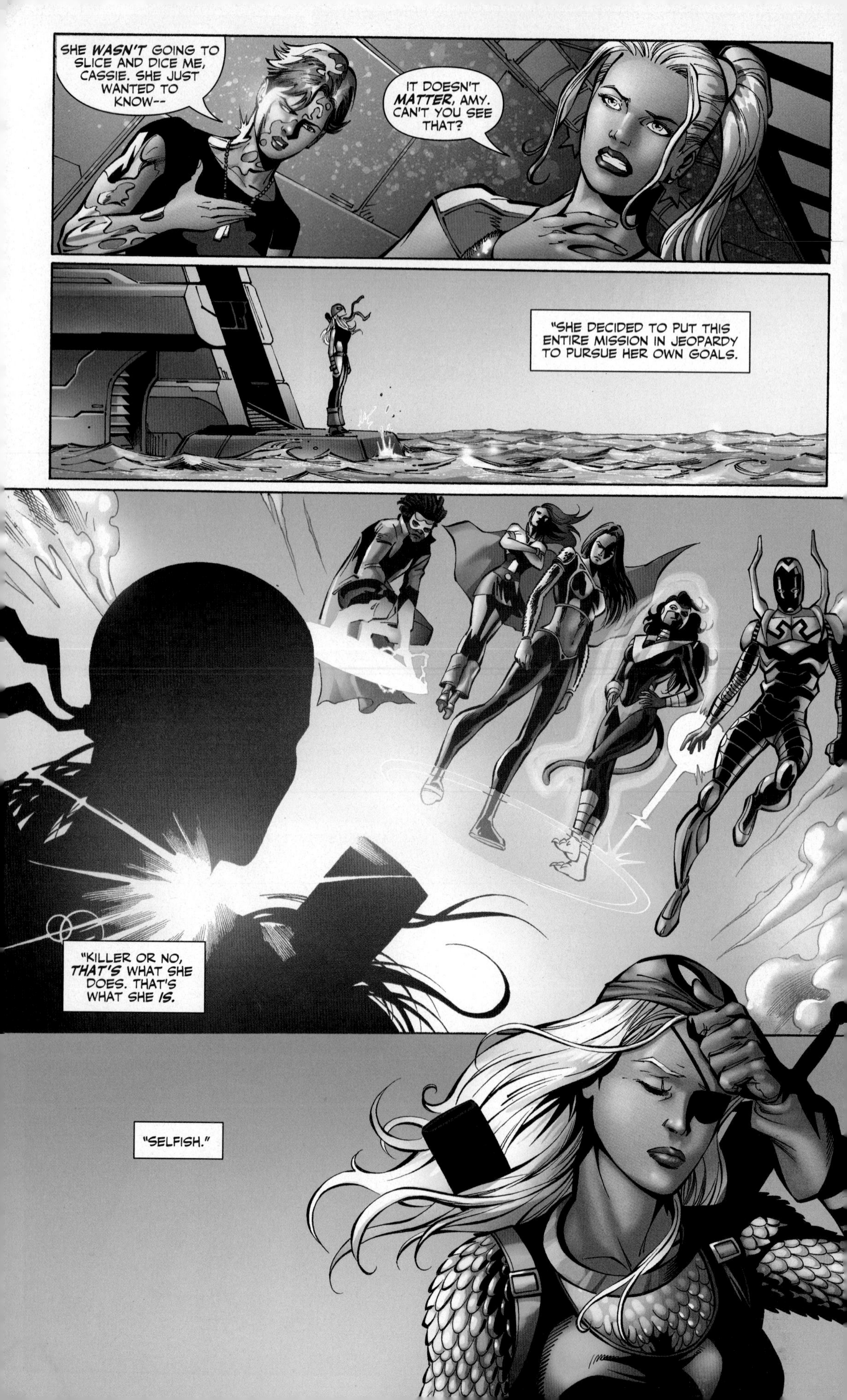
SHE *WASN'T* GOING TO SLICE AND DICE ME, CASSIE. SHE JUST WANTED TO KNOW--
IT DOESN'T *MATTER*, AMY. CAN'T YOU SEE THAT?
"SHE DECIDED TO PUT THIS ENTIRE MISSION IN JEOPARDY TO PURSUE HER OWN GOALS.
"KILLER OR NO, *THAT'S* WHAT SHE DOES. THAT'S WHAT SHE *IS*.
"SELFISH."

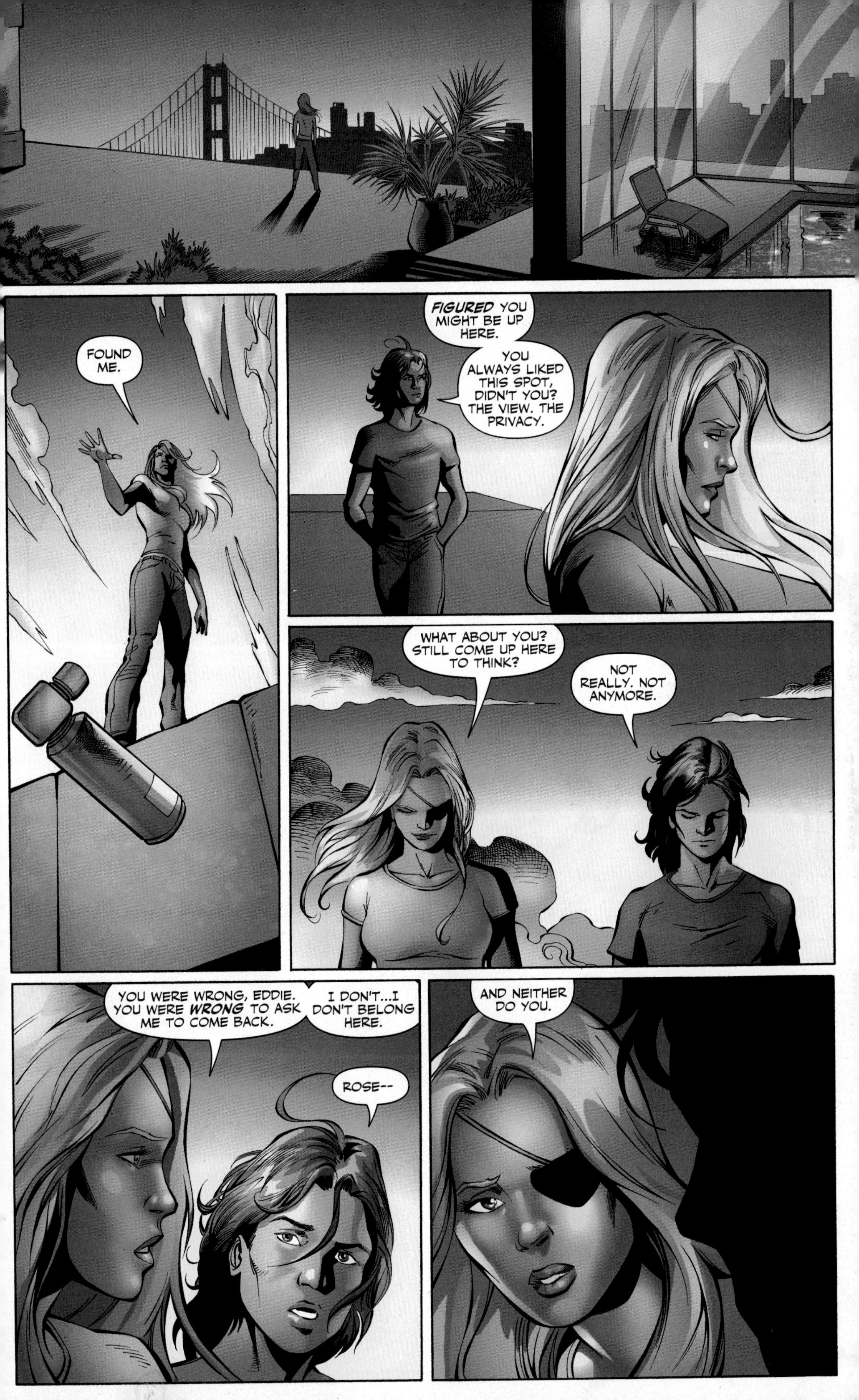
FOUND ME.
FIGURED YOU MIGHT BE UP HERE.
YOU ALWAYS LIKED THIS SPOT, DIDN'T YOU? THE VIEW. THE PRIVACY.
WHAT ABOUT YOU? STILL COME UP HERE TO THINK?
NOT REALLY. NOT ANYMORE.
YOU WERE WRONG, EDDIE. YOU WERE WRONG TO ASK ME TO COME BACK.
I DON'T...I DON'T BELONG HERE.
ROSE--
AND NEITHER DO YOU.

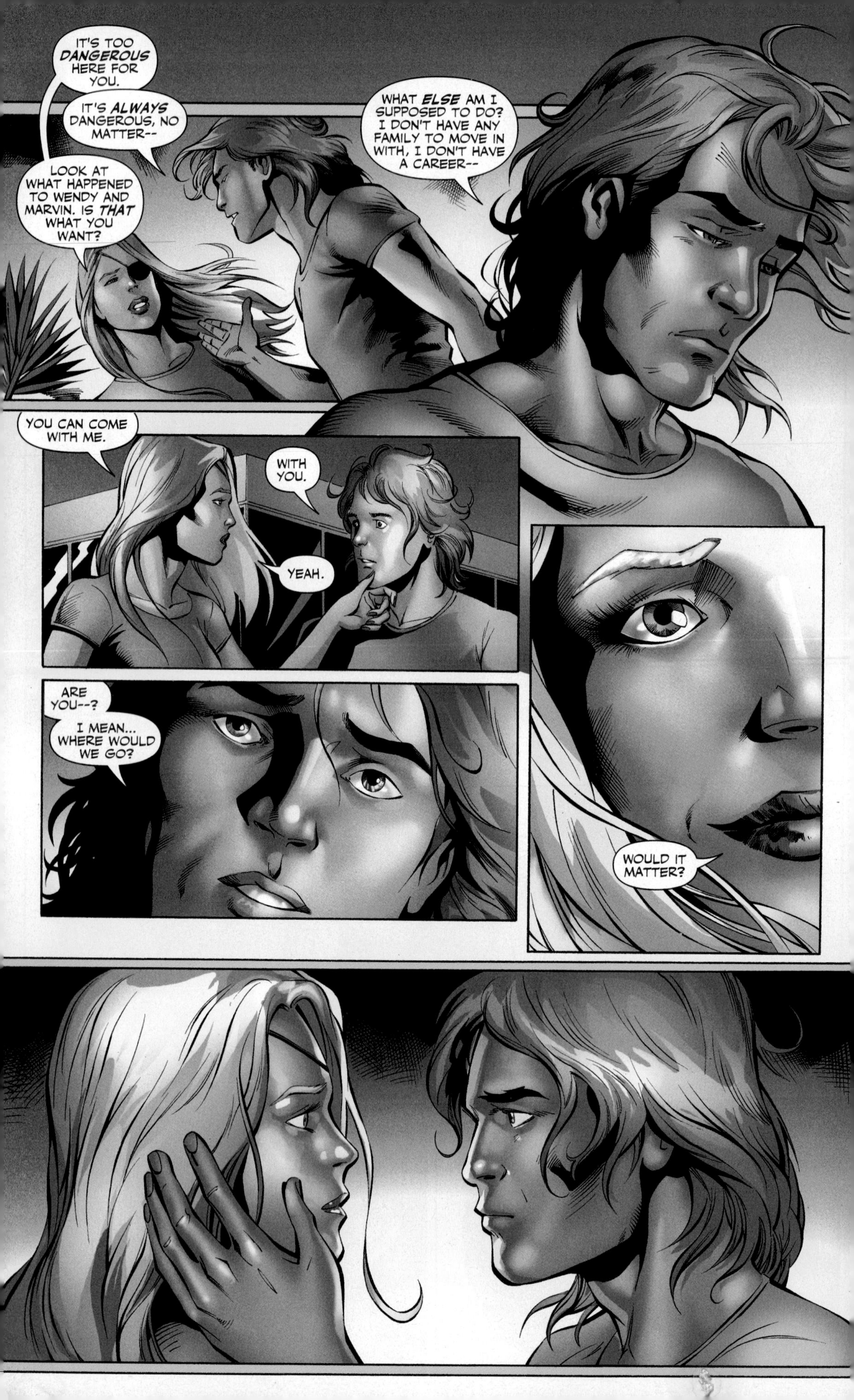
IT'S TOO DANGEROUS HERE FOR YOU.
IT'S ALWAYS DANGEROUS, NO MATTER--
LOOK AT WHAT HAPPENED TO WENDY AND MARVIN. IS THAT WHAT YOU WANT?
WHAT ELSE AM I SUPPOSED TO DO? I DON'T HAVE ANY FAMILY TO MOVE IN WITH, I DON'T HAVE A CAREER--
YOU CAN COME WITH ME.
WITH YOU.
YEAH.
ARE YOU--?
I MEAN... WHERE WOULD WE GO?
WOULD IT MATTER?

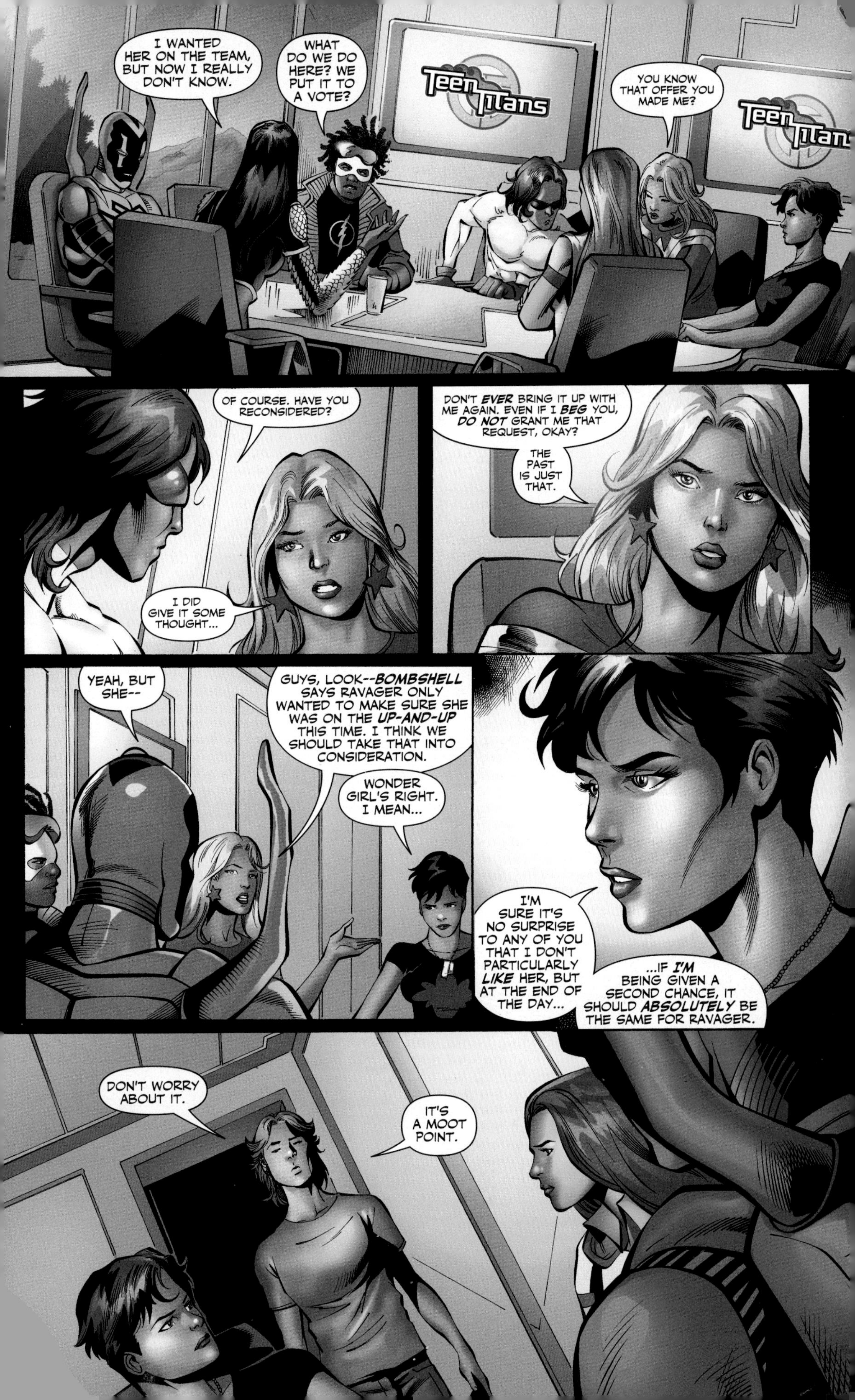

I WANTED HER ON THE TEAM, BUT NOW I REALLY DON'T KNOW.
WHAT DO WE DO HERE? WE PUT IT TO A VOTE?
Teen Titans
YOU KNOW THAT OFFER YOU MADE ME?
Teen Titans
OF COURSE. HAVE YOU RECONSIDERED?
I DID GIVE IT SOME THOUGHT...
DON'T EVER BRING IT UP WITH ME AGAIN. EVEN IF I BEG YOU, DO NOT GRANT ME THAT REQUEST, OKAY?
THE PAST IS JUST THAT.
YEAH, BUT SHE--
GUYS, LOOK--BOMBSHELL SAYS RAVAGER ONLY WANTED TO MAKE SURE SHE WAS ON THE UP-AND-UP THIS TIME. I THINK WE SHOULD TAKE THAT INTO CONSIDERATION.
WONDER GIRL'S RIGHT. I MEAN...
I'M SURE IT'S NO SURPRISE TO ANY OF YOU THAT I DON'T PARTICULARLY LIKE HER, BUT AT THE END OF THE DAY...
...IF I'M BEING GIVEN A SECOND CHANCE, IT SHOULD ABSOLUTELY BE THE SAME FOR RAVAGER.
DON'T WORRY ABOUT IT.
IT'S A MOOT POINT.

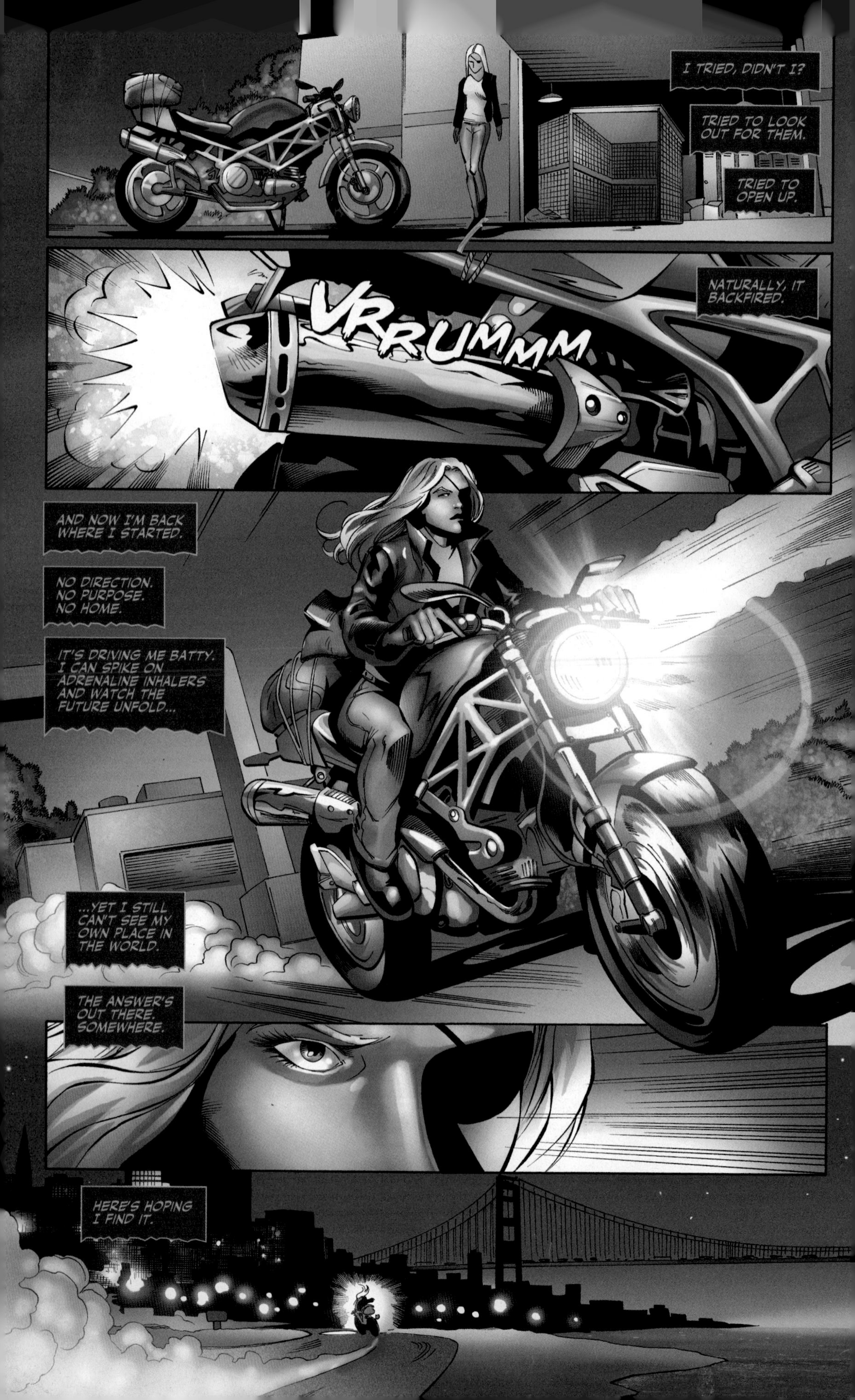

I TRIED, DIDN'T I?
TRIED TO LOOK OUT FOR THEM.
TRIED TO OPEN UP.
VRRUMMM
NATURALLY, IT BACKFIRED.
AND NOW I'M BACK WHERE I STARTED.
NO DIRECTION. NO PURPOSE. NO HOME.
IT'S DRIVING ME BATTY. I CAN SPIKE ON ADRENALINE INHALERS AND WATCH THE FUTURE UNFOLD...
...YET I STILL CAN'T SEE MY OWN PLACE IN THE WORLD.
THE ANSWER'S OUT THERE. SOMEWHERE.
HERE'S HOPING I FIND IT.

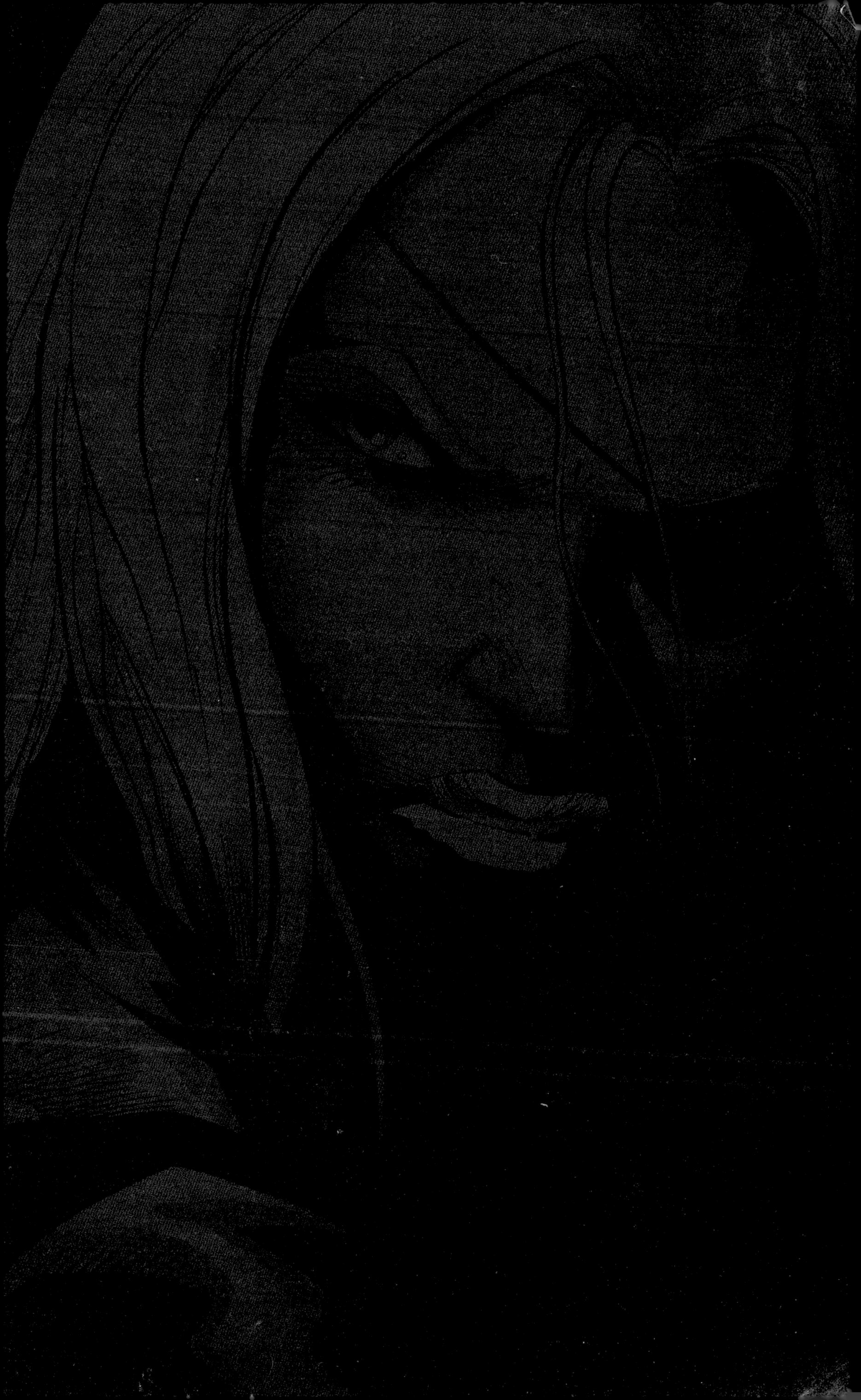

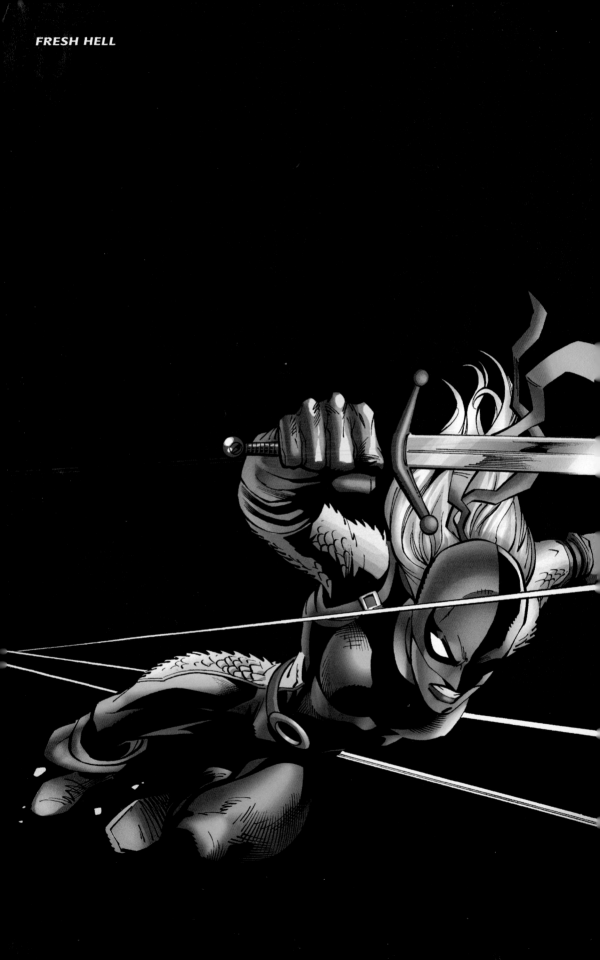

RAVAGER IN FRESH HELL

YILDIRAY CINAR draws
SEAN McKEEVER writes
JULIO FERREIRA inks

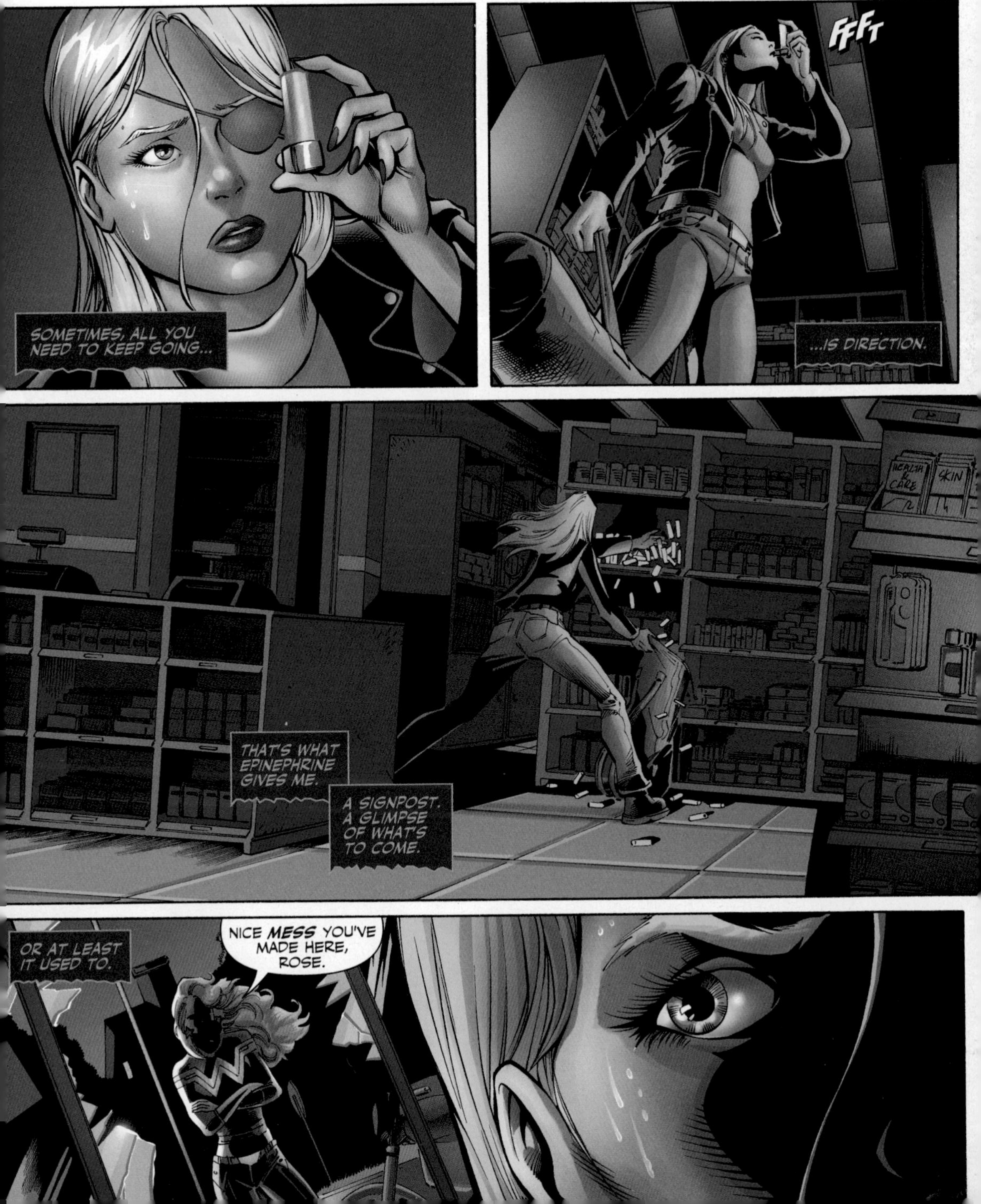
SOMETIMES, ALL YOU NEED TO KEEP GOING...
FFFT
...IS DIRECTION.
HEALTH & CARE
SKIN
THAT'S WHAT EPINEPHRINE GIVES ME.
A SIGNPOST. A GLIMPSE OF WHAT'S TO COME.
OR AT LEAST IT USED TO.
NICE MESS YOU'VE MADE HERE, ROSE.

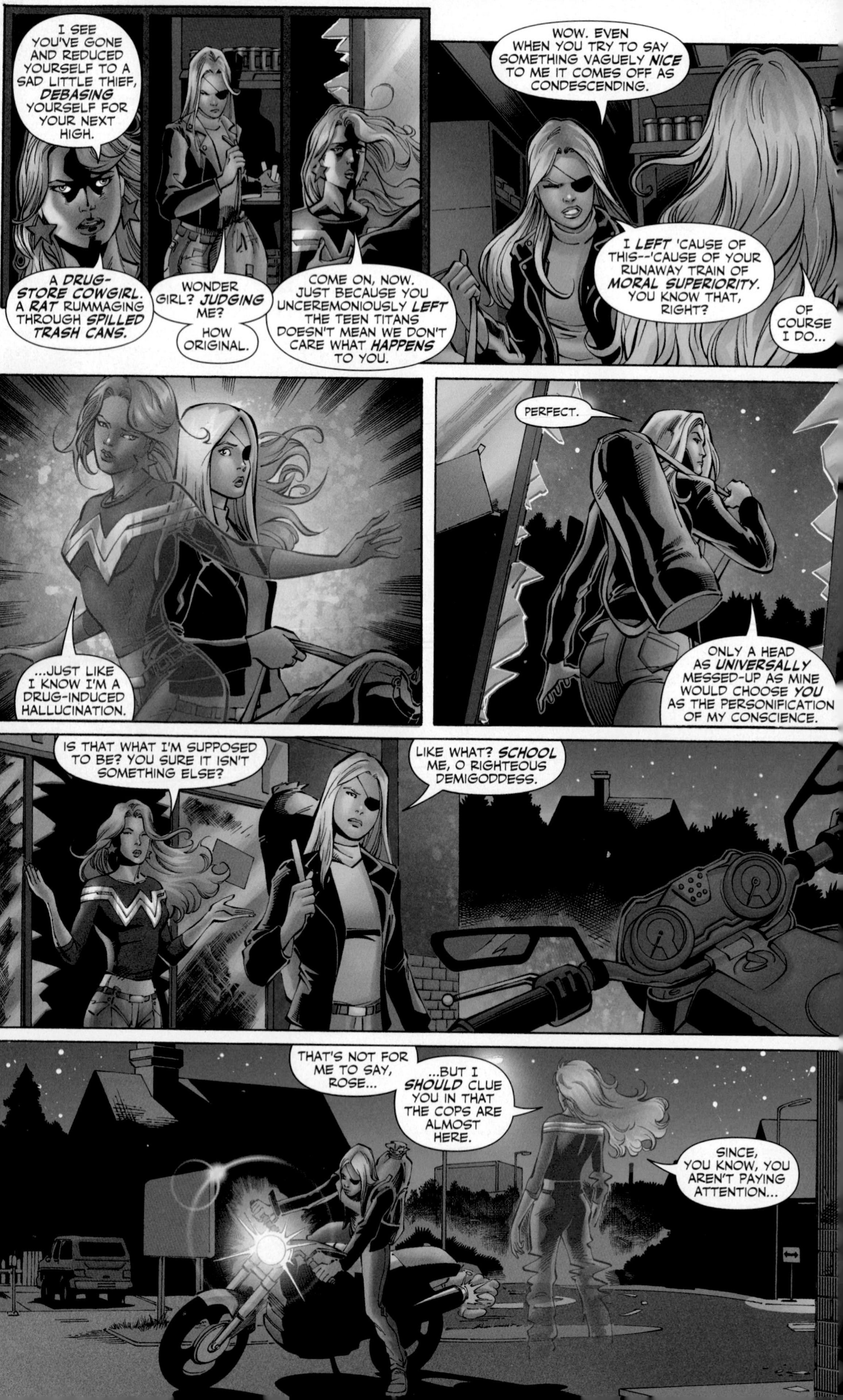
I SEE YOU'VE GONE AND REDUCED YOURSELF TO A SAD LITTLE THIEF, DEBASING YOURSELF FOR YOUR NEXT HIGH.
A DRUG-STORE COWGIRL. A RAT RUMMAGING THROUGH SPILLED TRASH CANS.
WONDER GIRL? JUDGING ME?
HOW ORIGINAL.
COME ON, NOW. JUST BECAUSE YOU UNCEREMONIOUSLY LEFT THE TEEN TITANS DOESN'T MEAN WE DON'T CARE WHAT HAPPENS TO YOU.
WOW. EVEN WHEN YOU TRY TO SAY SOMETHING VAGUELY NICE TO ME IT COMES OFF AS CONDESCENDING.
I LEFT 'CAUSE OF THIS--'CAUSE OF YOUR RUNAWAY TRAIN OF MORAL SUPERIORITY. YOU KNOW THAT, RIGHT?
OF COURSE I DO...
...JUST LIKE I KNOW I'M A DRUG-INDUCED HALLUCINATION.
PERFECT.
ONLY A HEAD AS UNIVERSALLY MESSED-UP AS MINE WOULD CHOOSE YOU AS THE PERSONIFICATION OF MY CONSCIENCE.
IS THAT WHAT I'M SUPPOSED TO BE? YOU SURE IT ISN'T SOMETHING ELSE?
LIKE WHAT? SCHOOL ME, O RIGHTEOUS DEMIGODDESS.
THAT'S NOT FOR ME TO SAY, ROSE...
...BUT I SHOULD CLUE YOU IN THAT THE COPS ARE ALMOST HERE.
SINCE, YOU KNOW, YOU AREN'T PAYING ATTENTION...

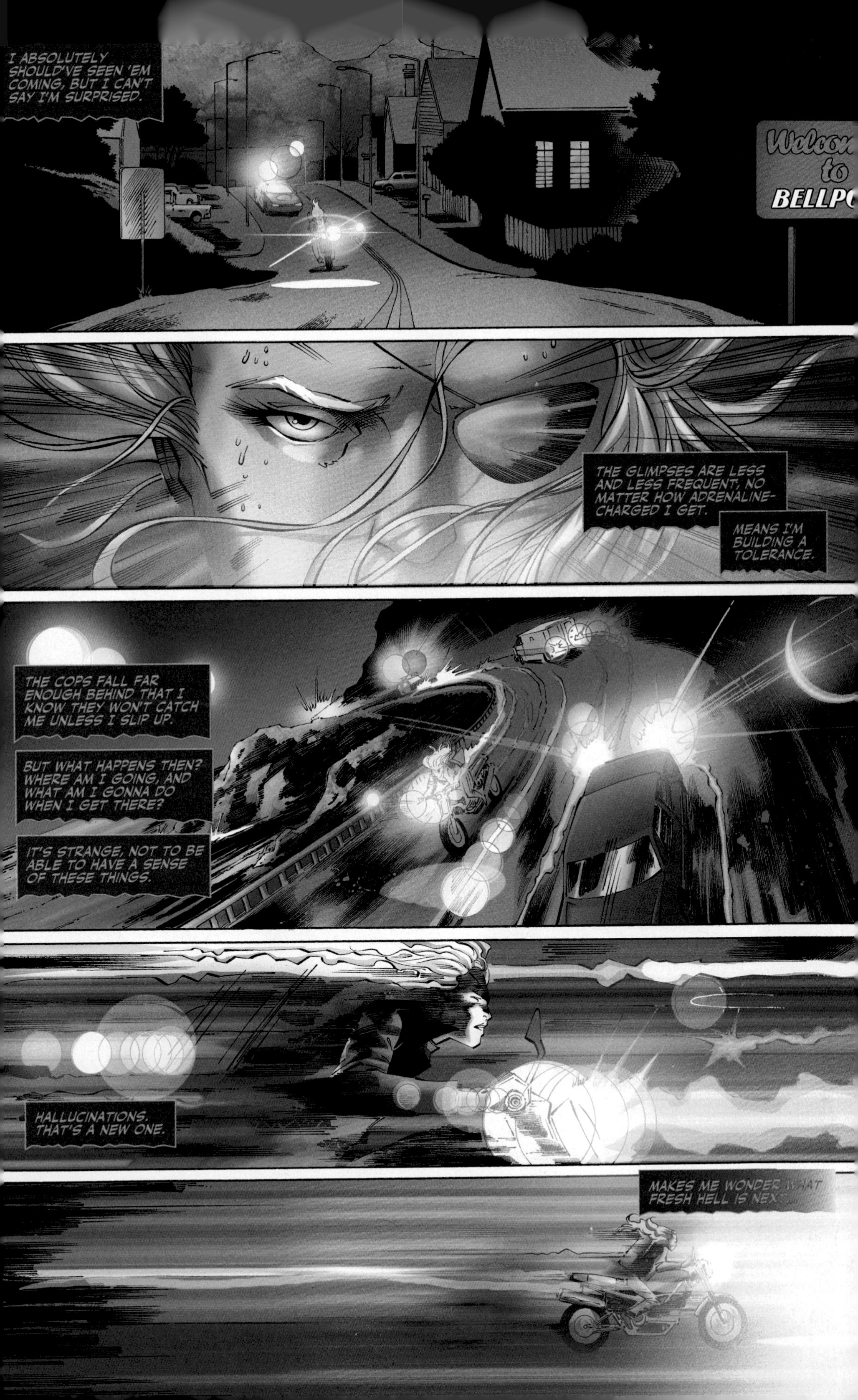
I ABSOLUTELY SHOULD'VE SEEN 'EM COMING, BUT I CAN'T SAY I'M SURPRISED.
Welcom to BELLPO
THE GLIMPSES ARE LESS AND LESS FREQUENT, NO MATTER HOW ADRENALINE-CHARGED I GET.
MEANS I'M BUILDING A TOLERANCE.
THE COPS FALL FAR ENOUGH BEHIND THAT I KNOW THEY WON'T CATCH ME UNLESS I SLIP UP.
BUT WHAT HAPPENS THEN? WHERE AM I GOING, AND WHAT AM I GONNA DO WHEN I GET THERE?
IT'S STRANGE, NOT TO BE ABLE TO HAVE A SENSE OF THESE THINGS.
HALLUCINATIONS. THAT'S A NEW ONE.
MAKES ME WONDER WHAT FRESH HELL IS NEXT...

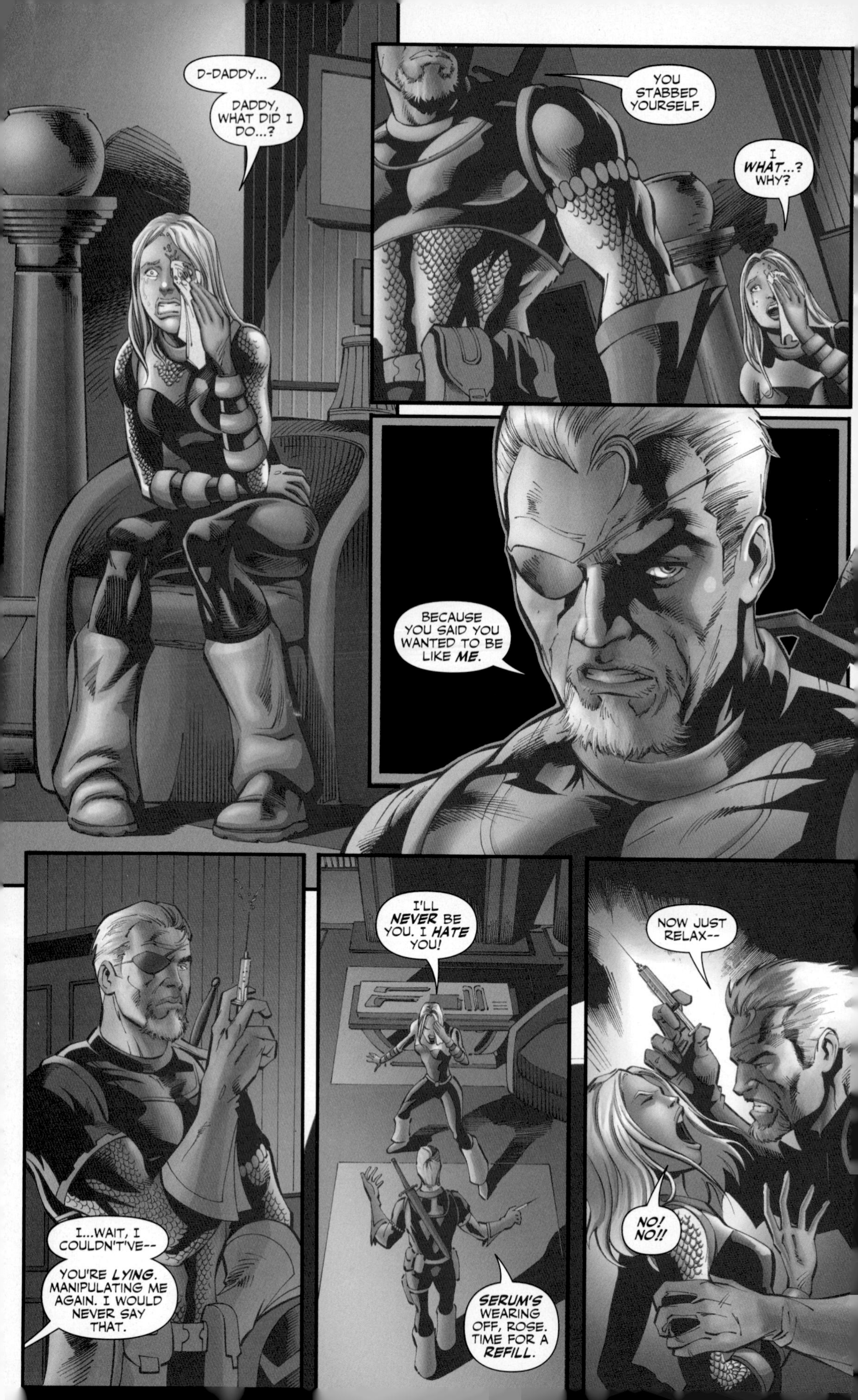
D-DADDY...
DADDY, WHAT DID I DO...?
YOU STABBED YOURSELF.
I *WHAT*...? WHY?
BECAUSE YOU SAID YOU WANTED TO BE LIKE *ME*.
I...WAIT, I COULDN'T'VE--
YOU'RE *LYING*. MANIPULATING ME AGAIN. I WOULD NEVER SAY THAT.
I'LL *NEVER* BE YOU. I *HATE* YOU!
SERUM'S WEARING OFF, ROSE. TIME FOR A *REFILL*.
NOW JUST RELAX--
NO! NO!!

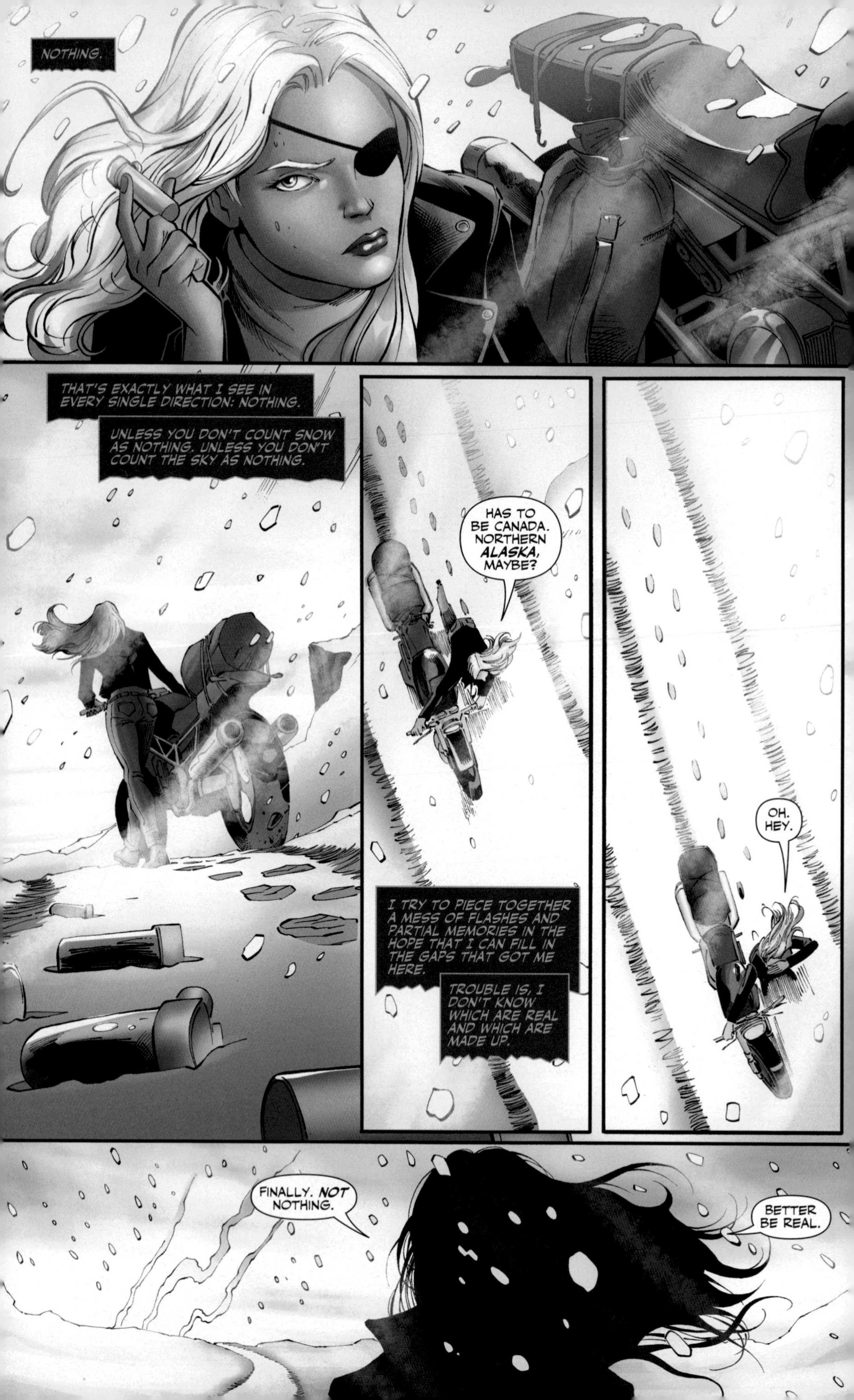
NOTHING.
THAT'S EXACTLY WHAT I SEE IN EVERY SINGLE DIRECTION: NOTHING.
UNLESS YOU DON'T COUNT SNOW AS NOTHING. UNLESS YOU DON'T COUNT THE SKY AS NOTHING.
HAS TO BE CANADA. NORTHERN *ALASKA*, MAYBE?
I TRY TO PIECE TOGETHER A MESS OF FLASHES AND PARTIAL MEMORIES IN THE HOPE THAT I CAN FILL IN THE GAPS THAT GOT ME HERE.
TROUBLE IS, I DON'T KNOW WHICH ARE REAL AND WHICH ARE MADE UP.
OH. HEY.
FINALLY. *NOT* NOTHING.
BETTER BE REAL.

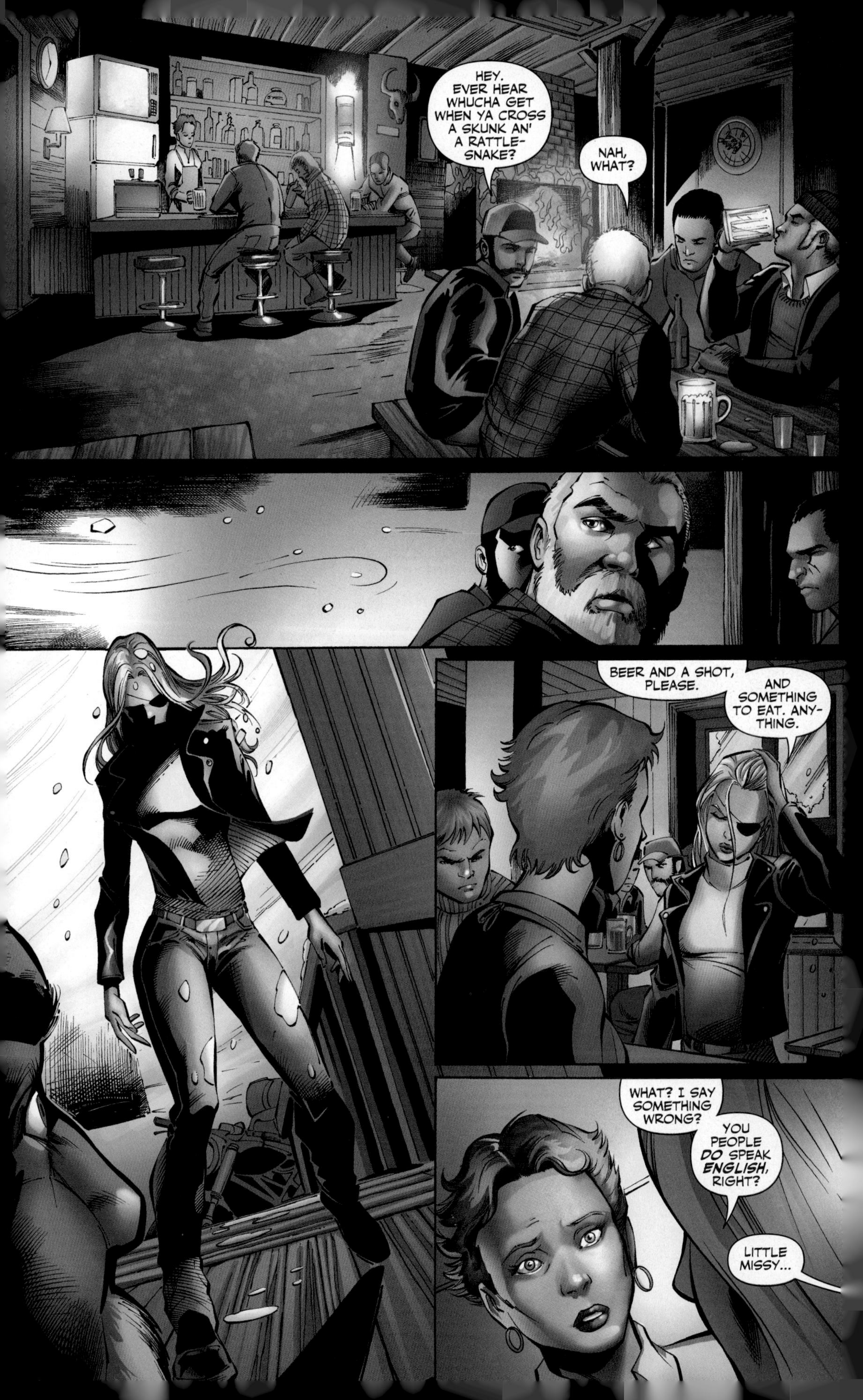
HEY. EVER HEAR WHUCHA GET WHEN YA CROSS A SKUNK AN' A RATTLE-SNAKE?
NAH, WHAT?
BEER AND A SHOT, PLEASE.
AND SOMETHING TO EAT. ANY-THING.
WHAT? I SAY SOMETHING WRONG?
YOU PEOPLE *DO* SPEAK *ENGLISH*, RIGHT?
LITTLE MISSY...

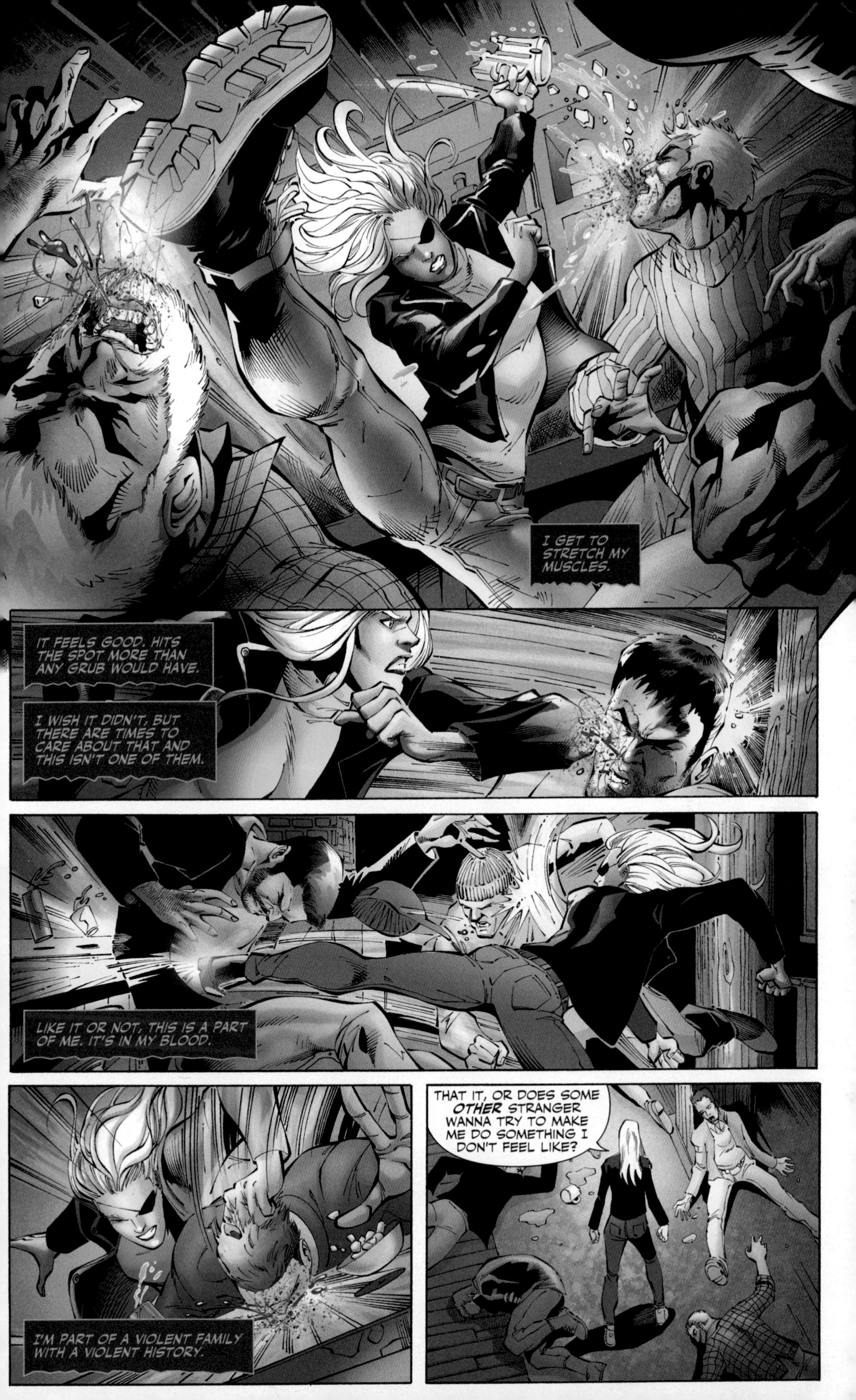
I GET TO STRETCH MY MUSCLES.
IT FEELS GOOD. HITS THE SPOT MORE THAN ANY GRUB WOULD HAVE.
I WISH IT DIDN'T, BUT THERE ARE TIMES TO CARE ABOUT THAT AND THIS ISN'T ONE OF THEM.
LIKE IT OR NOT, THIS IS A PART OF ME. IT'S IN MY BLOOD.
I'M PART OF A VIOLENT FAMILY WITH A VIOLENT HISTORY.
THAT IT, OR DOES SOME OTHER STRANGER WANNA TRY TO MAKE ME DO SOMETHING I DON'T FEEL LIKE?

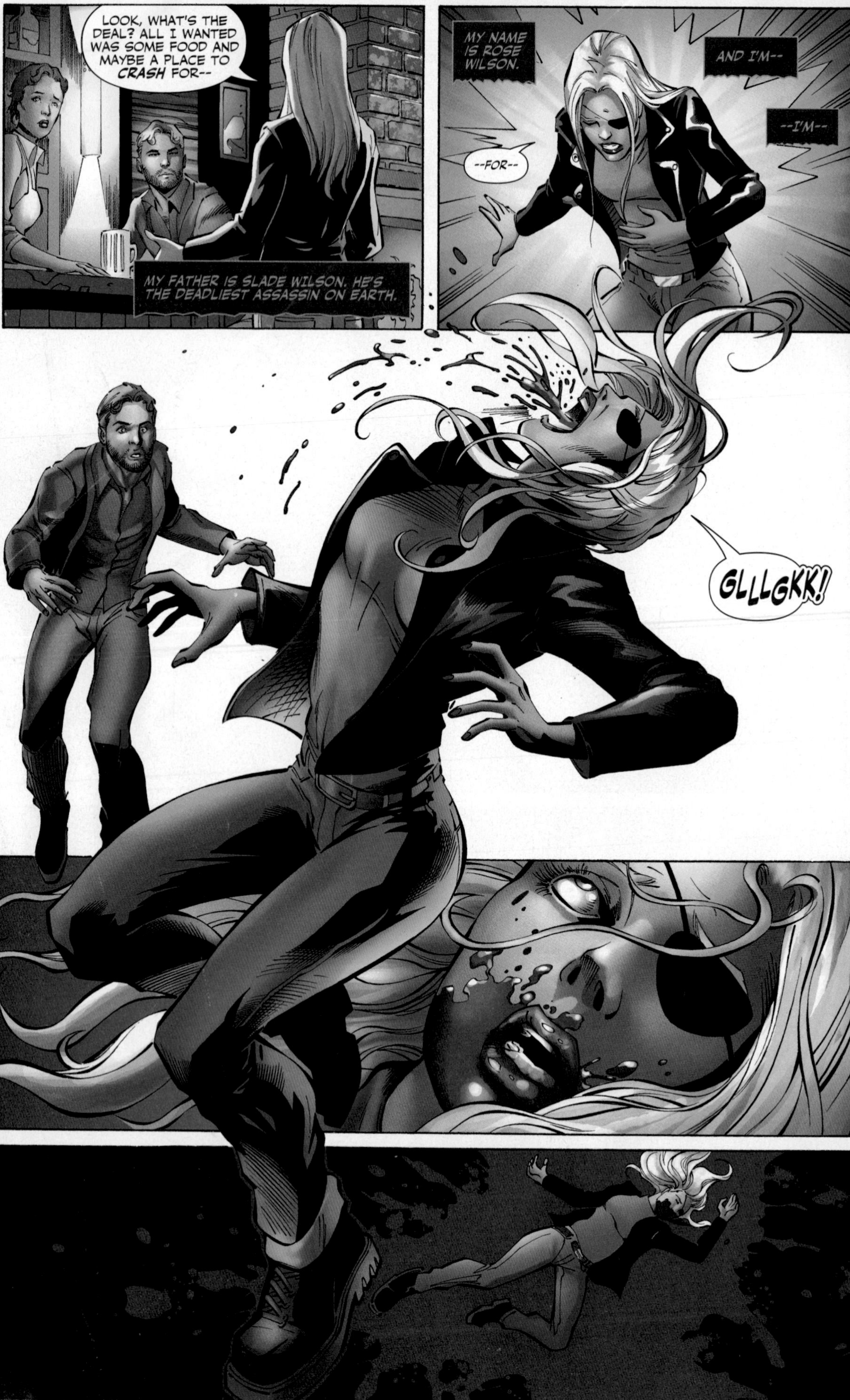
LOOK, WHAT'S THE DEAL? ALL I WANTED WAS SOME FOOD AND MAYBE A PLACE TO CRASH FOR--
MY FATHER IS SLADE WILSON. HE'S THE DEADLIEST ASSASSIN ON EARTH.
MY NAME IS ROSE WILSON.
--FOR--
AND I'M--
--I'M--
GLLLGKK!

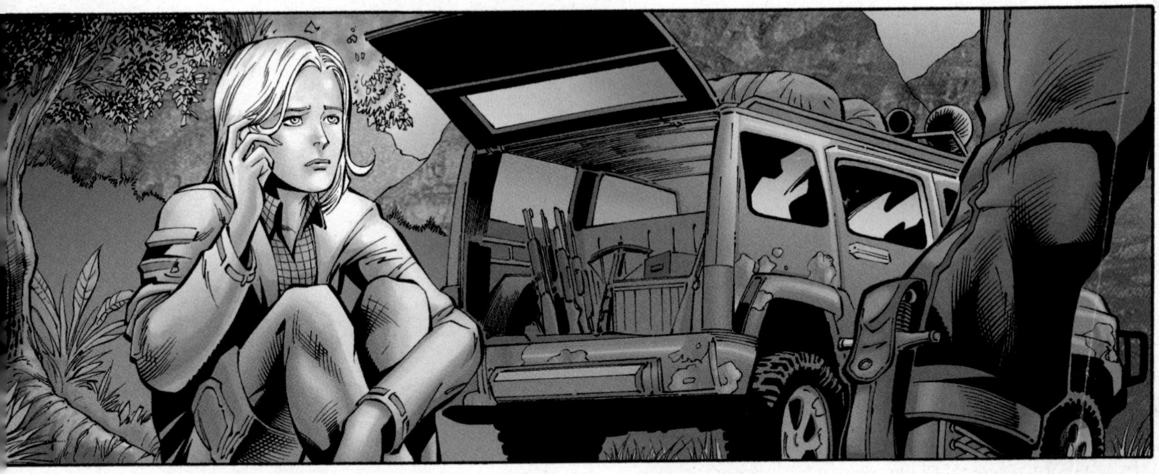

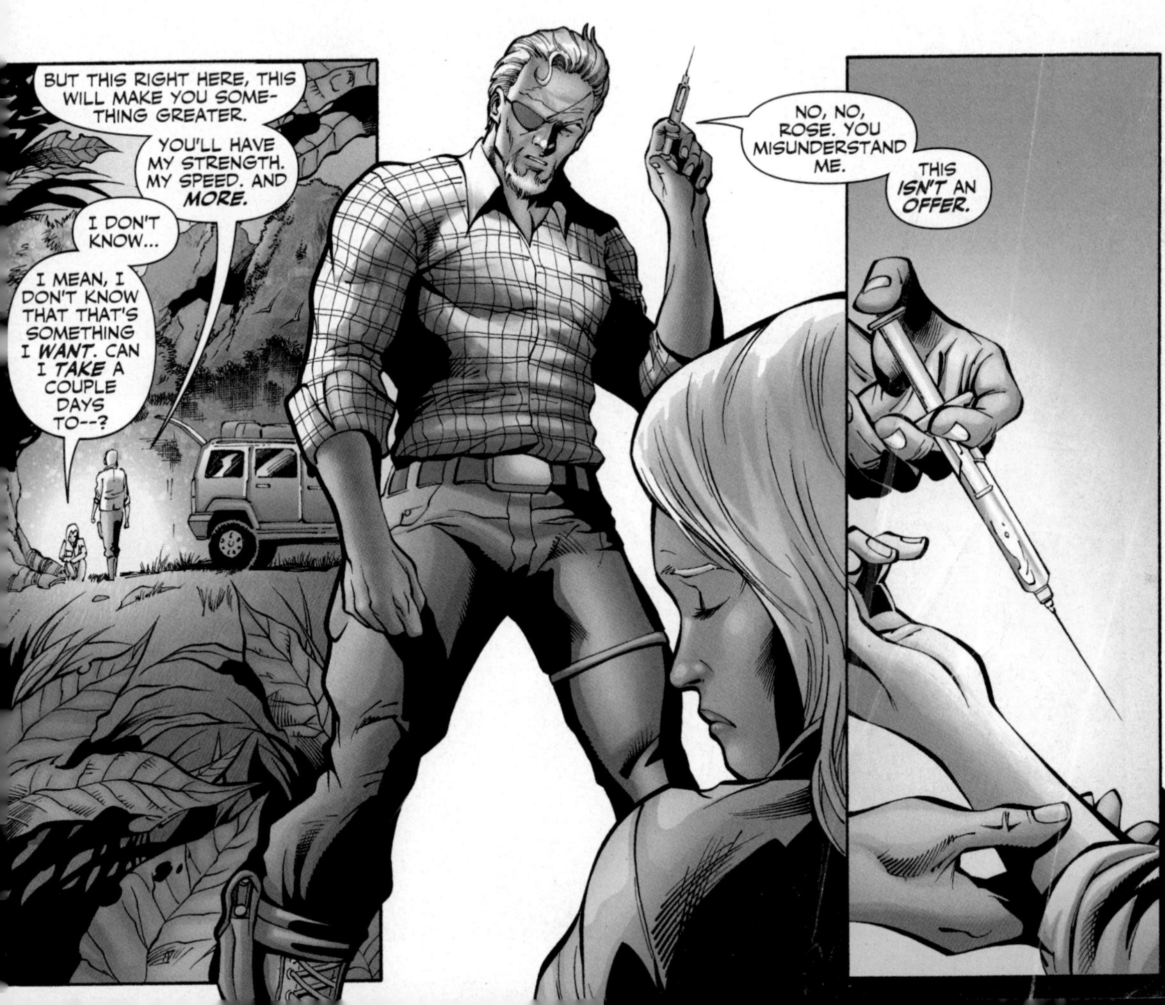
BUT THIS RIGHT HERE, THIS WILL MAKE YOU SOMETHING GREATER.
YOU'LL HAVE MY STRENGTH. MY SPEED. AND ***MORE.***
I DON'T KNOW...
I MEAN, I DON'T KNOW THAT THAT'S SOMETHING I *WANT*. CAN I *TAKE* A COUPLE DAYS TO--?
NO, NO, ROSE. YOU MISUNDERSTAND ME.
THIS *ISN'T* AN *OFFER.*

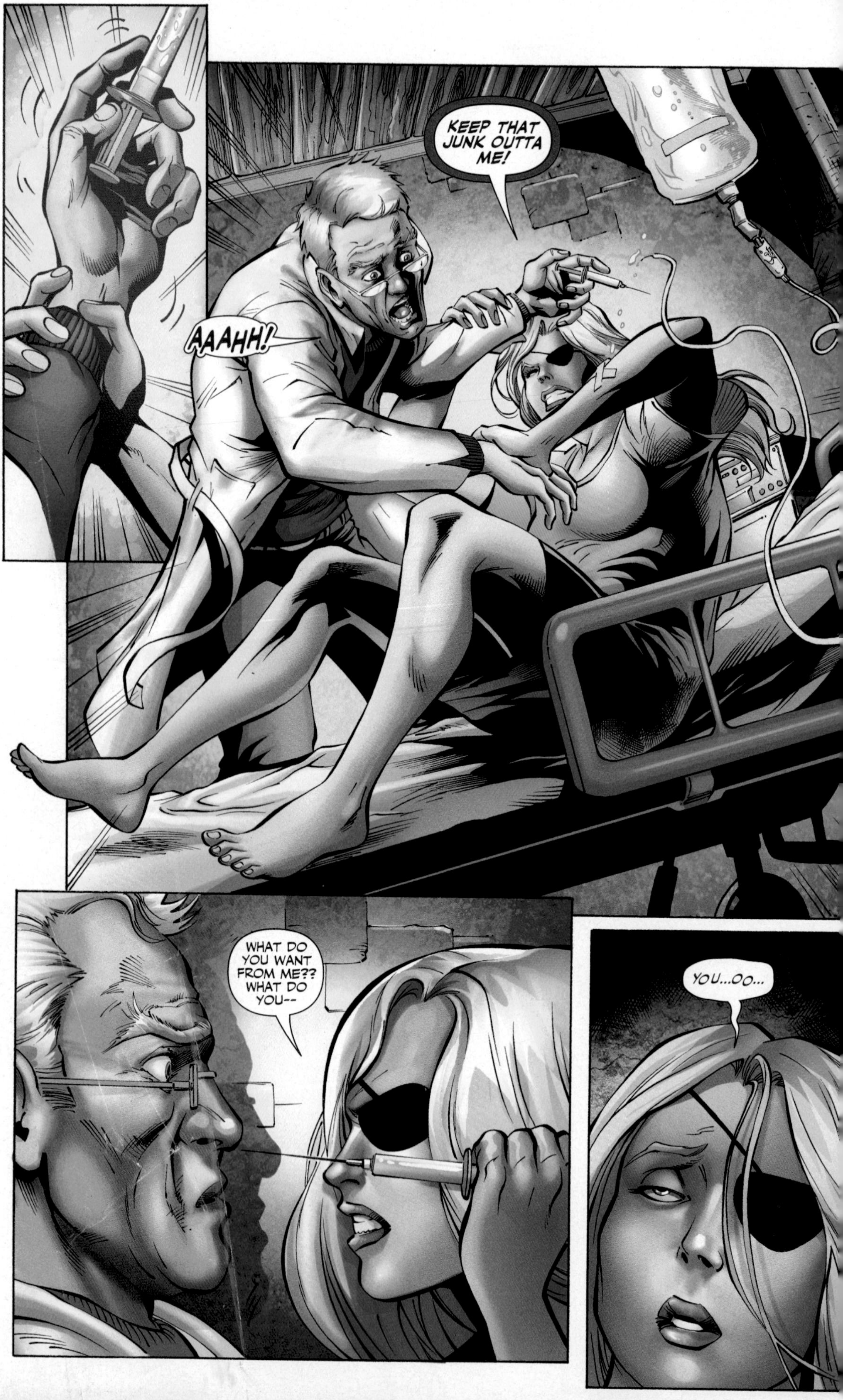
KEEP THAT JUNK OUTTA ME!
AAAHH!
WHAT DO YOU WANT FROM ME?? WHAT DO YOU--
YOU...OO...

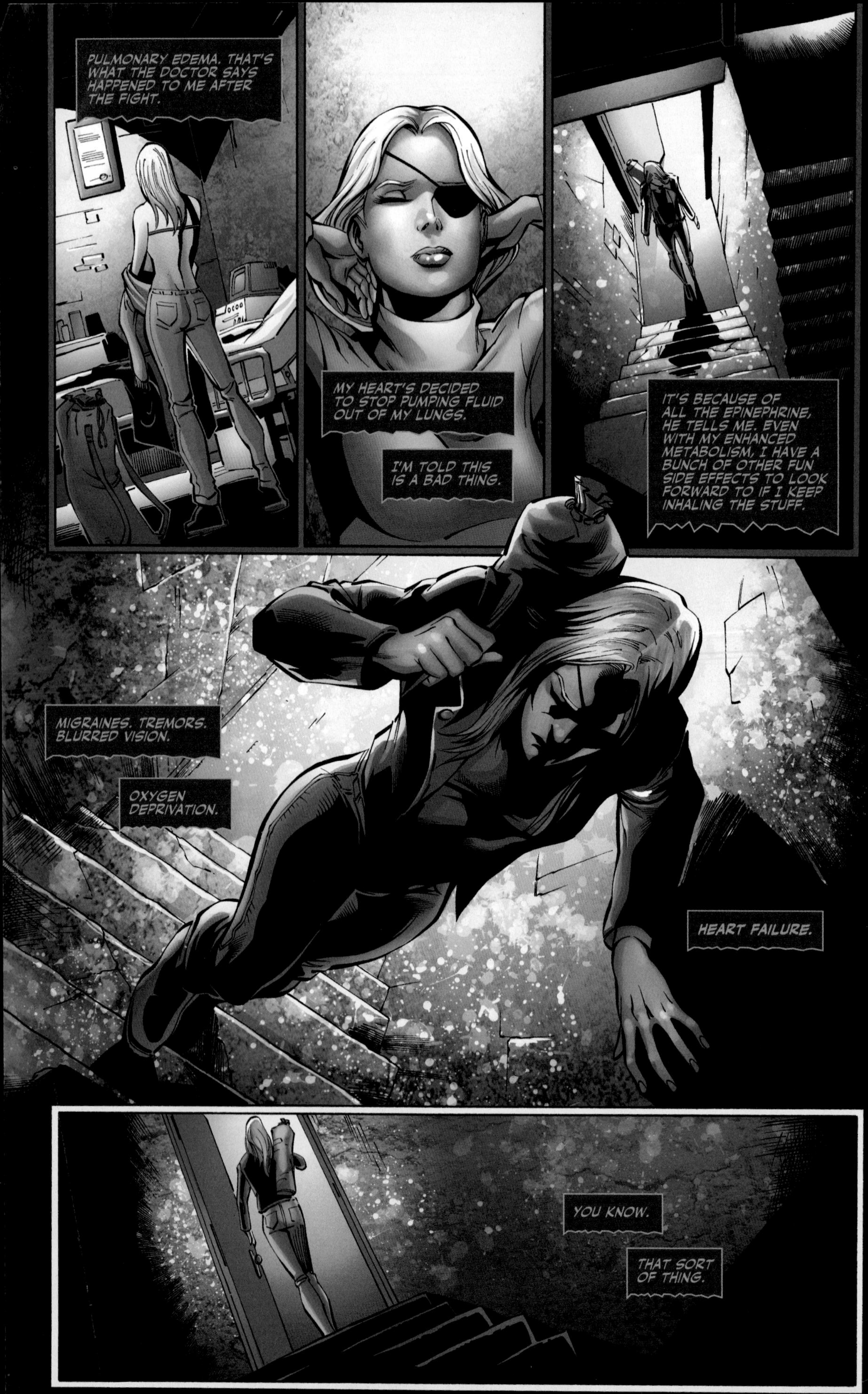
PULMONARY EDEMA. THAT'S WHAT THE DOCTOR SAYS HAPPENED TO ME AFTER THE FIGHT.
MY HEART'S DECIDED TO STOP PUMPING FLUID OUT OF MY LUNGS.
I'M TOLD THIS IS A BAD THING.
IT'S BECAUSE OF ALL THE EPINEPHRINE, HE TELLS ME. EVEN WITH MY ENHANCED METABOLISM, I HAVE A BUNCH OF OTHER FUN SIDE EFFECTS TO LOOK FORWARD TO IF I KEEP INHALING THE STUFF.
MIGRAINES. TREMORS. BLURRED VISION.
OXYGEN DEPRIVATION.
HEART FAILURE.
YOU KNOW.
THAT SORT OF THING.

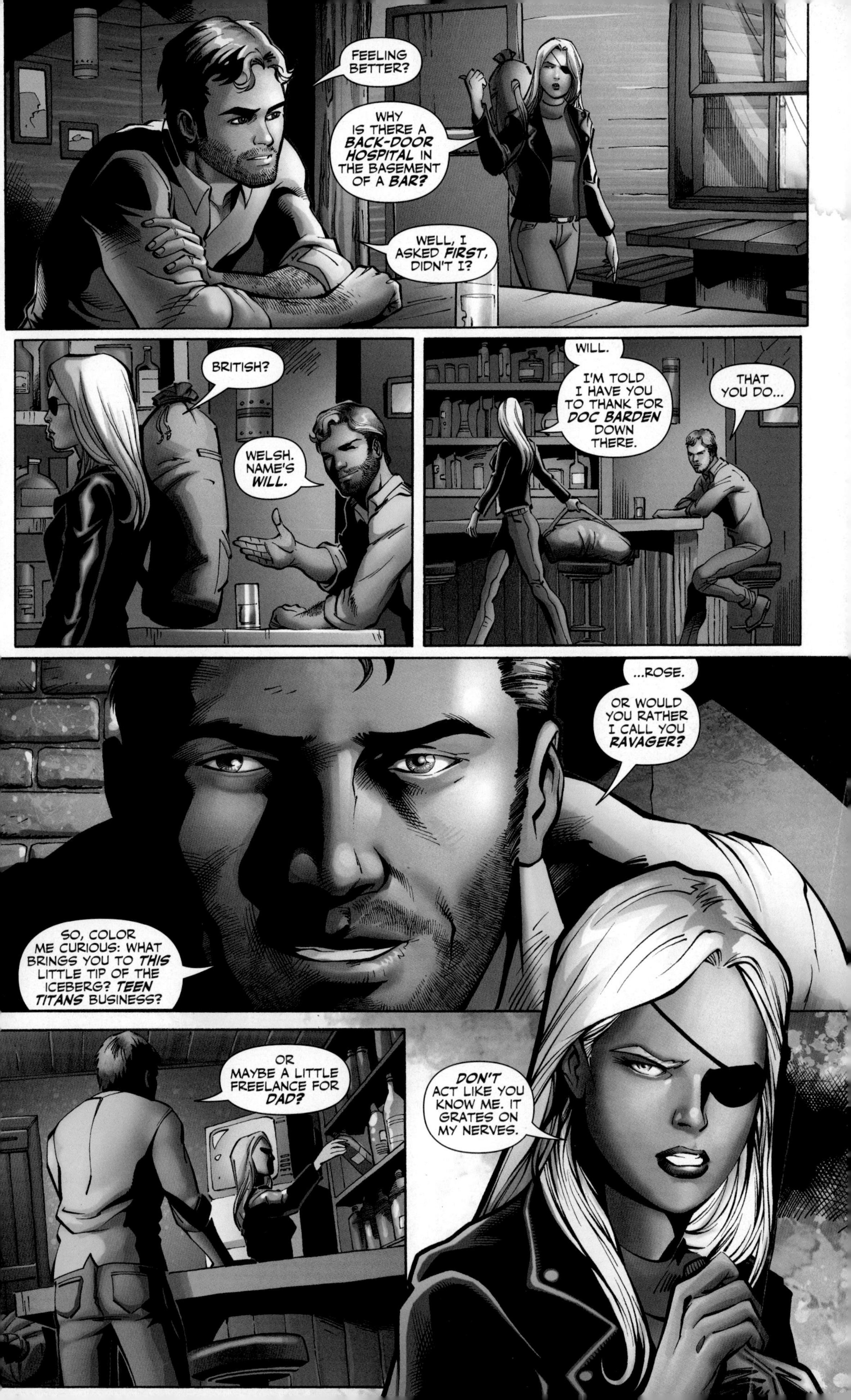

FEELING BETTER?
WHY IS THERE A BACK-DOOR HOSPITAL IN THE BASEMENT OF A BAR?
WELL, I ASKED FIRST, DIDN'T I?
BRITISH?
WELSH. NAME'S WILL.
WILL.
I'M TOLD I HAVE YOU TO THANK FOR DOC BARDEN DOWN THERE.
THAT YOU DO...
...ROSE.
OR WOULD YOU RATHER I CALL YOU RAVAGER?
SO, COLOR ME CURIOUS: WHAT BRINGS YOU TO THIS LITTLE TIP OF THE ICEBERG? TEEN TITANS BUSINESS?
OR MAYBE A LITTLE FREELANCE FOR DAD?
DON'T ACT LIKE YOU KNOW ME. IT GRATES ON MY NERVES.

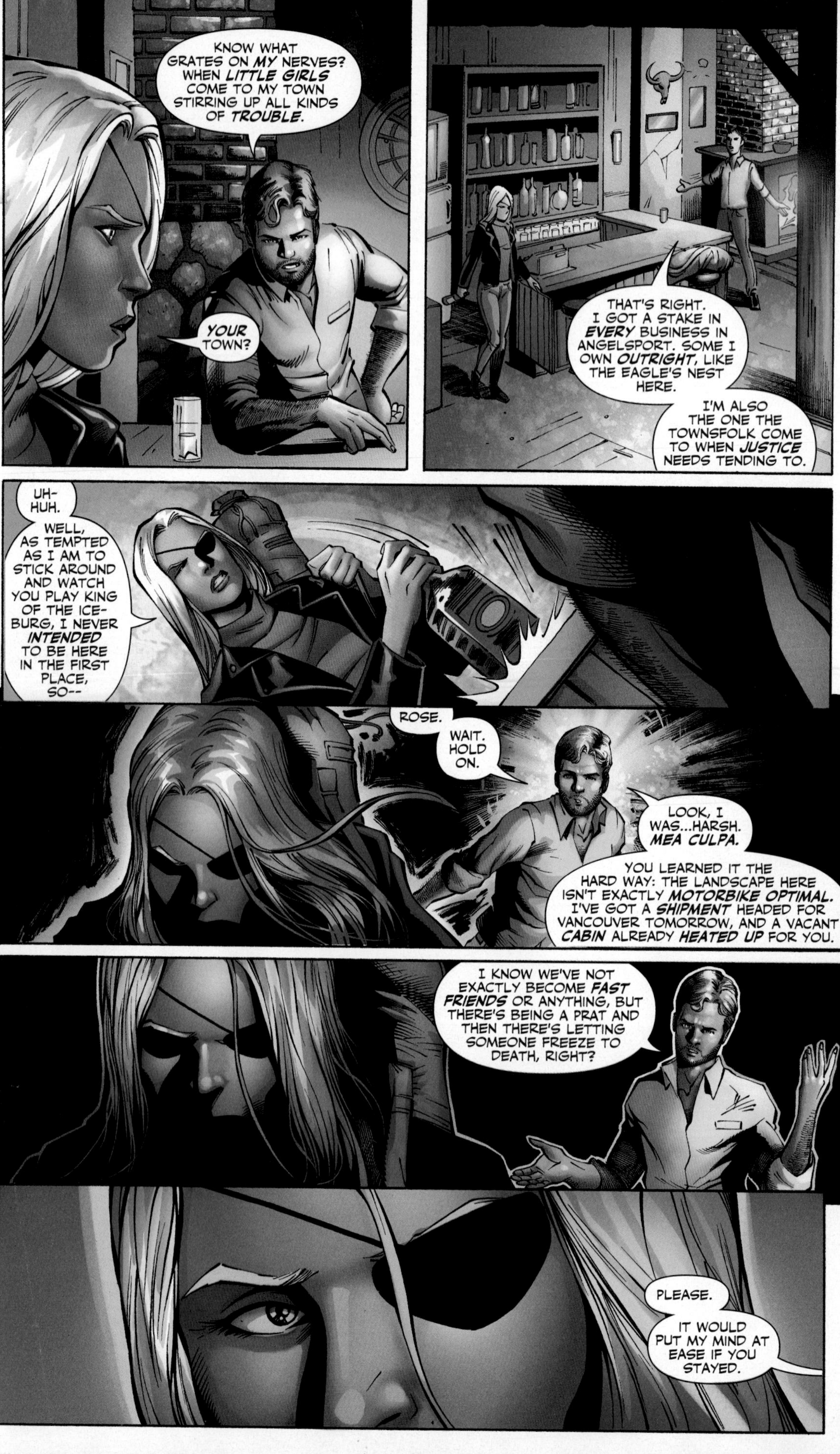
KNOW WHAT GRATES ON *MY* NERVES? WHEN *LITTLE GIRLS* COME TO MY TOWN STIRRING UP ALL KINDS OF *TROUBLE*.
YOUR TOWN?
THAT'S RIGHT. I GOT A STAKE IN *EVERY* BUSINESS IN ANGELSPORT. SOME I OWN *OUTRIGHT*, LIKE THE EAGLE'S NEST HERE.
I'M ALSO THE ONE THE TOWNSFOLK COME TO WHEN *JUSTICE* NEEDS TENDING TO.
UH-HUH.
WELL, AS TEMPTED AS I AM TO STICK AROUND AND WATCH YOU PLAY KING OF THE ICE-BURG, I NEVER *INTENDED* TO BE HERE IN THE FIRST PLACE, SO--
ROSE.
WAIT. HOLD ON.
LOOK, I WAS...HARSH. *MEA CULPA.*
YOU LEARNED IT THE HARD WAY: THE LANDSCAPE HERE ISN'T EXACTLY *MOTORBIKE OPTIMAL.* I'VE GOT A *SHIPMENT* HEADED FOR VANCOUVER TOMORROW, AND A VACANT *CABIN* ALREADY *HEATED UP* FOR YOU.
I KNOW WE'VE NOT EXACTLY BECOME *FAST FRIENDS* OR ANYTHING, BUT THERE'S BEING A PRAT AND THEN THERE'S LETTING SOMEONE FREEZE TO DEATH, RIGHT?
PLEASE.
IT WOULD PUT MY MIND AT EASE IF YOU STAYED.

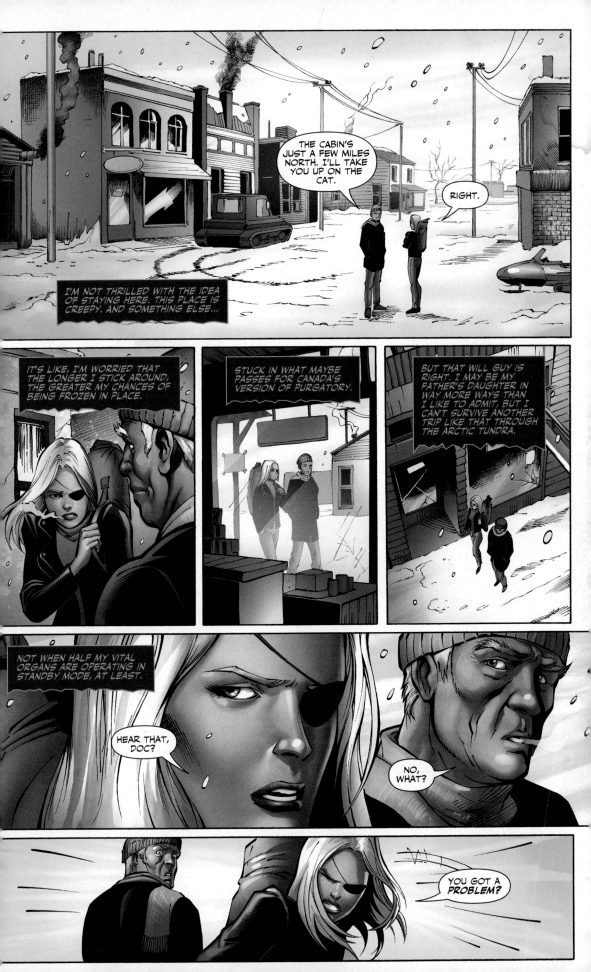

"GET 'ER OUTTA HERE."

PFFT. AMEN TO THAT.

STILL, AS MUCH AS THIS LITTLE SLICE OF NOWHERE SUCKS AWAY WHAT'S LEFT OF MY SOUL...

...I'VE GOT TO ADMIT THAT IT'S ODDLY *SOOTHING.*

AS LONG AS I'M HERE, MY LIFE IS ON HOLD.

ONCE I LEAVE...WHERE IS IT I'M HEADED? WHAT IS IT I'M SUPPOSED TO DO? OR BE?

IT'S NOT THE PEACE AND QUIET, 'CAUSE THOSE TWO TEND TO BRING ME ANYTHING BUT. IT'S NOT THE RUSTIC AMBIANCE.

IT'S THAT I'M UNACCOUNTED FOR.

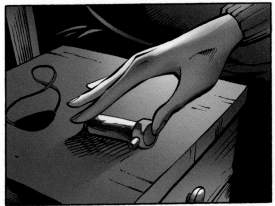

JUST THE SAME, WHATEVER TIME I SPEND HERE IS SURE TO BE FAR FROM PLEASANT. I GUESS THAT ALL I CAN REALLY HOPE FOR...

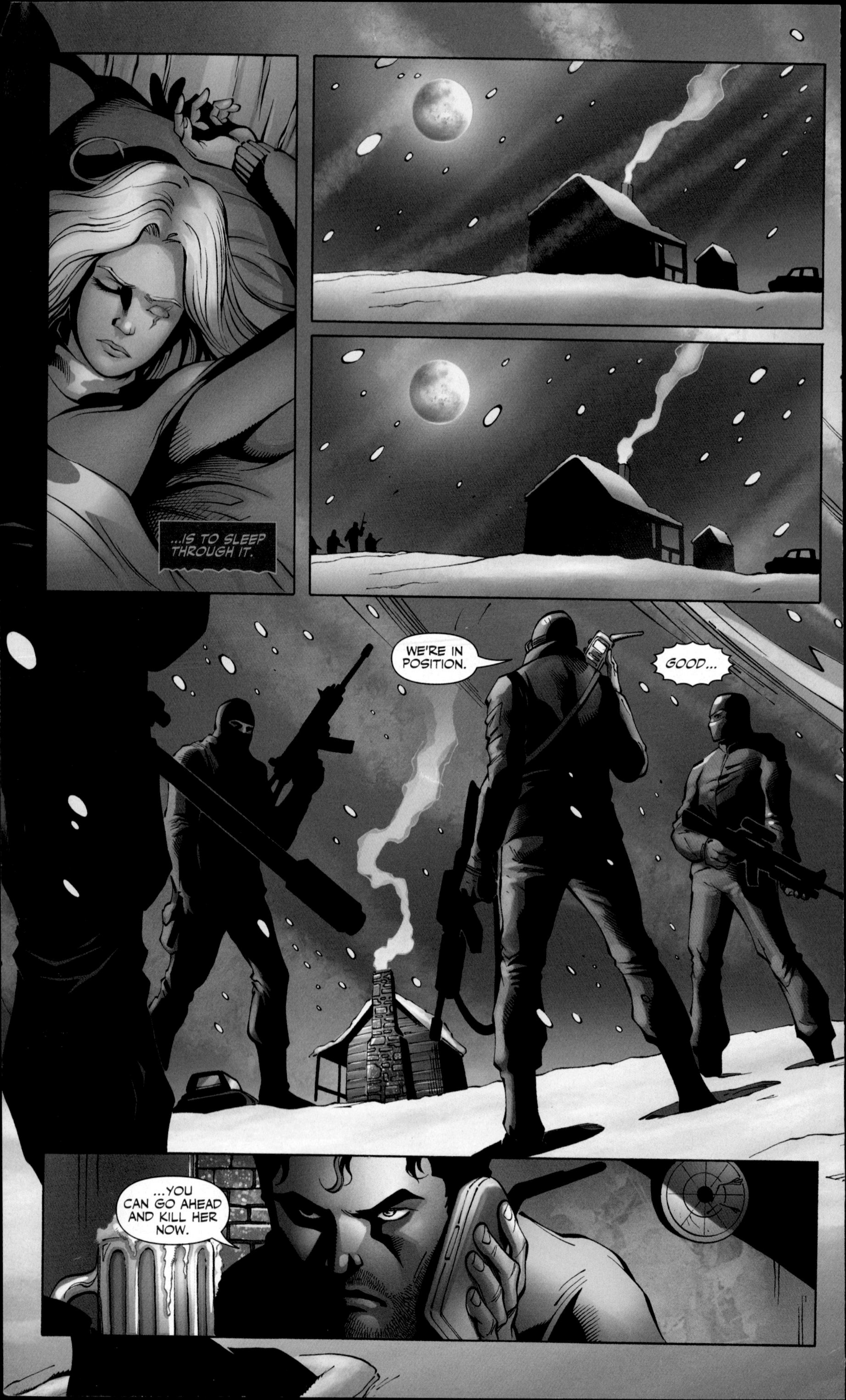
...IS TO SLEEP THROUGH IT.
WE'RE IN POSITION.
GOOD...
...YOU CAN GO AHEAD AND KILL HER NOW.

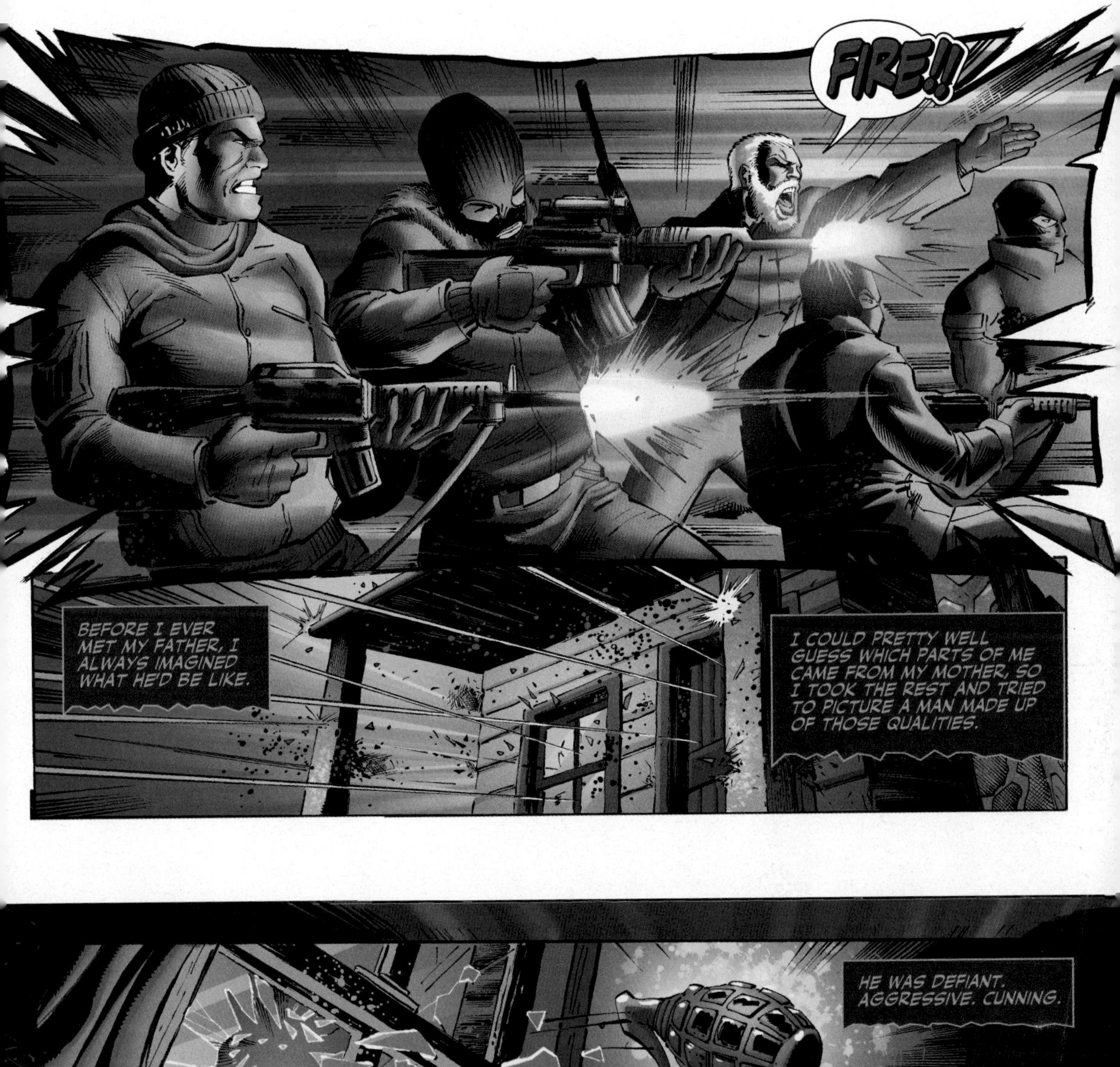
FIRE!!
BEFORE I EVER MET MY FATHER, I ALWAYS IMAGINED WHAT HE'D BE LIKE.
I COULD PRETTY WELL GUESS WHICH PARTS OF ME CAME FROM MY MOTHER, SO I TOOK THE REST AND TRIED TO PICTURE A MAN MADE UP OF THOSE QUALITIES.

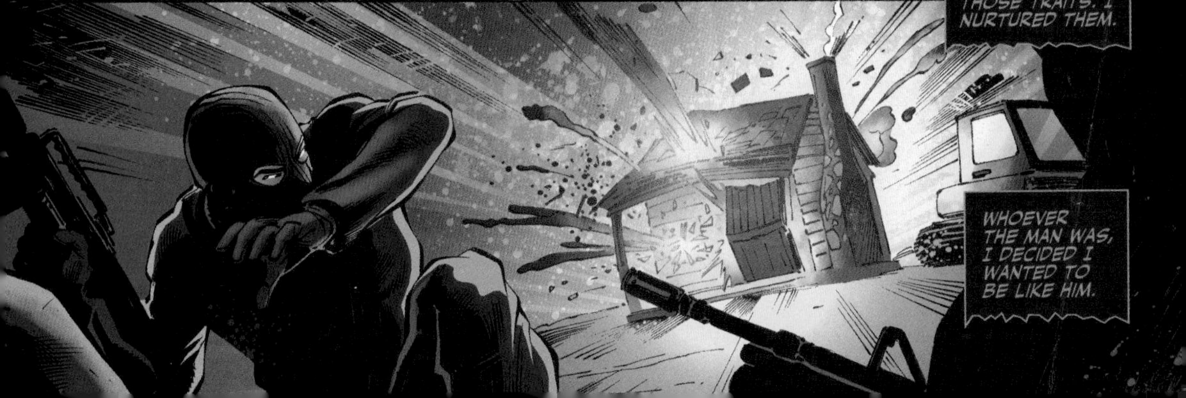
HE WAS DEFIANT. AGGRESSIVE. CUNNING.
I TOOK TO THOSE TRAITS. I NURTURED THEM.
WHOEVER THE MAN WAS, I DECIDED I WANTED TO BE LIKE HIM.

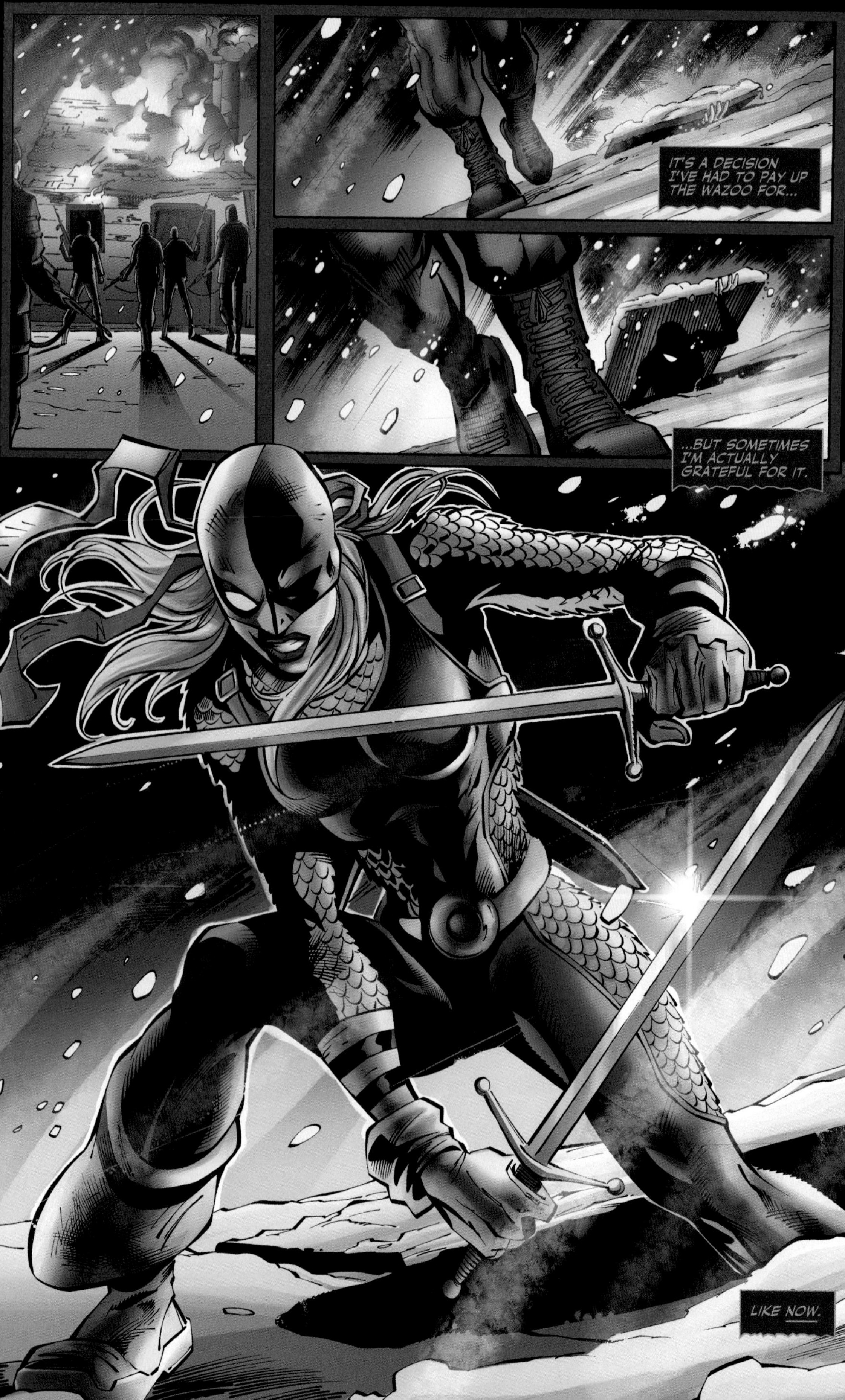
IT'S A DECISION I'VE HAD TO PAY UP THE WAZOO FOR...
...BUT SOMETIMES I'M ACTUALLY GRATEFUL FOR IT.
LIKE NOW.

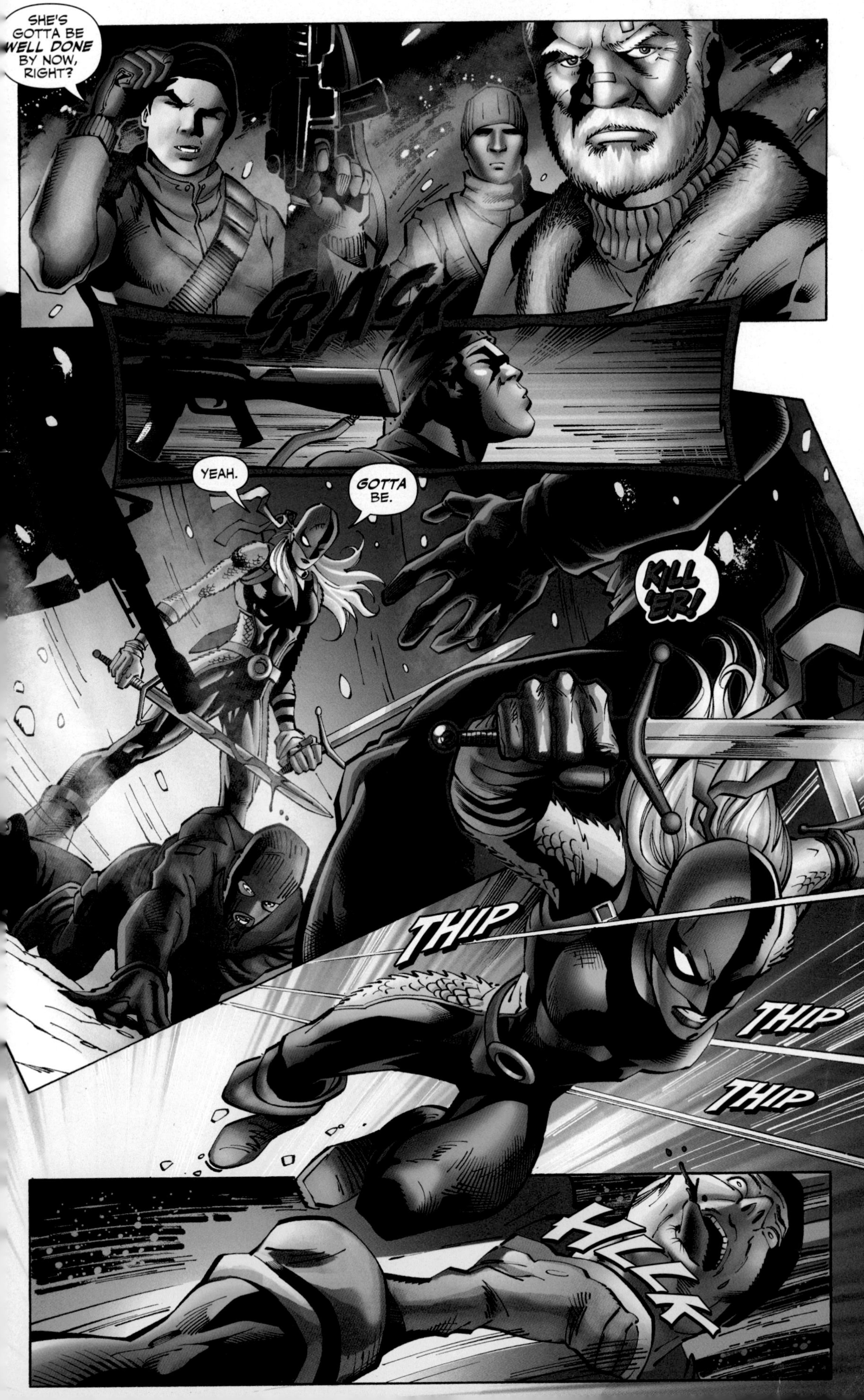
SHE'S GOTTA BE WELL DONE BY NOW, RIGHT?
CRACK
YEAH.
GOTTA BE.
KILL 'ER!
THIP
THIP
THIP
HLLK

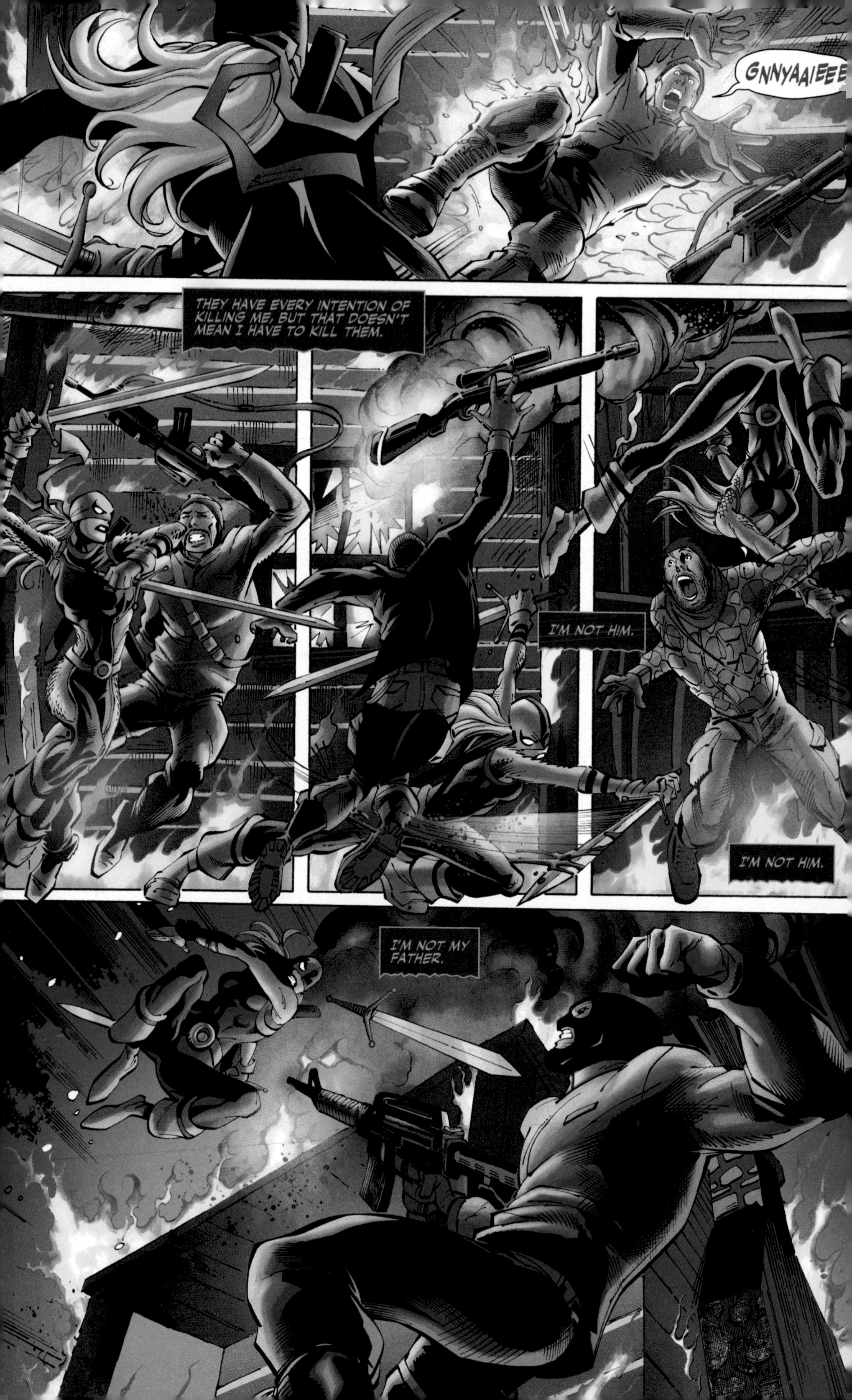
GNNYAAIEEE
THEY HAVE EVERY INTENTION OF KILLING ME, BUT THAT DOESN'T MEAN I HAVE TO KILL THEM.
I'M NOT HIM.
I'M NOT HIM.
I'M NOT MY FATHER.

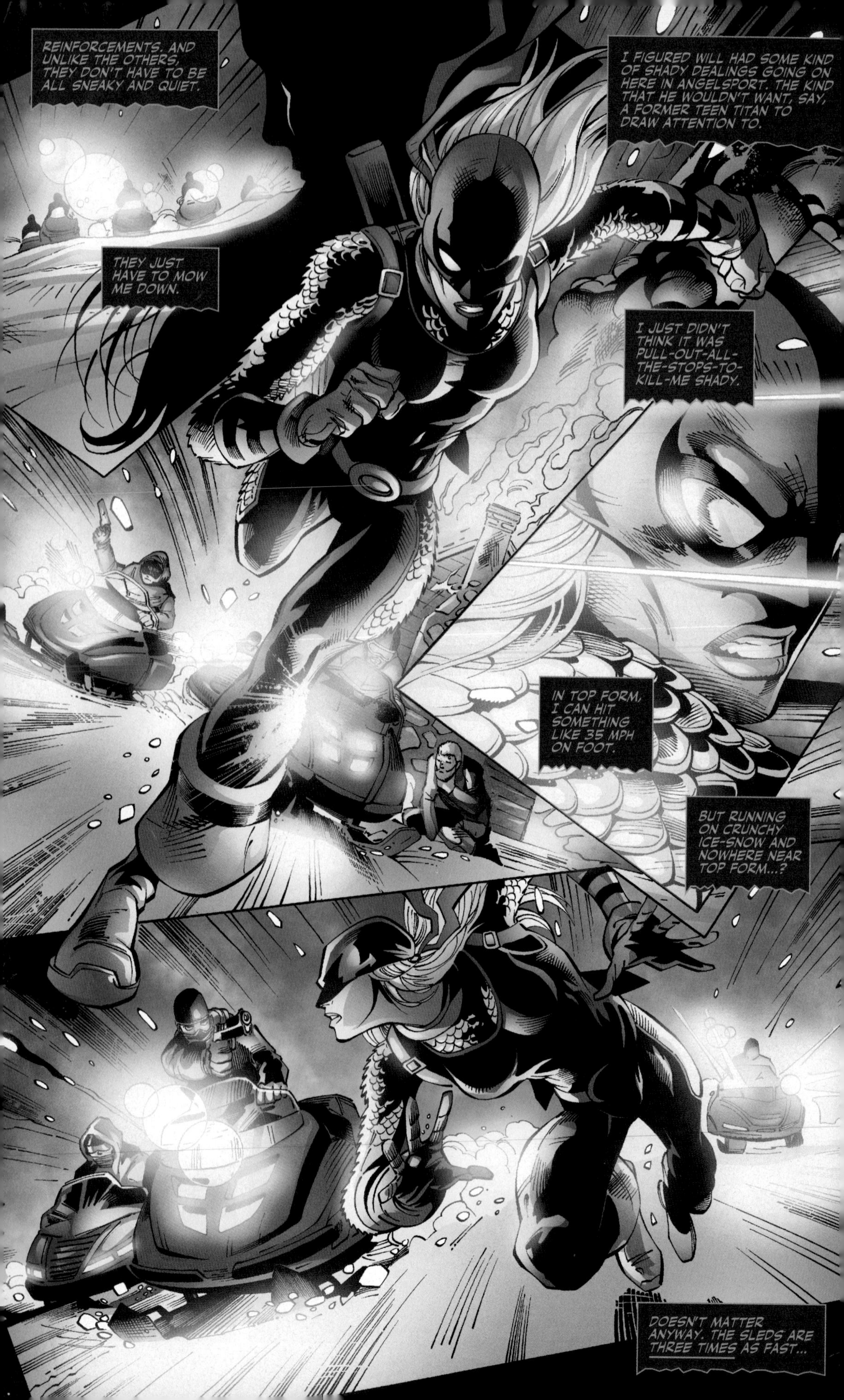
REINFORCEMENTS. AND UNLIKE THE OTHERS, THEY DON'T HAVE TO BE ALL SNEAKY AND QUIET.
THEY JUST HAVE TO MOW ME DOWN.
I FIGURED WILL HAD SOME KIND OF SHADY DEALINGS GOING ON HERE IN ANGELSPORT. THE KIND THAT HE WOULDN'T WANT, SAY, A FORMER TEEN TITAN TO DRAW ATTENTION TO.
I JUST DIDN'T THINK IT WAS PULL-OUT-ALL-THE-STOPS-TO-KILL-ME SHADY.
IN TOP FORM, I CAN HIT SOMETHING LIKE 35 MPH ON FOOT.
BUT RUNNING ON CRUNCHY ICE-SNOW AND NOWHERE NEAR TOP FORM...?
DOESN'T MATTER ANYWAY. THE SLEDS ARE THREE TIMES AS FAST...

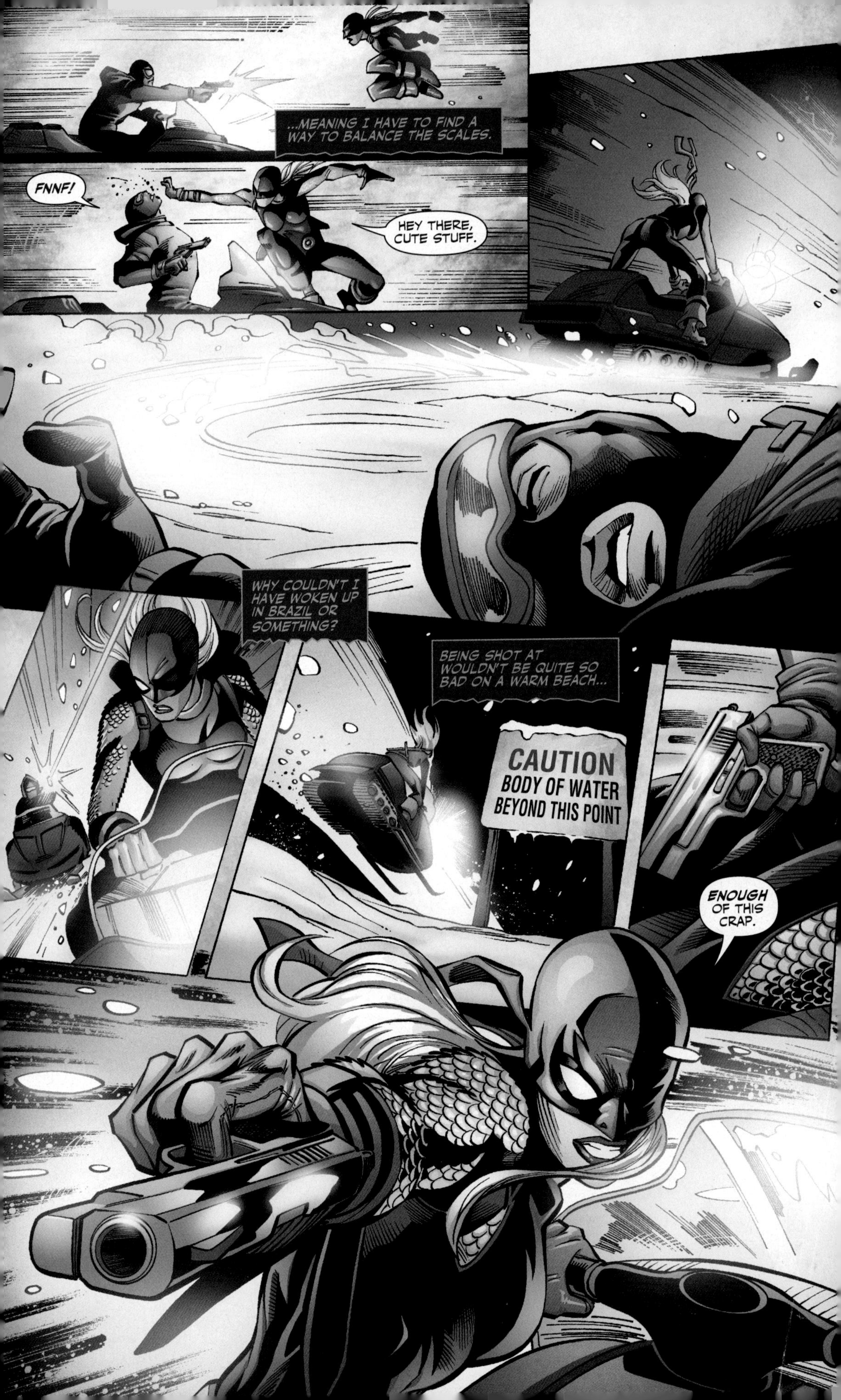
...MEANING I HAVE TO FIND A WAY TO BALANCE THE SCALES.
FNNF!
HEY THERE, CUTE STUFF.
WHY COULDN'T I HAVE WOKEN UP IN BRAZIL OR SOMETHING?
BEING SHOT AT WOULDN'T BE QUITE SO BAD ON A WARM BEACH...
CAUTION
BODY OF WATER
BEYOND THIS POINT
ENOUGH OF THIS CRAP.

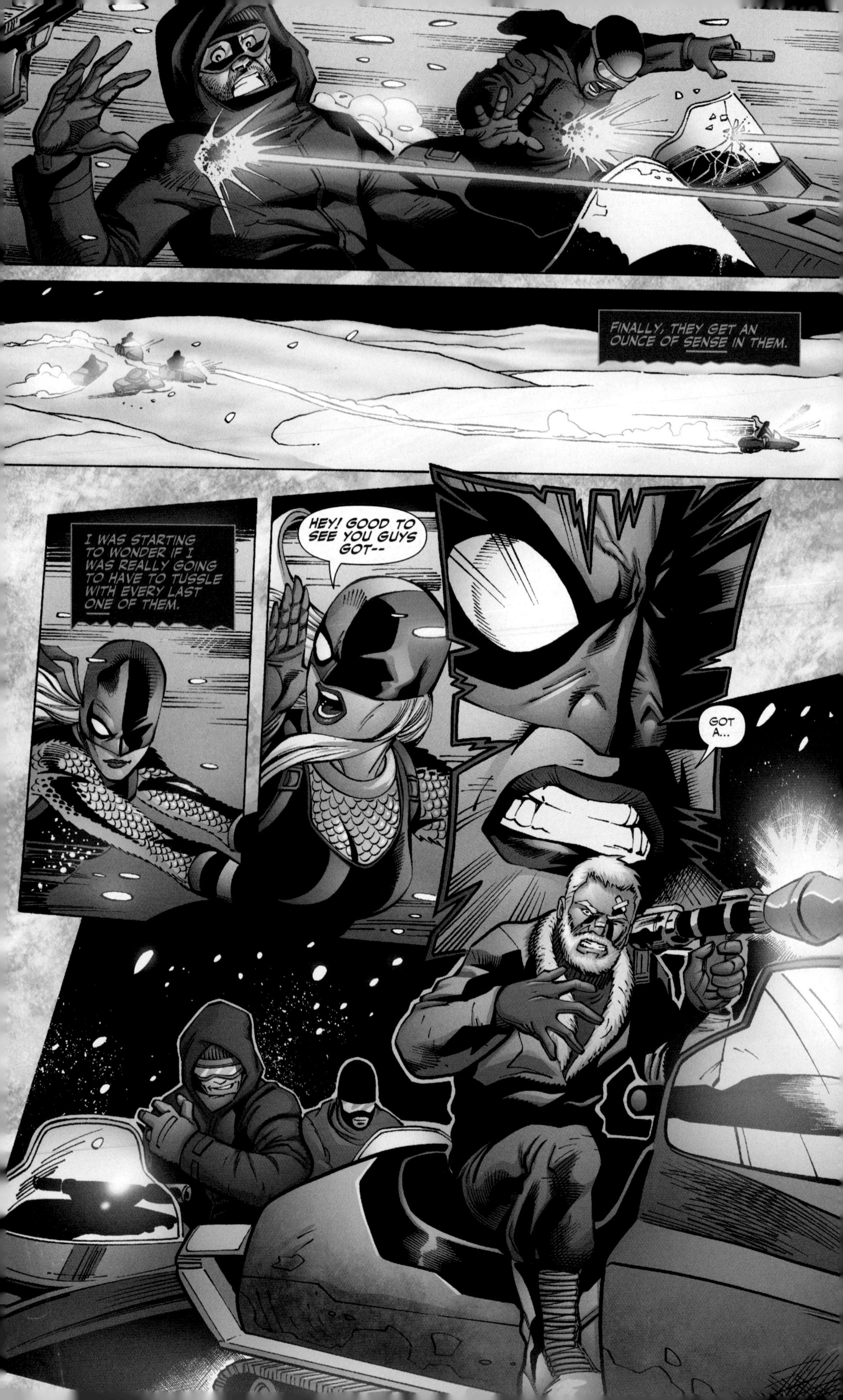

FINALLY, THEY GET AN OUNCE OF SENSE IN THEM.
I WAS STARTING TO WONDER IF I WAS REALLY GOING TO HAVE TO TUSSLE WITH EVERY LAST ONE OF THEM.
HEY! GOOD TO SEE YOU GUYS GOT--
GOT A...

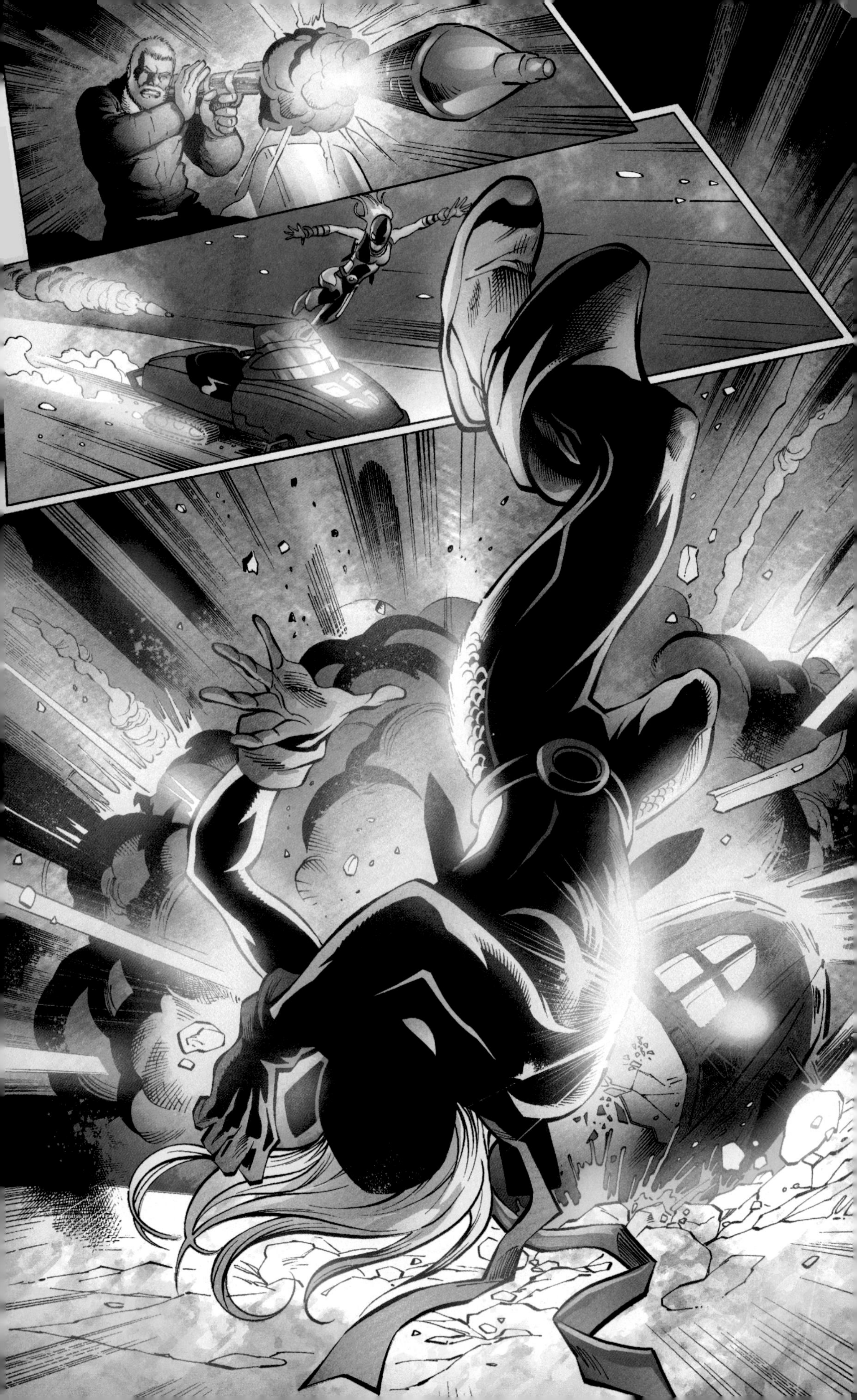

THAT'S IT.
IF SHE AIN'T
DEAD...

LONG'S IT
BEEN?

THREE
MINUTES AN'
CHANGE.

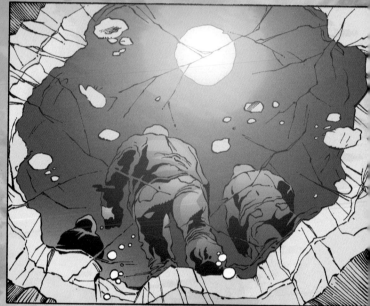

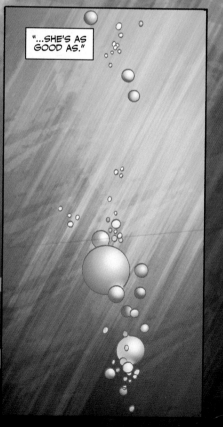
"...SHE'S AS
GOOD AS."

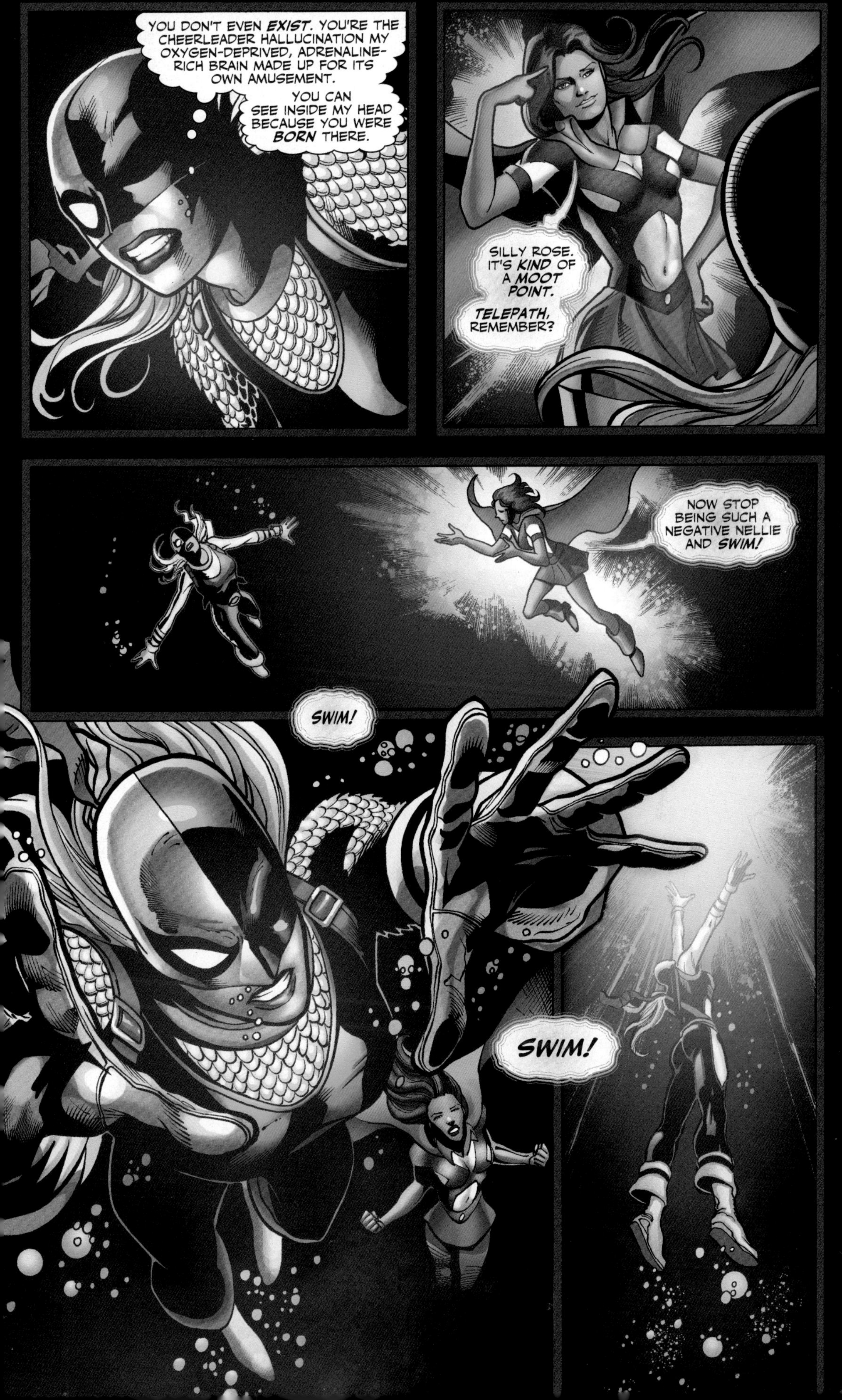
YOU DON'T EVEN EXIST. YOU'RE THE CHEERLEADER HALLUCINATION MY OXYGEN-DEPRIVED, ADRENALINE-RICH BRAIN MADE UP FOR ITS OWN AMUSEMENT.
YOU CAN SEE INSIDE MY HEAD BECAUSE YOU WERE BORN THERE.
SILLY ROSE. IT'S KIND OF A MOOT POINT.
TELEPATH, REMEMBER?
NOW STOP BEING SUCH A NEGATIVE NELLIE AND SWIM!
SWIM!
SWIM!

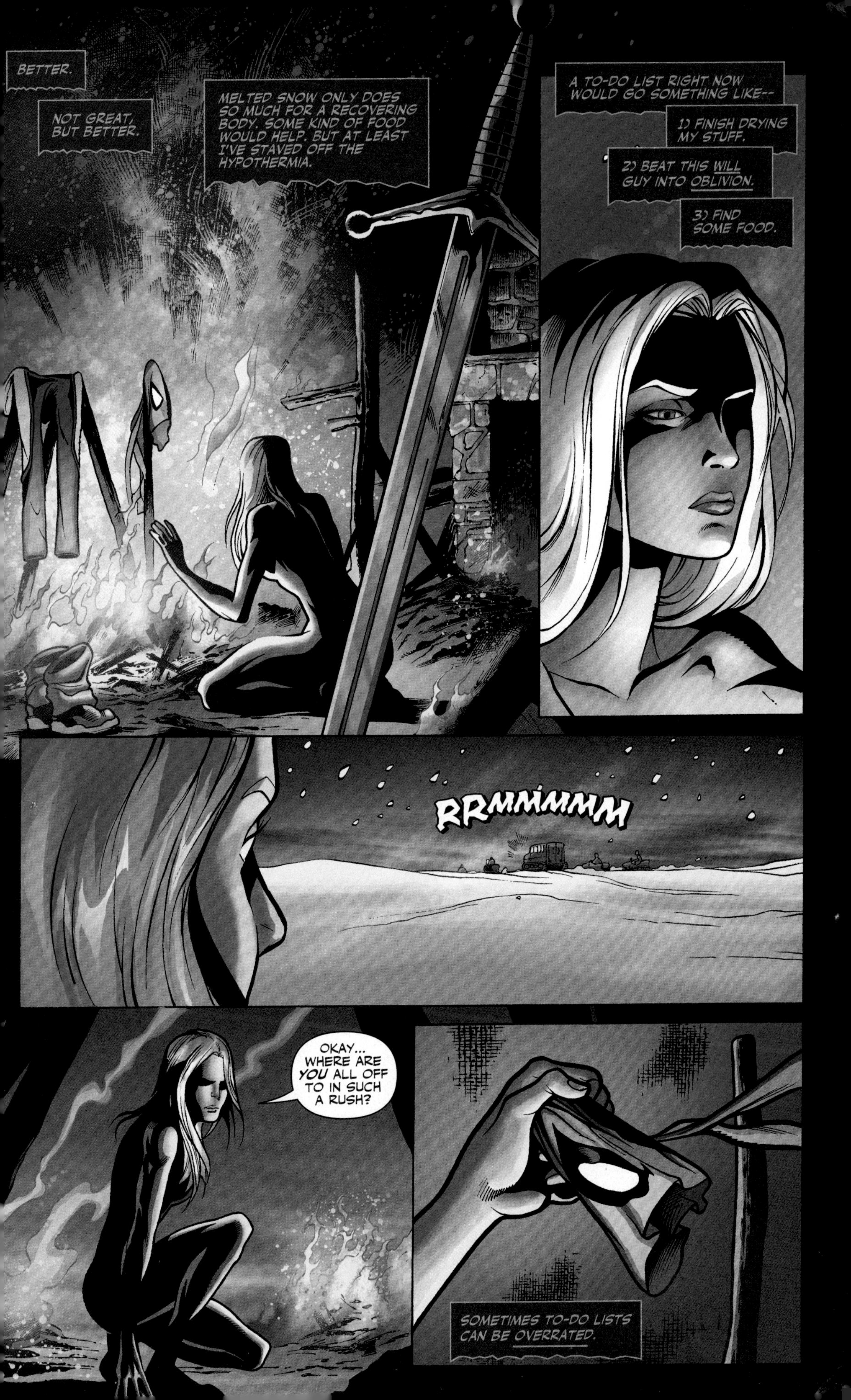

BETTER.
NOT GREAT, BUT BETTER.
MELTED SNOW ONLY DOES SO MUCH FOR A RECOVERING BODY. SOME KIND OF FOOD WOULD HELP. BUT AT LEAST I'VE STAVED OFF THE HYPOTHERMIA.
A TO-DO LIST RIGHT NOW WOULD GO SOMETHING LIKE--
1) FINISH DRYING MY STUFF.
2) BEAT THIS WILL GUY INTO OBLIVION.
3) FIND SOME FOOD.
RRMMMMM
OKAY... WHERE ARE YOU ALL OFF TO IN SUCH A RUSH?
SOMETIMES TO-DO LISTS CAN BE OVERRATED.

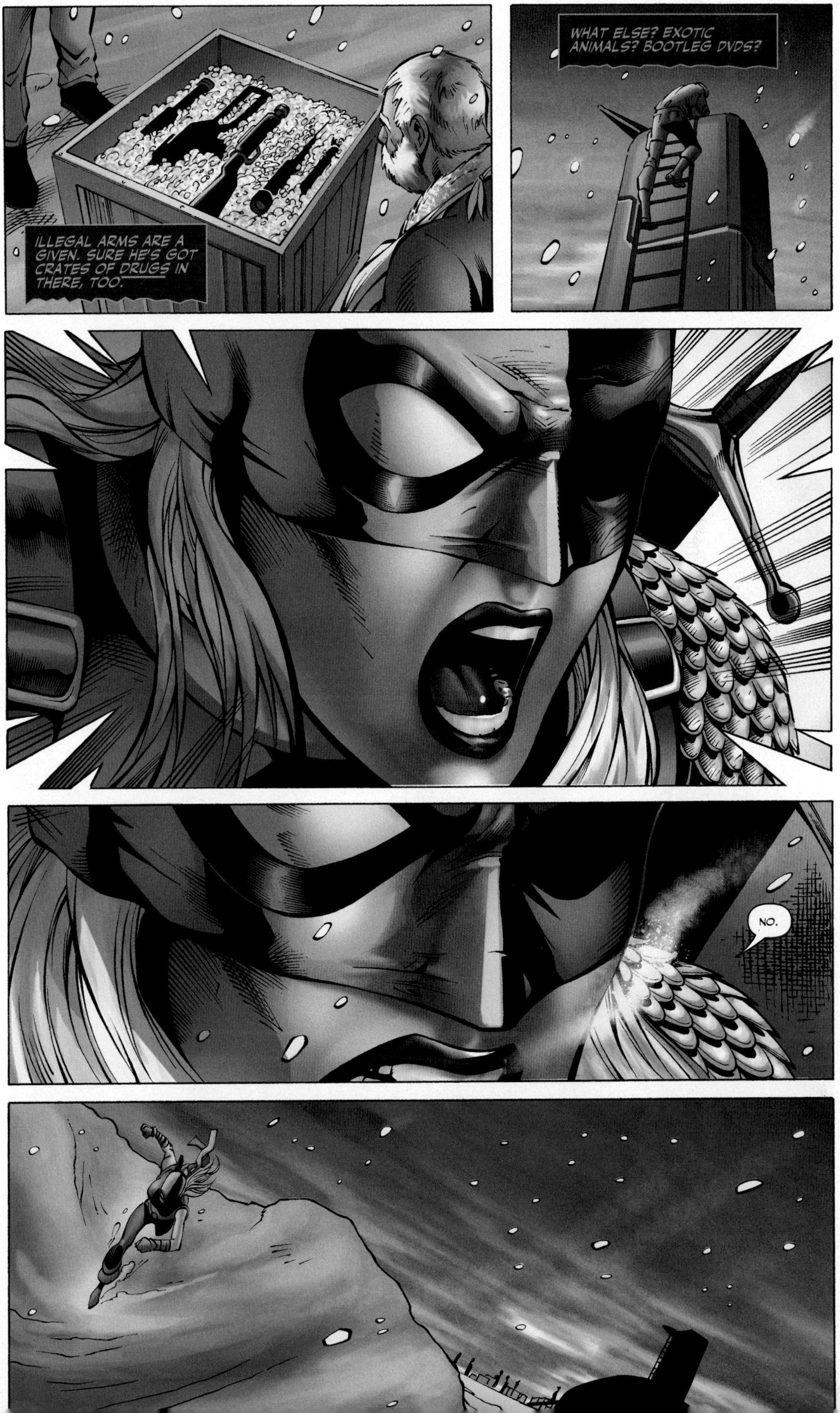
ILLEGAL ARMS ARE A GIVEN. SURE HE'S GOT CRATES OF DRUGS IN THERE, TOO.
WHAT ELSE? EXOTIC ANIMALS? BOOTLEG DVDS?
NO.

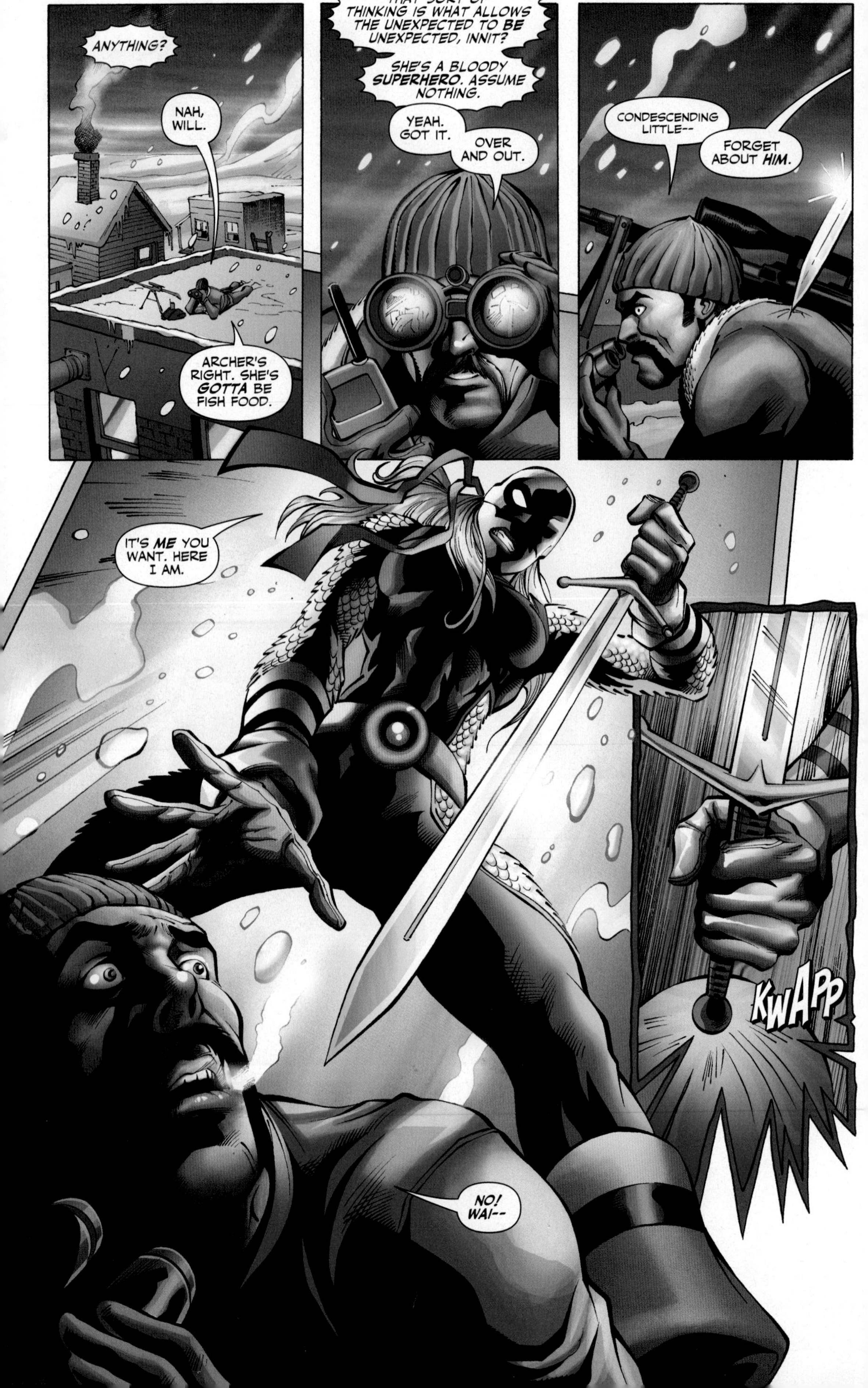
ANYTHING?
NAH, WILL.
ARCHER'S RIGHT. SHE'S GOTTA BE FISH FOOD.
THAT SORT OF THINKING IS WHAT ALLOWS THE UNEXPECTED TO BE UNEXPECTED, INNIT?
SHE'S A BLOODY SUPERHERO. ASSUME NOTHING.
YEAH. GOT IT.
OVER AND OUT.
CONDESCENDING LITTLE--
FORGET ABOUT HIM.
IT'S ME YOU WANT. HERE I AM.
KWAPP
NO! WAI--

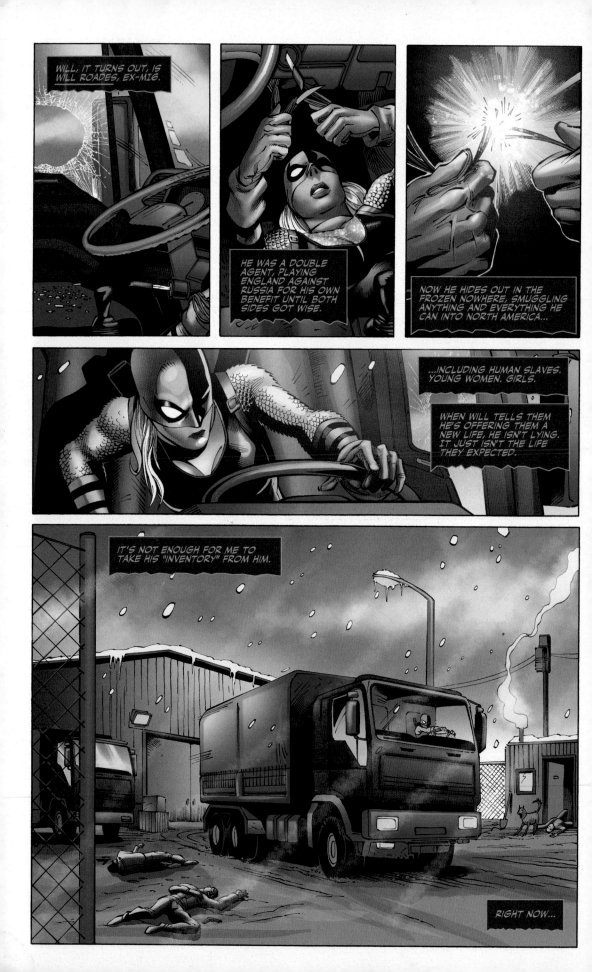

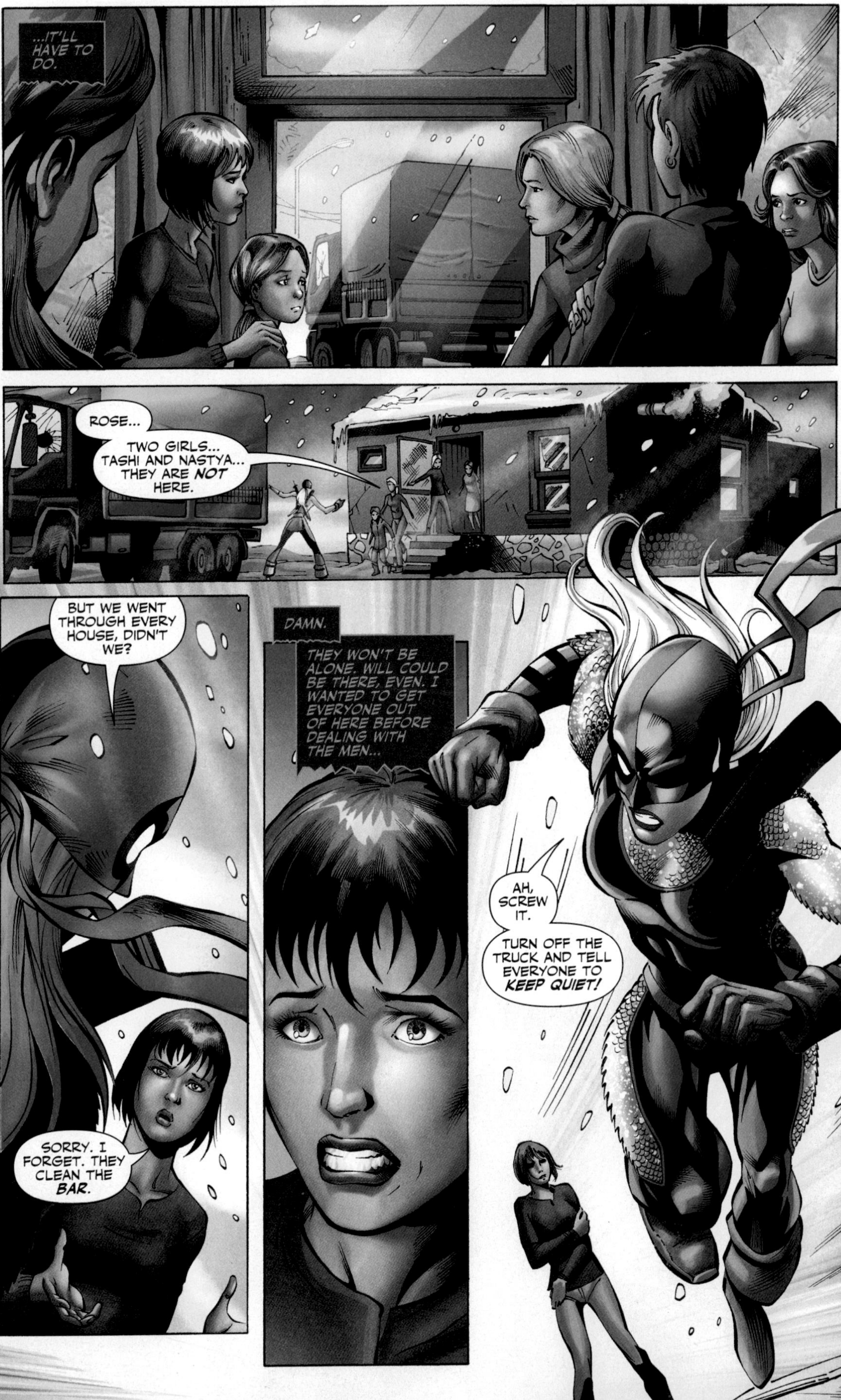
...IT'LL HAVE TO DO.
ROSE... TWO GIRLS... TASHI AND NASTYA... THEY ARE NOT HERE.
BUT WE WENT THROUGH EVERY HOUSE, DIDN'T WE?
SORRY. I FORGET. THEY CLEAN THE BAR.
DAMN.
THEY WON'T BE ALONE. WILL COULD BE THERE, EVEN. I WANTED TO GET EVERYONE OUT OF HERE BEFORE DEALING WITH THE MEN...
AH, SCREW IT.
TURN OFF THE TRUCK AND TELL EVERYONE TO KEEP QUIET!

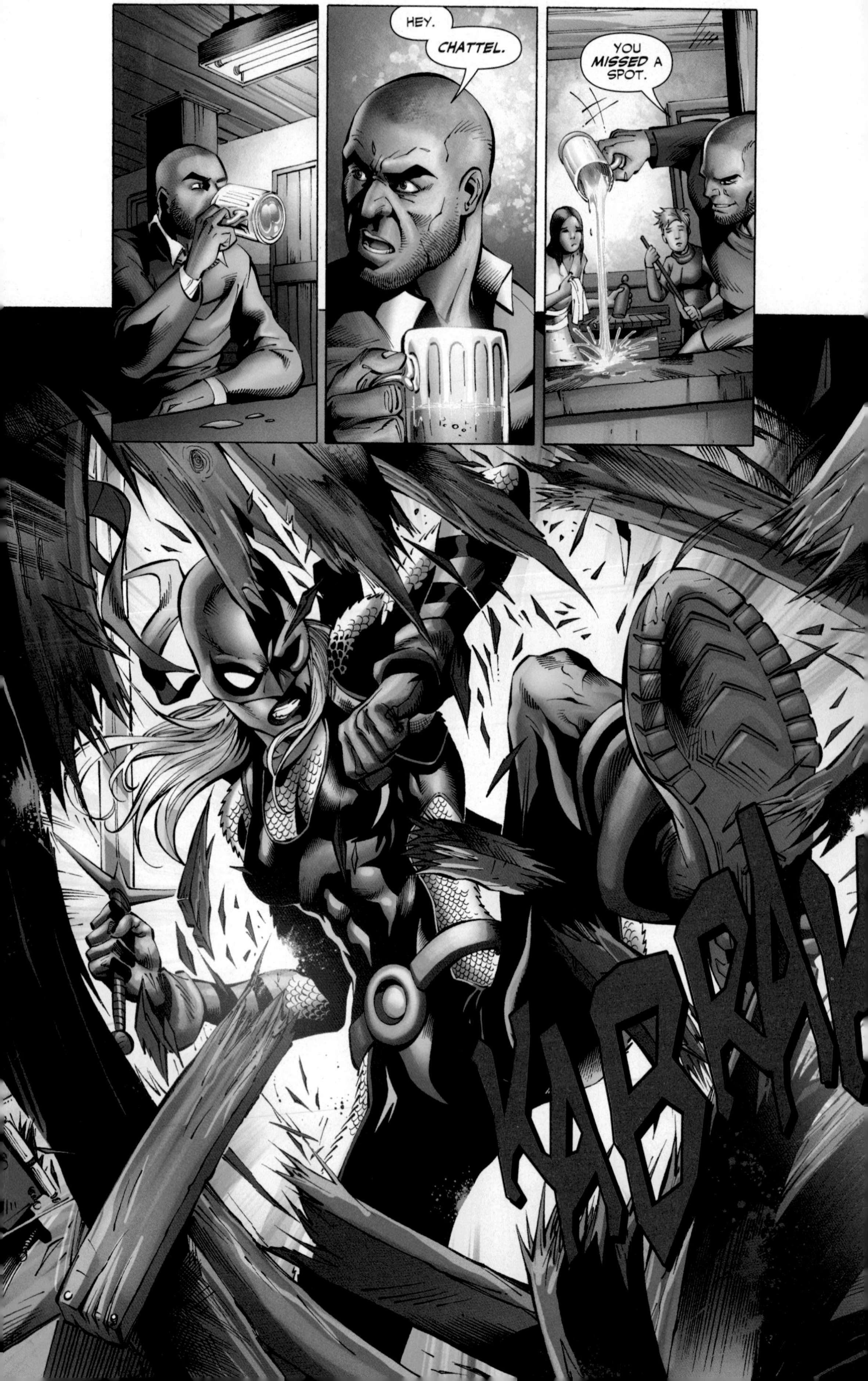
HEY.
CHATTEL.
YOU MISSED A SPOT.
KABRA

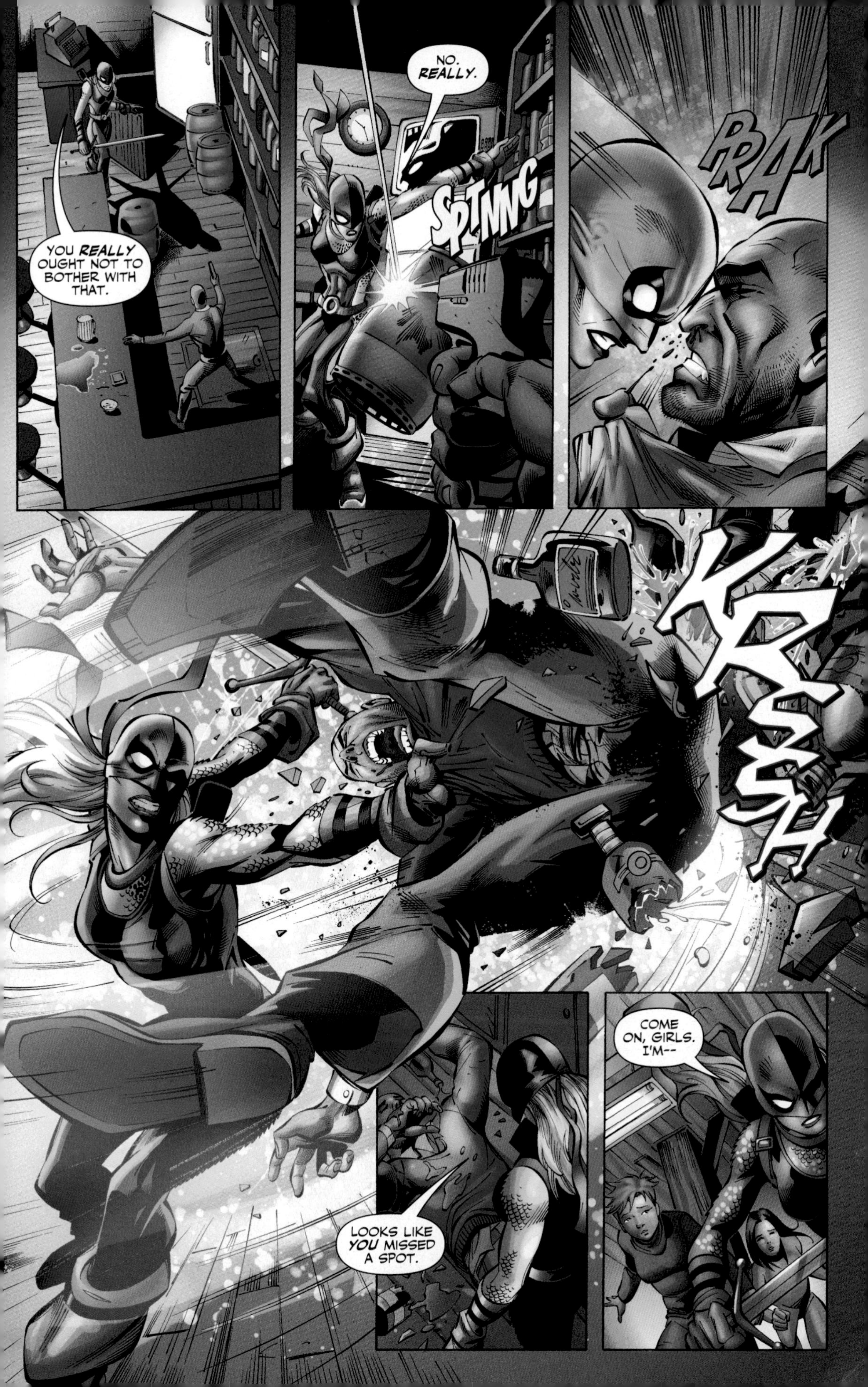
YOU REALLY OUGHT NOT TO BOTHER WITH THAT.
NO. REALLY.
SPTNNG
PRAK
KRSSH
LOOKS LIKE YOU MISSED A SPOT.
COME ON, GIRLS. I'M--

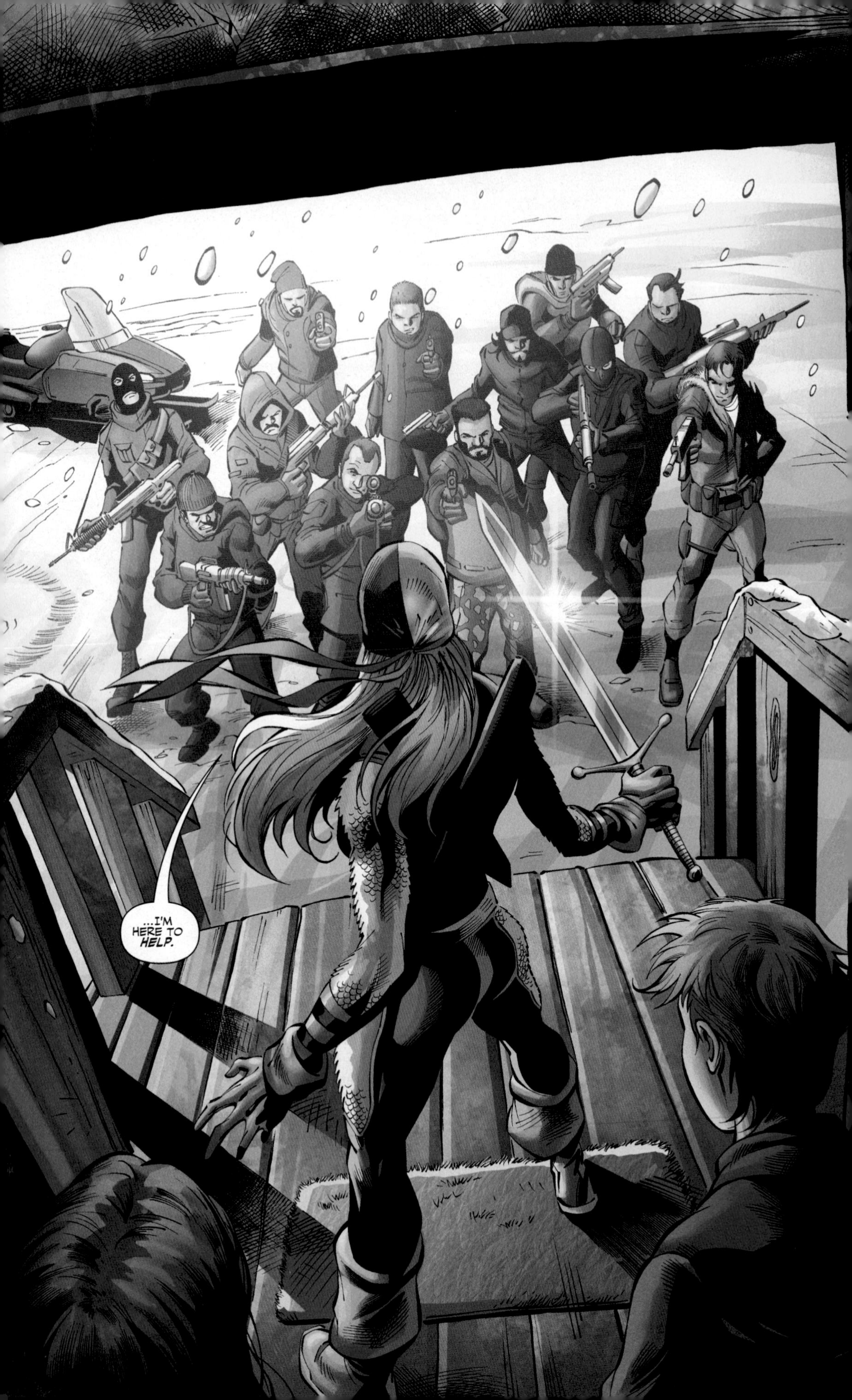
...I'M HERE TO HELP.

NO. NOT TODAY.

NOT ANYTIME SOON.

WELL, NOW...

THAT WAS WORTH EVERY *BIT* OF TROUBLE SHE'S CAUSED.

CR!K

YOU TWO TAKE HER INSIDE. AND SOMEONE CALL *DOC BARDEN.*

TIME TO CONSCRIPT MYSELF A *SUPER-SOLDIER.*

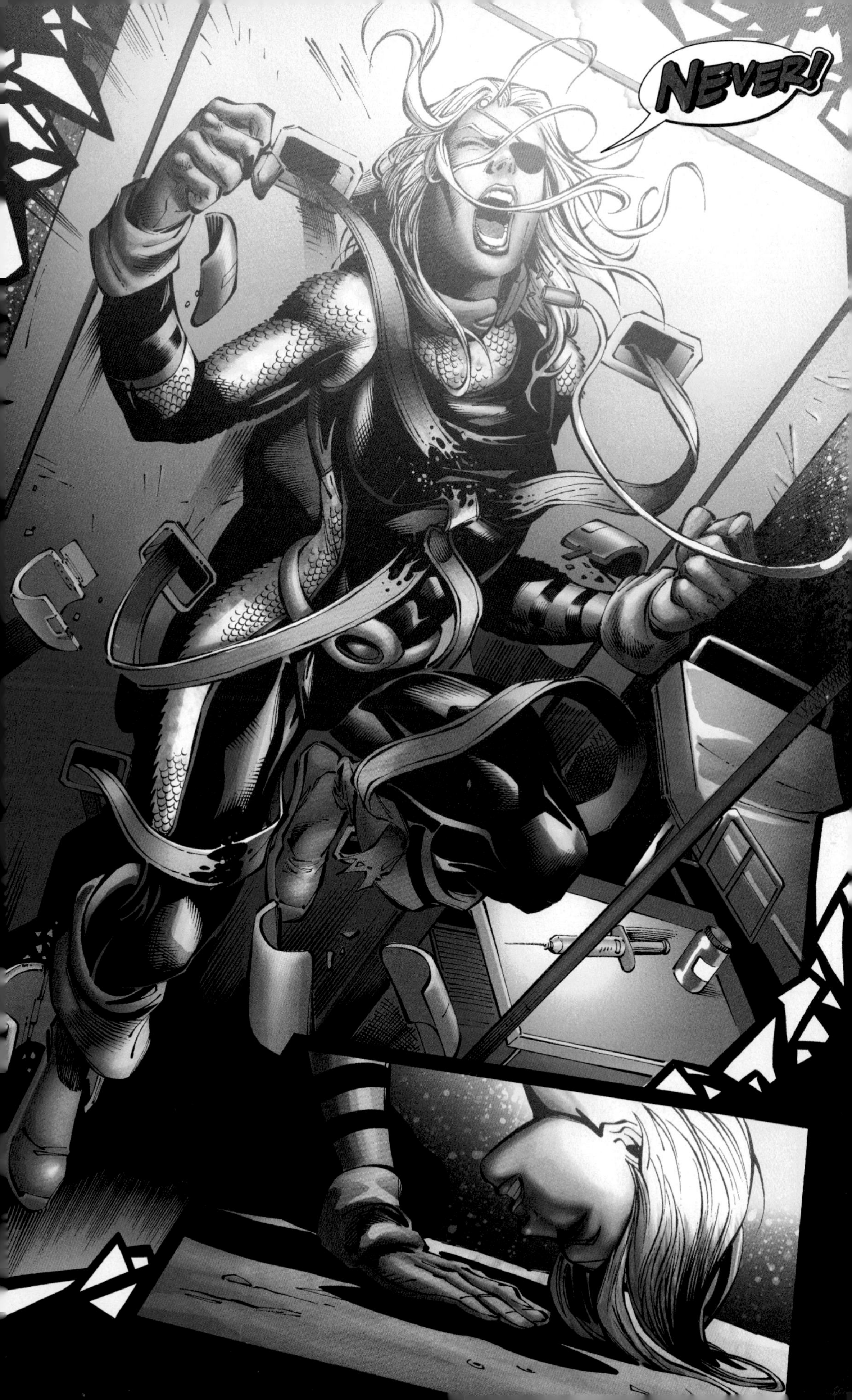
NEVER!

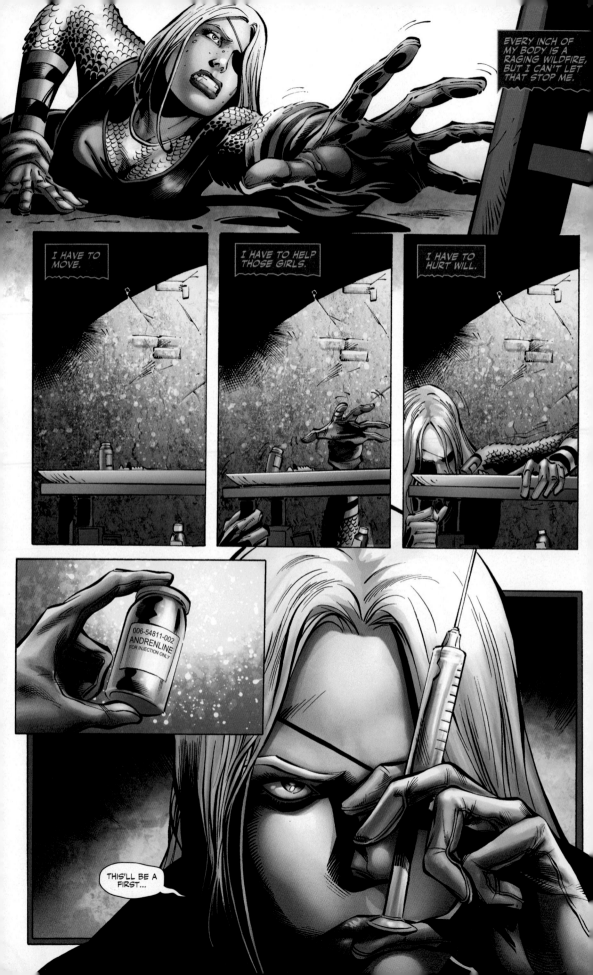

EVERY INCH OF MY BODY IS A RAGING WILDFIRE, BUT I CAN'T LET THAT STOP ME.

I HAVE TO MOVE.

I HAVE TO HELP THOSE GIRLS.

I HAVE TO HURT WILL.

006-54811-002
ANDRENLINE
FOR INJECTION ONLY

THIS'LL BE A FIRST...

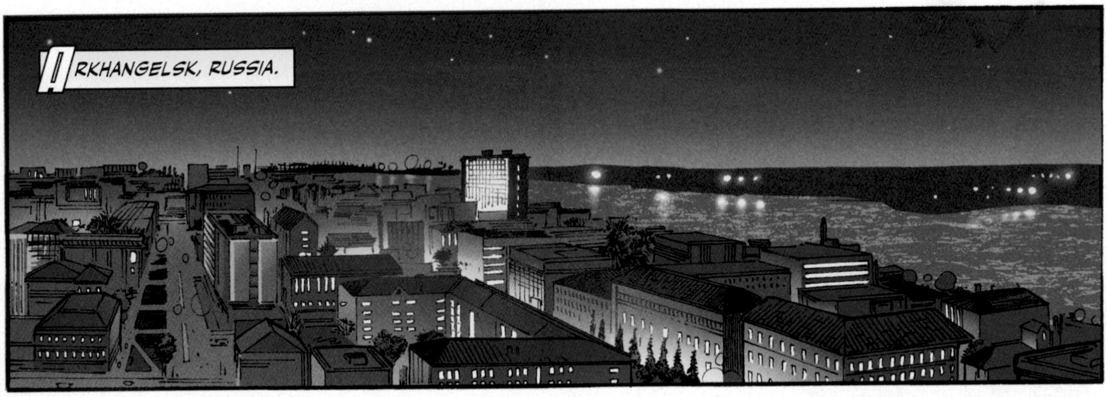
ARKHANGELSK, RUSSIA.

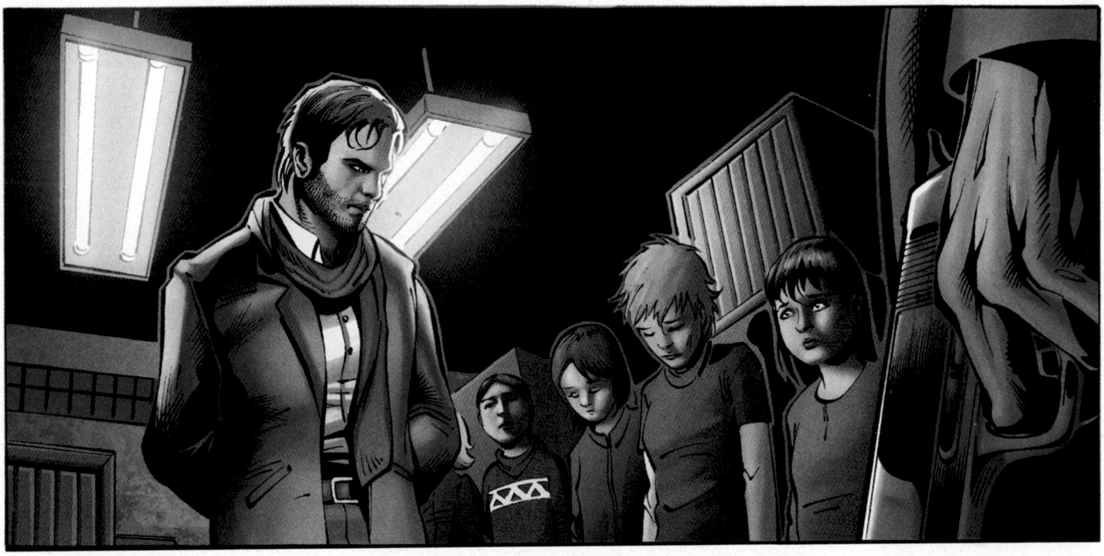

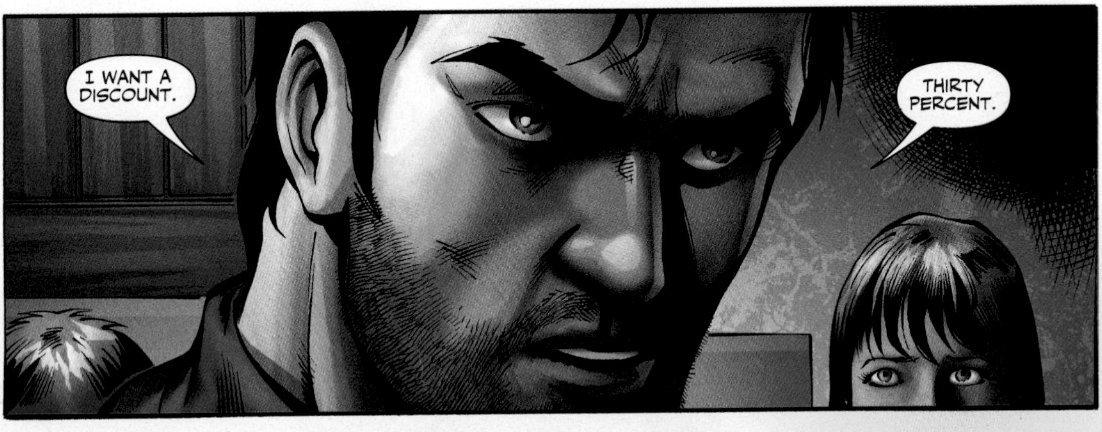
I WANT A DISCOUNT.
THIRTY PERCENT.

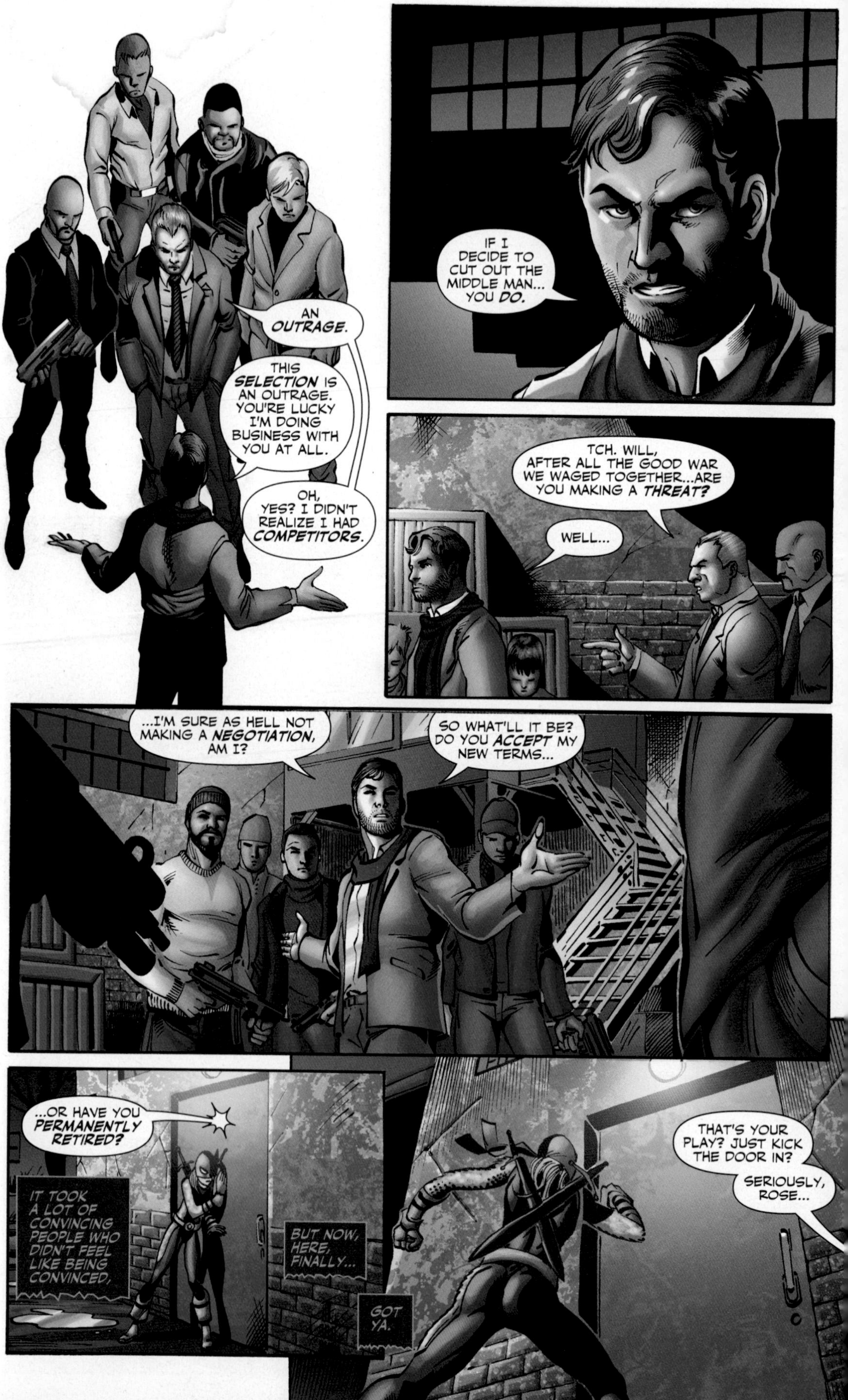
AN OUTRAGE.
THIS SELECTION IS AN OUTRAGE. YOU'RE LUCKY I'M DOING BUSINESS WITH YOU AT ALL.
OH, YES? I DIDN'T REALIZE I HAD COMPETITORS.
IF I DECIDE TO CUT OUT THE MIDDLE MAN... YOU DO.
TCH. WILL, AFTER ALL THE GOOD WAR WE WAGED TOGETHER...ARE YOU MAKING A THREAT?
WELL...
...I'M SURE AS HELL NOT MAKING A NEGOTIATION, AM I?
SO WHAT'LL IT BE? DO YOU ACCEPT MY NEW TERMS...
...OR HAVE YOU PERMANENTLY RETIRED?
IT TOOK A LOT OF CONVINCING PEOPLE WHO DIDN'T FEEL LIKE BEING CONVINCED,
BUT NOW, HERE, FINALLY...
GOT YA.
THAT'S YOUR PLAY? JUST KICK THE DOOR IN?
SERIOUSLY, ROSE...

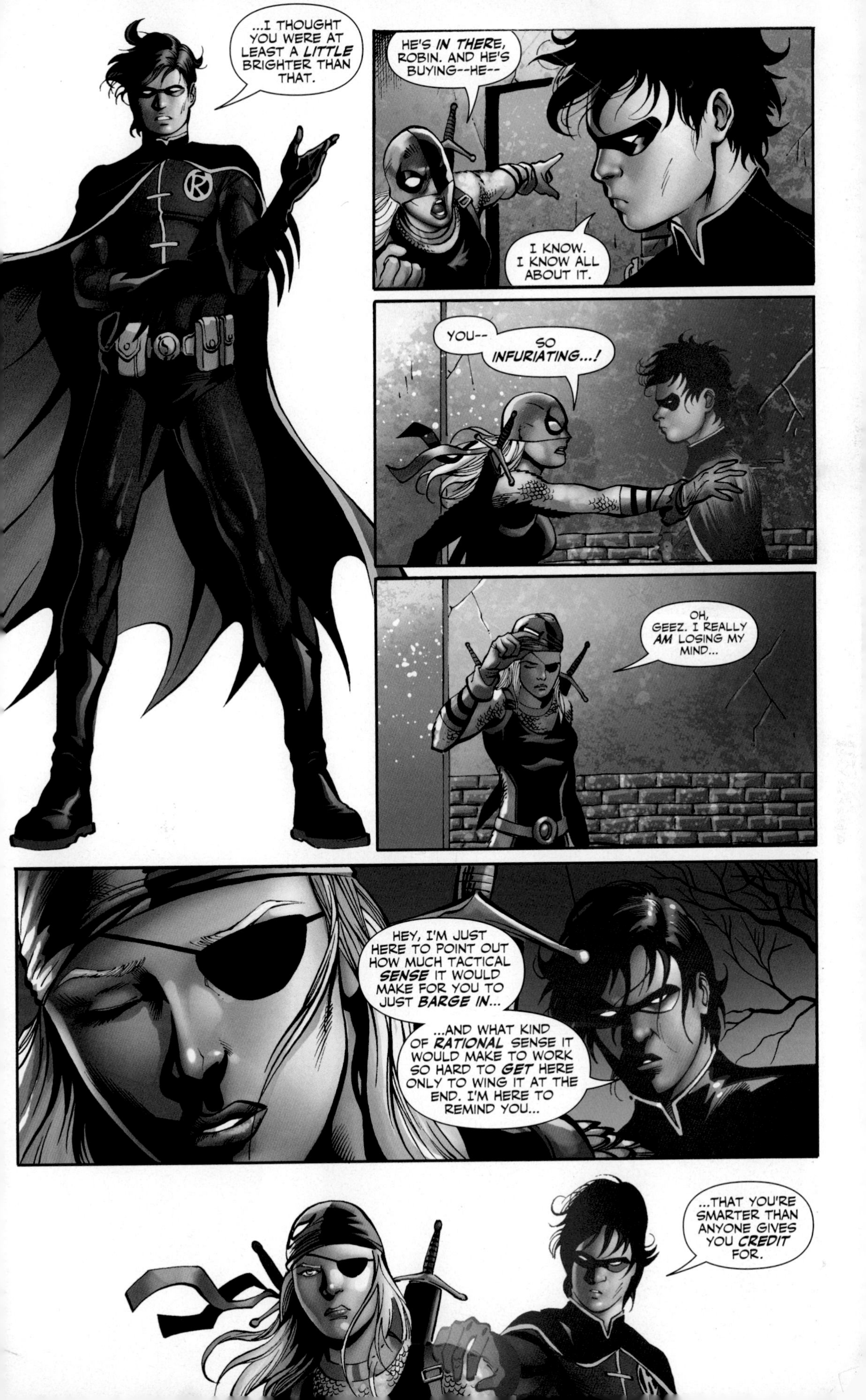
...I THOUGHT YOU WERE AT LEAST A LITTLE BRIGHTER THAN THAT.
HE'S IN THERE, ROBIN. AND HE'S BUYING--HE--
I KNOW. I KNOW ALL ABOUT IT.
YOU--
SO INFURIATING...!
OH, GEEZ. I REALLY AM LOSING MY MIND...
HEY, I'M JUST HERE TO POINT OUT HOW MUCH TACTICAL SENSE IT WOULD MAKE FOR YOU TO JUST BARGE IN...
...AND WHAT KIND OF RATIONAL SENSE IT WOULD MAKE TO WORK SO HARD TO GET HERE ONLY TO WING IT AT THE END. I'M HERE TO REMIND YOU...
...THAT YOU'RE SMARTER THAN ANYONE GIVES YOU CREDIT FOR.

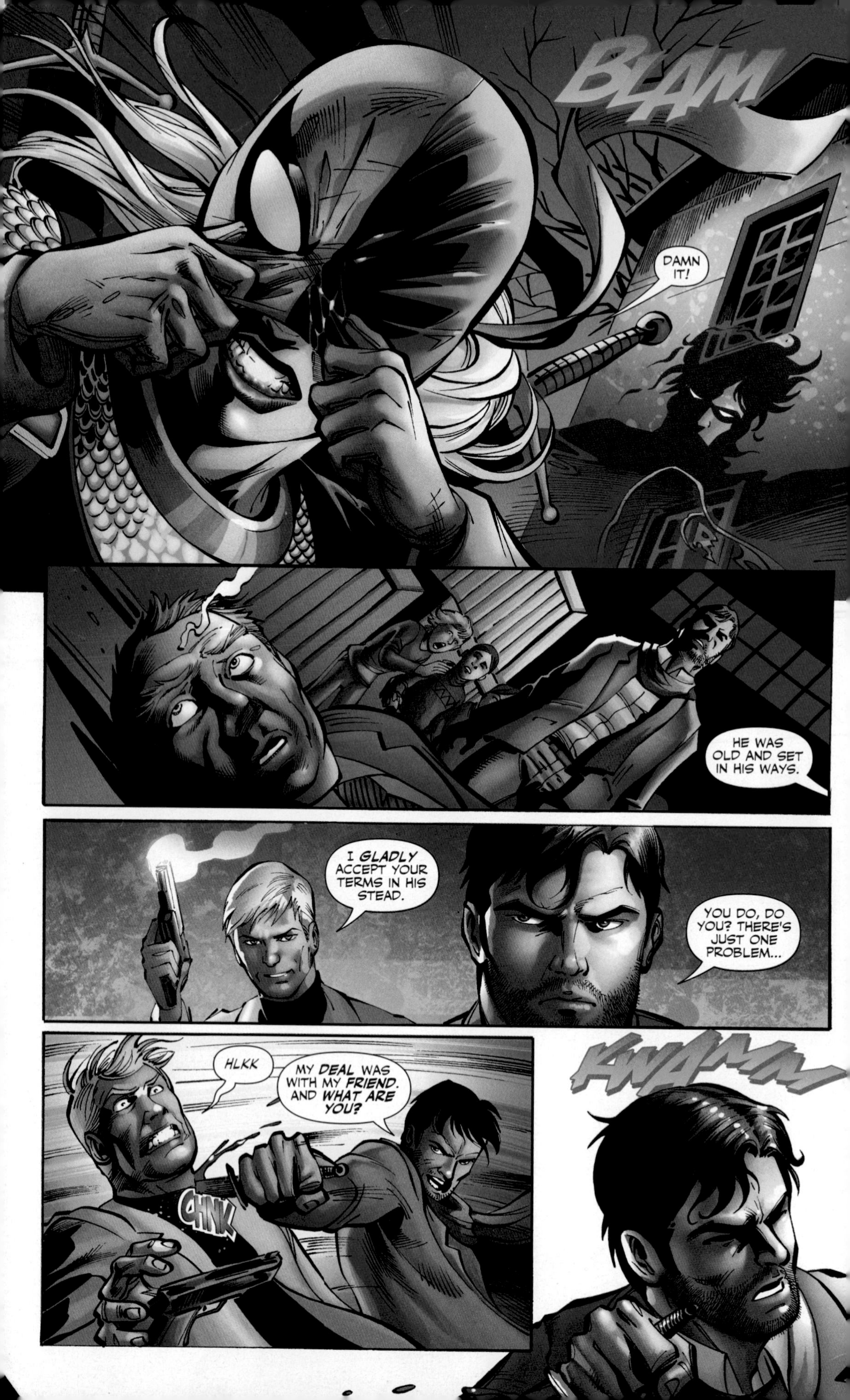
BLAM
DAMN IT!
HE WAS OLD AND SET IN HIS WAYS.
I GLADLY ACCEPT YOUR TERMS IN HIS STEAD.
YOU DO, DO YOU? THERE'S JUST ONE PROBLEM...
HLKK
MY DEAL WAS WITH MY FRIEND. AND WHAT ARE YOU?
CHNK
KWAMM

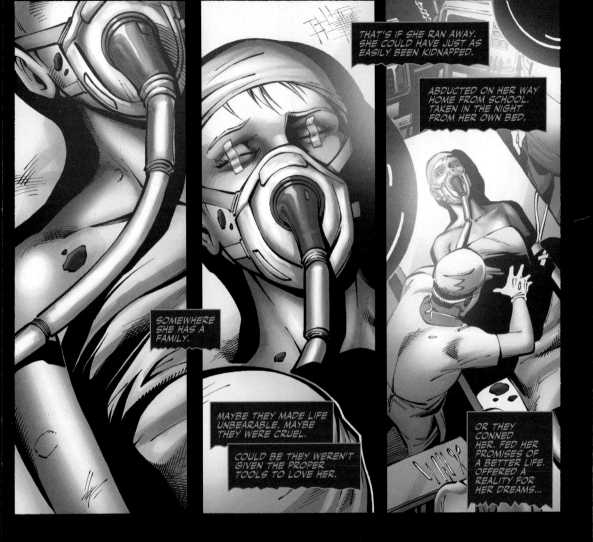

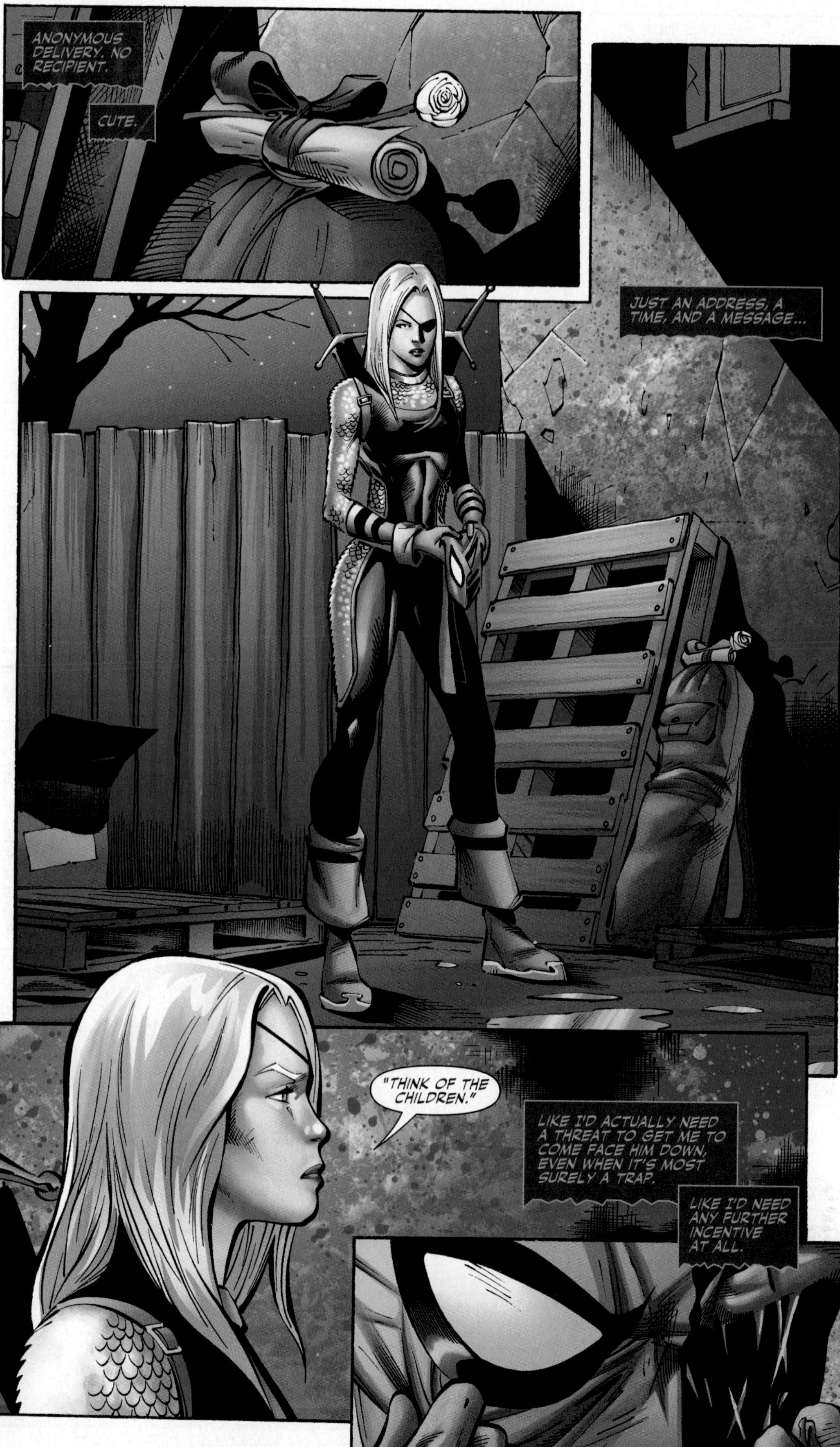
ANONYMOUS DELIVERY. NO RECIPIENT.
CUTE.
JUST AN ADDRESS, A TIME, AND A MESSAGE...
"THINK OF THE CHILDREN."
LIKE I'D ACTUALLY NEED A THREAT TO GET ME TO COME FACE HIM DOWN, EVEN WHEN IT'S MOST SURELY A TRAP.
LIKE I'D NEED ANY FURTHER INCENTIVE AT ALL.

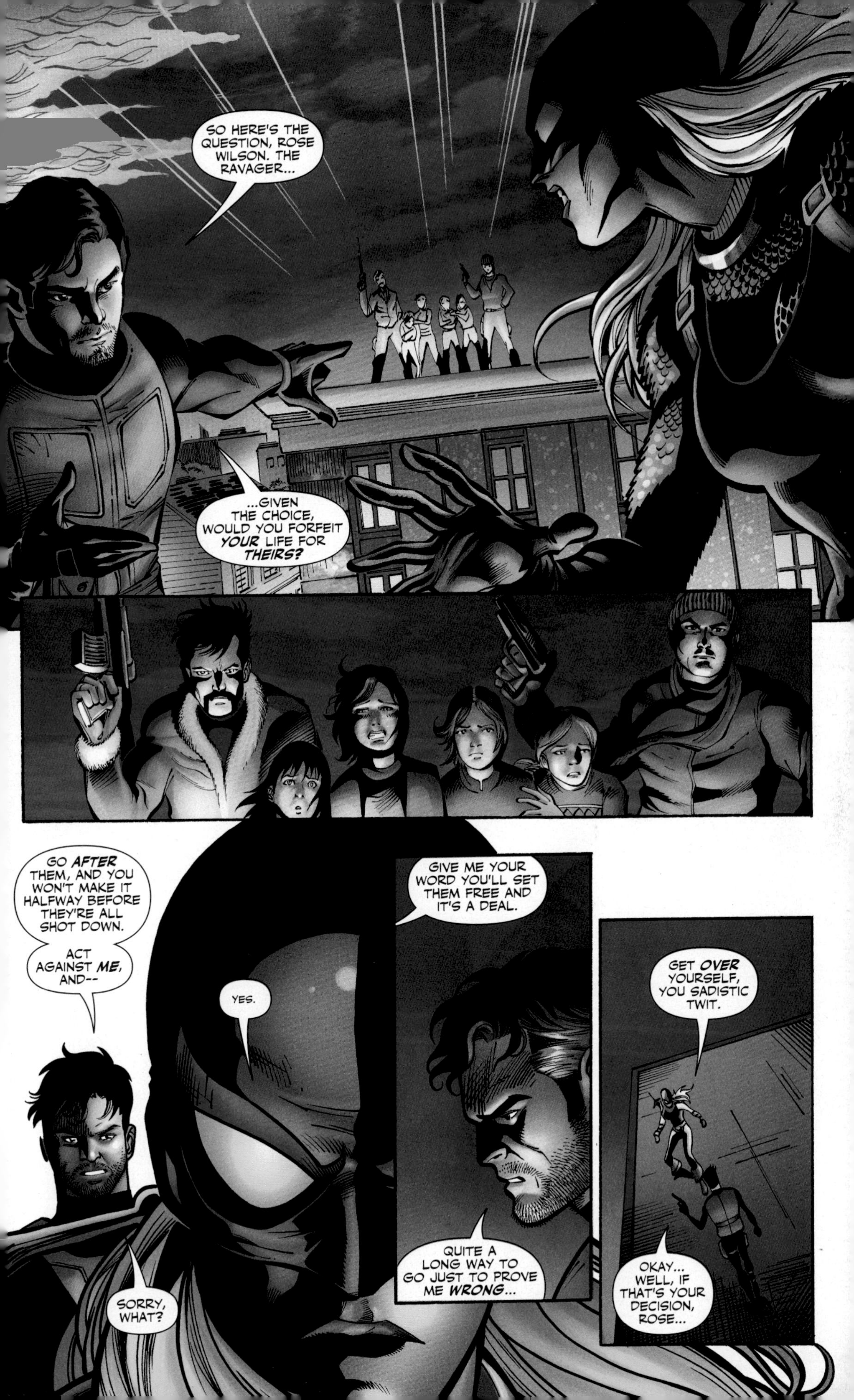
SO HERE'S THE QUESTION, ROSE WILSON. THE RAVAGER...
...GIVEN THE CHOICE, WOULD YOU FORFEIT YOUR LIFE FOR THEIRS?
GO AFTER THEM, AND YOU WON'T MAKE IT HALFWAY BEFORE THEY'RE ALL SHOT DOWN.
ACT AGAINST ME, AND--
YES.
SORRY, WHAT?
GIVE ME YOUR WORD YOU'LL SET THEM FREE AND IT'S A DEAL.
QUITE A LONG WAY TO GO JUST TO PROVE ME WRONG...
GET OVER YOURSELF, YOU SADISTIC TWIT.
OKAY... WELL, IF THAT'S YOUR DECISION, ROSE...

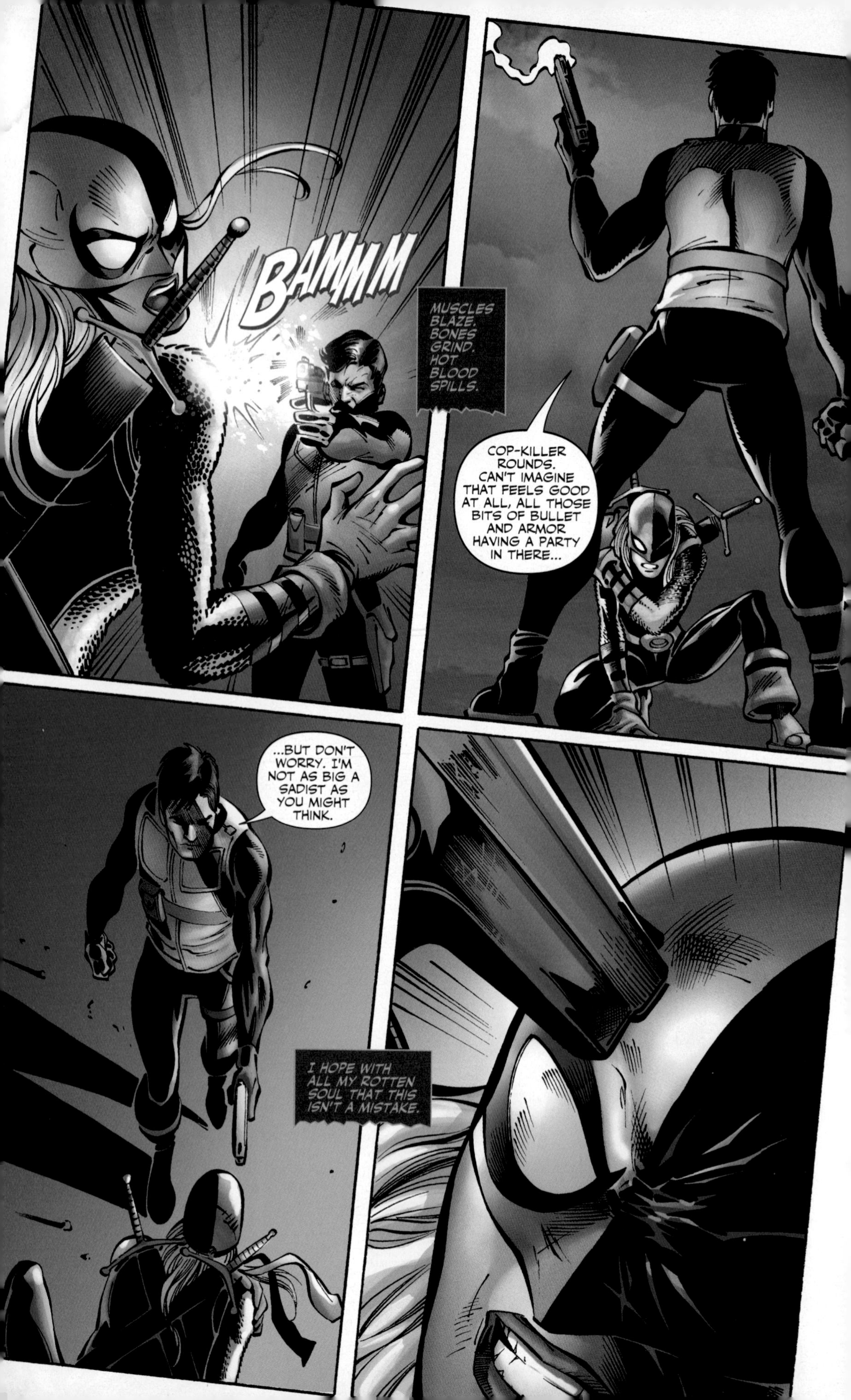
BAMMM
MUSCLES BLAZE. BONES GRIND. HOT BLOOD SPILLS.
COP-KILLER ROUNDS. CAN'T IMAGINE THAT FEELS GOOD AT ALL, ALL THOSE BITS OF BULLET AND ARMOR HAVING A PARTY IN THERE...
...BUT DON'T WORRY. I'M NOT AS BIG A SADIST AS YOU MIGHT THINK.
I HOPE WITH ALL MY ROTTEN SOUL THAT THIS ISN'T A MISTAKE.

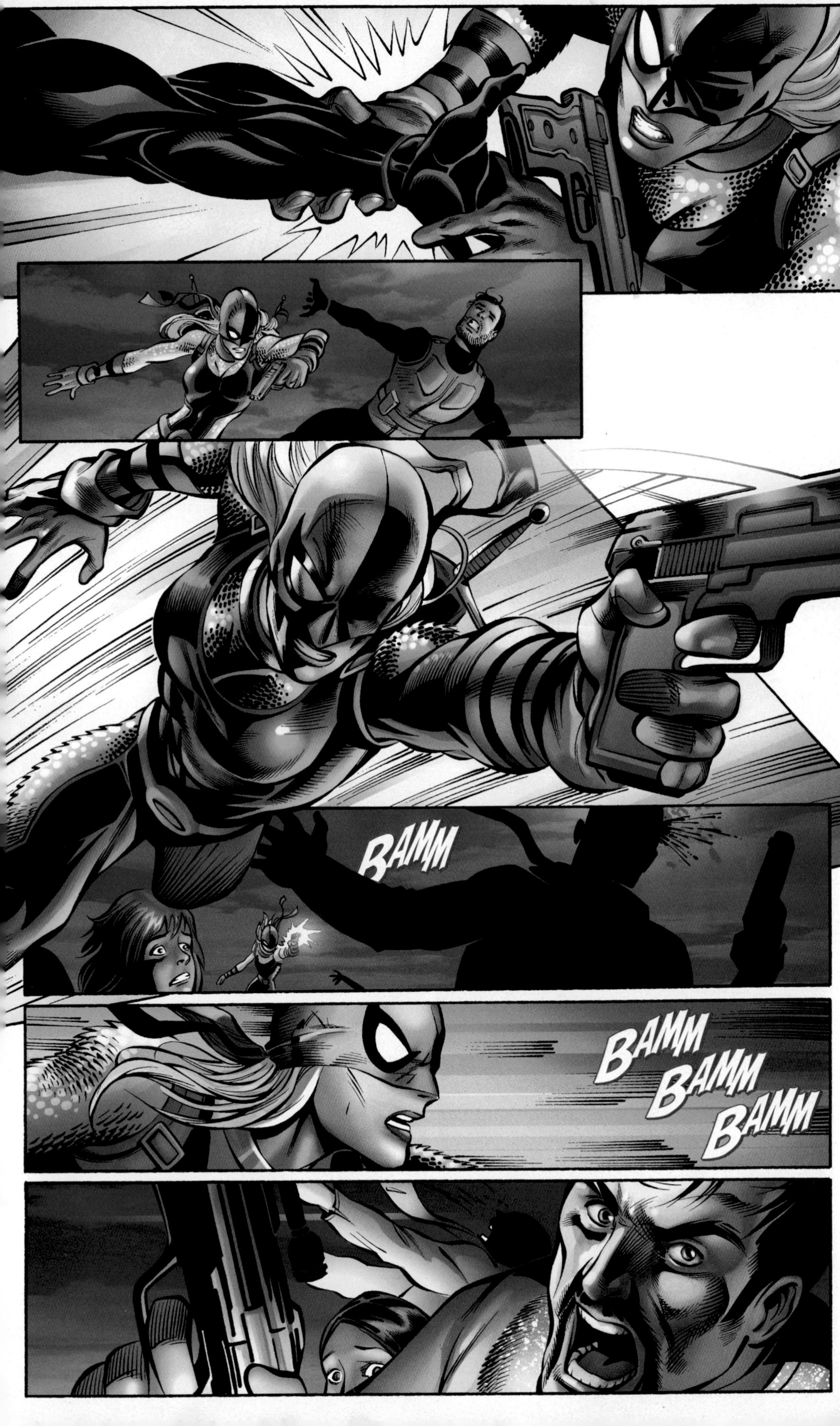
BAMM
BAMM
BAMM
BAMM

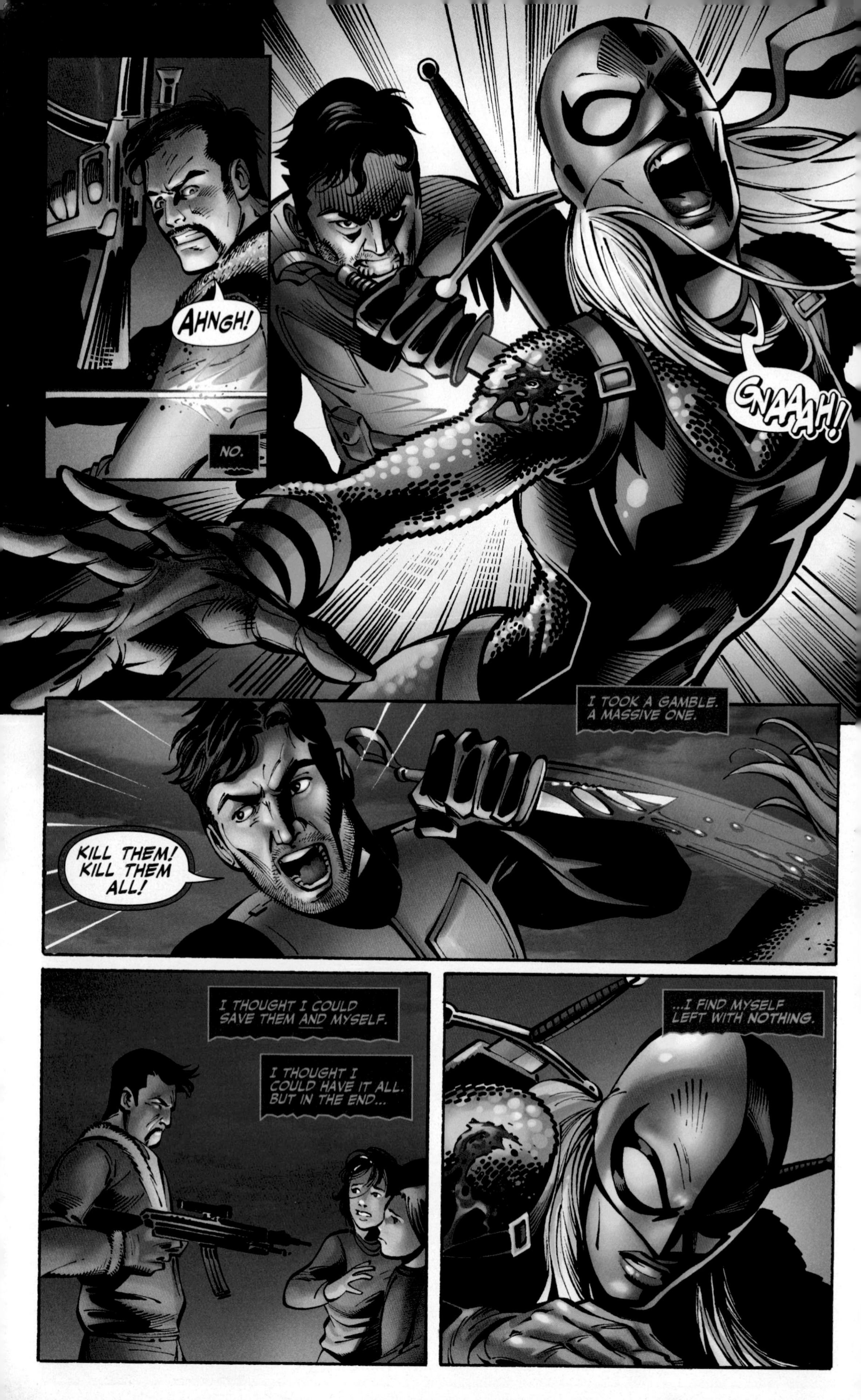
AHNGH!
NO.
GNAAAH!!
I TOOK A GAMBLE. A MASSIVE ONE.
KILL THEM! KILL THEM ALL!
I THOUGHT I COULD SAVE THEM AND MYSELF.
I THOUGHT I COULD HAVE IT ALL. BUT IN THE END...
...I FIND MYSELF LEFT WITH NOTHING.

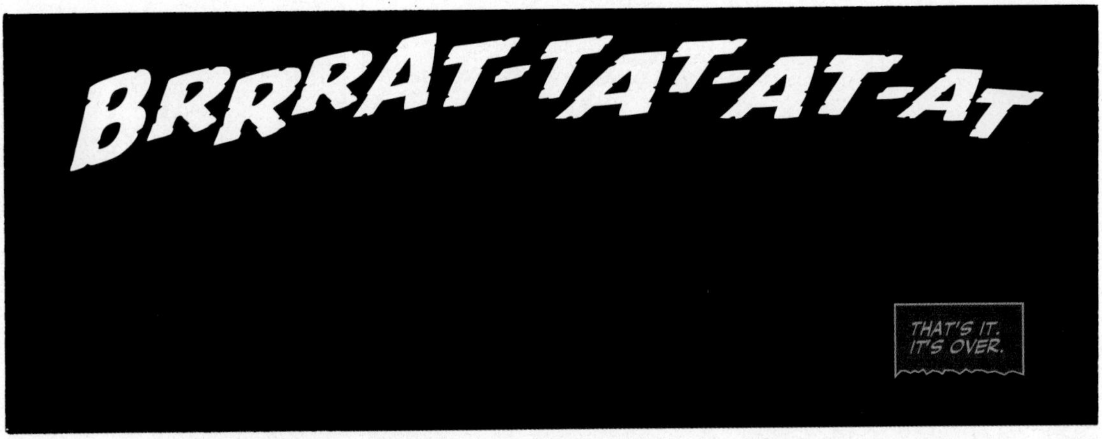
BRRRAT-TAT-AT-AT
THAT'S IT. IT'S OVER.

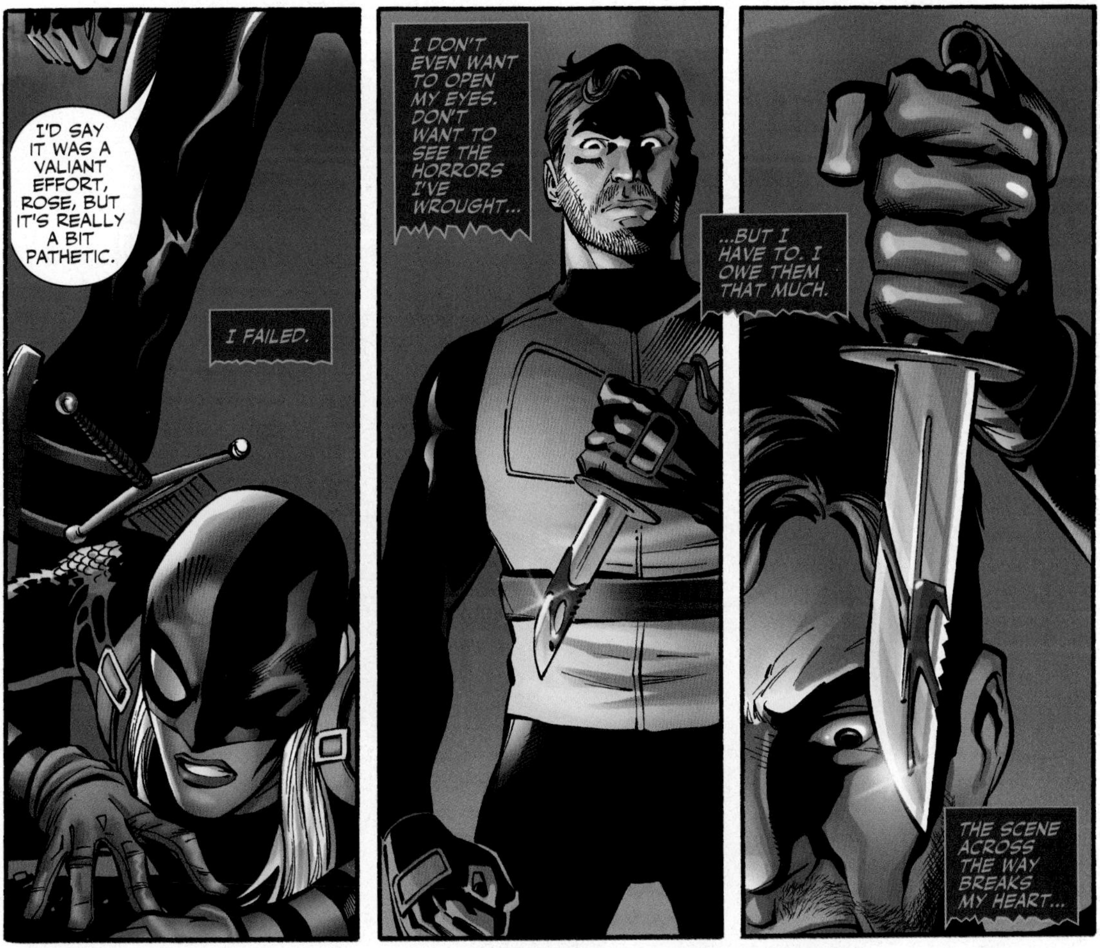
I'D SAY IT WAS A VALIANT EFFORT, ROSE, BUT IT'S REALLY A BIT PATHETIC.
I FAILED.
I DON'T EVEN WANT TO OPEN MY EYES. DON'T WANT TO SEE THE HORRORS I'VE WROUGHT...
...BUT I HAVE TO. I OWE THEM THAT MUCH.
THE SCENE ACROSS THE WAY BREAKS MY HEART...

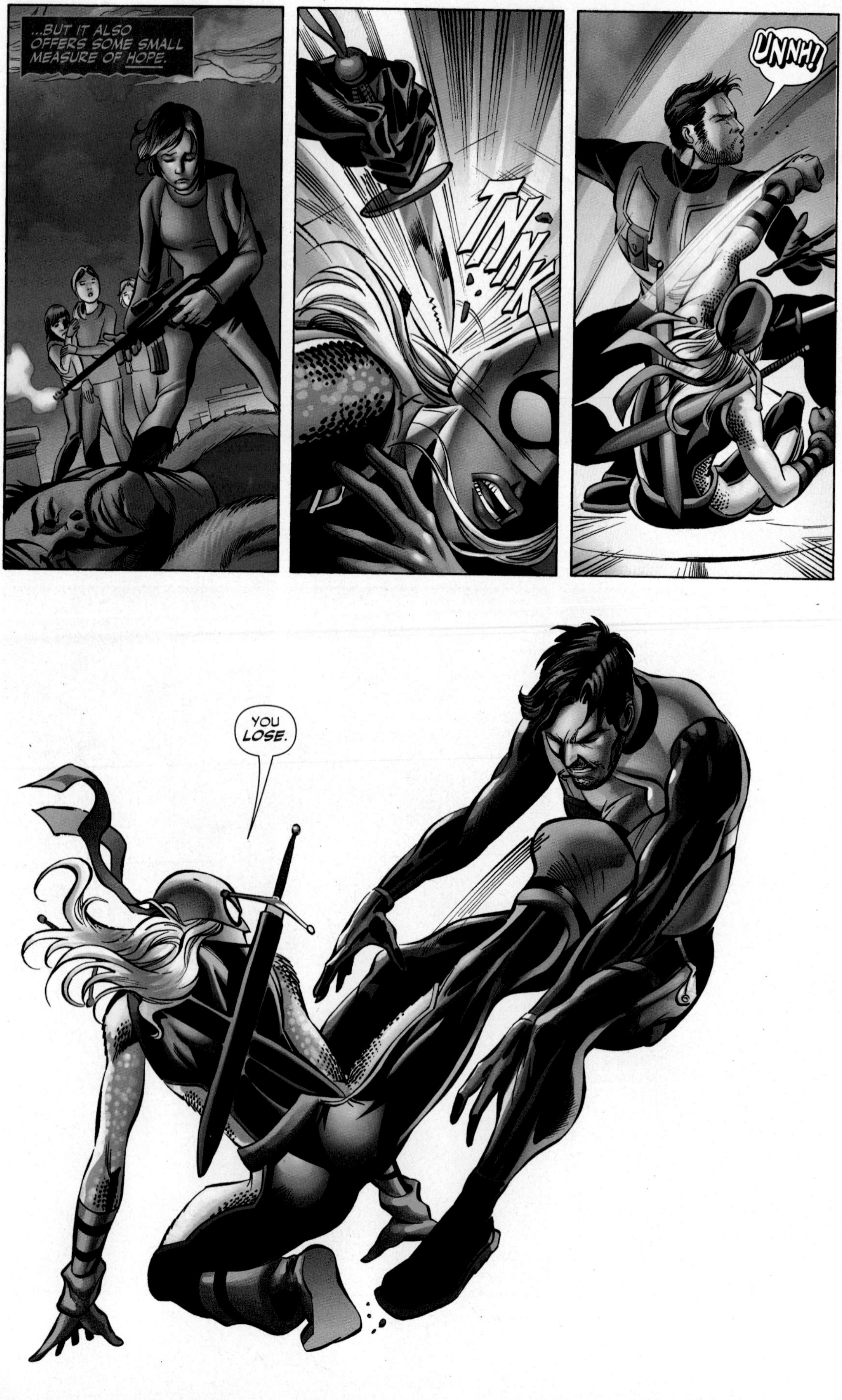
...BUT IT ALSO OFFERS SOME SMALL MEASURE OF HOPE.
TINK
UNNH!
YOU LOSE.

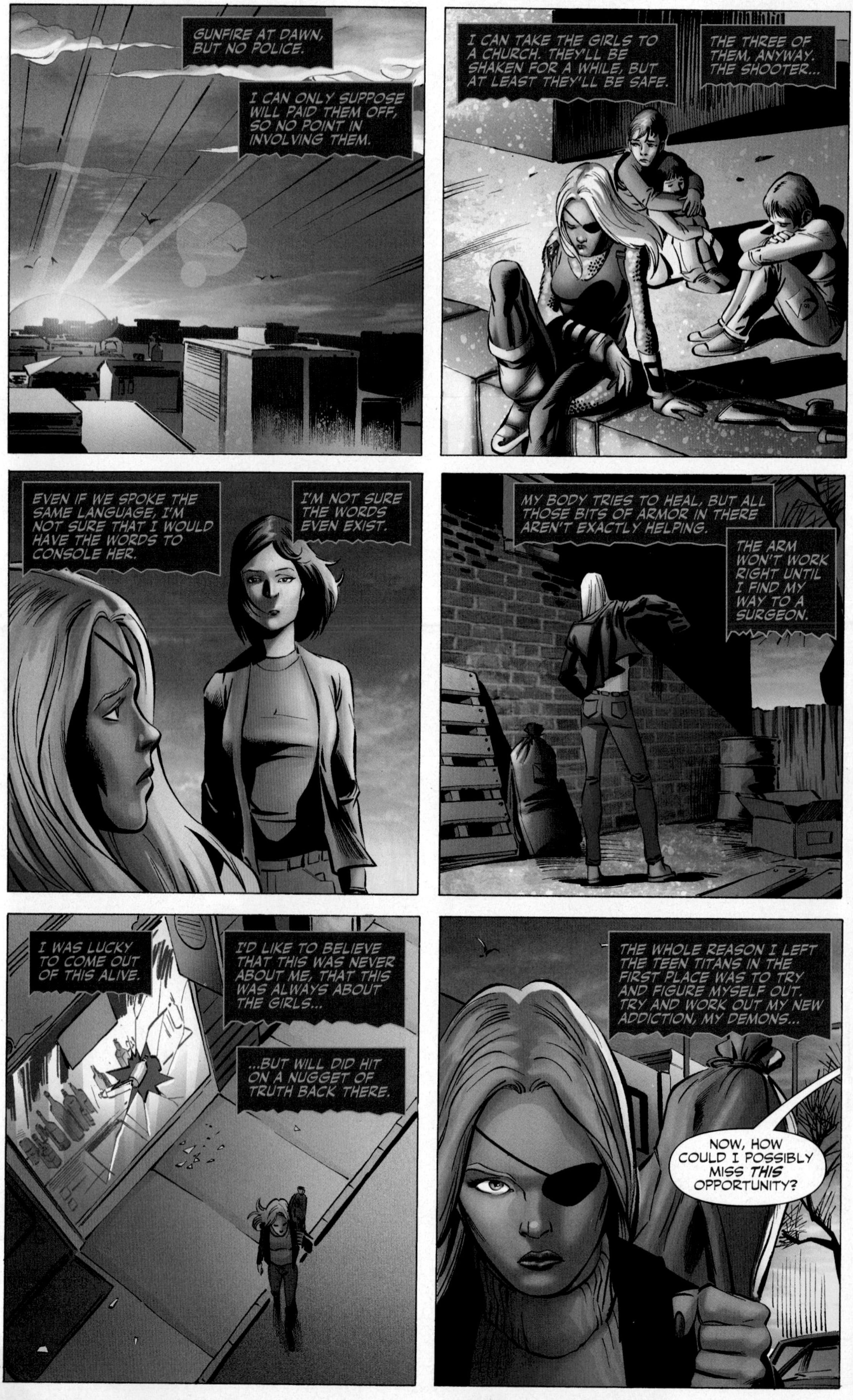
GUNFIRE AT DAWN, BUT NO POLICE.
I CAN ONLY SUPPOSE WILL PAID THEM OFF, SO NO POINT IN INVOLVING THEM.
I CAN TAKE THE GIRLS TO A CHURCH. THEY'LL BE SHAKEN FOR A WHILE, BUT AT LEAST THEY'LL BE SAFE.
THE THREE OF THEM, ANYWAY. THE SHOOTER...
EVEN IF WE SPOKE THE SAME LANGUAGE, I'M NOT SURE THAT I WOULD HAVE THE WORDS TO CONSOLE HER.
I'M NOT SURE THE WORDS EVEN EXIST.
MY BODY TRIES TO HEAL, BUT ALL THOSE BITS OF ARMOR IN THERE AREN'T EXACTLY HELPING.
THE ARM WON'T WORK RIGHT UNTIL I FIND MY WAY TO A SURGEON.
I WAS LUCKY TO COME OUT OF THIS ALIVE.
I'D LIKE TO BELIEVE THAT THIS WAS NEVER ABOUT ME, THAT THIS WAS ALWAYS ABOUT THE GIRLS...
...BUT WILL DID HIT ON A NUGGET OF TRUTH BACK THERE.
THE WHOLE REASON I LEFT THE TEEN TITANS IN THE FIRST PLACE WAS TO TRY AND FIGURE MYSELF OUT. TRY AND WORK OUT MY NEW ADDICTION, MY DEMONS...
NOW, HOW COULD I POSSIBLY MISS *THIS* OPPORTUNITY?

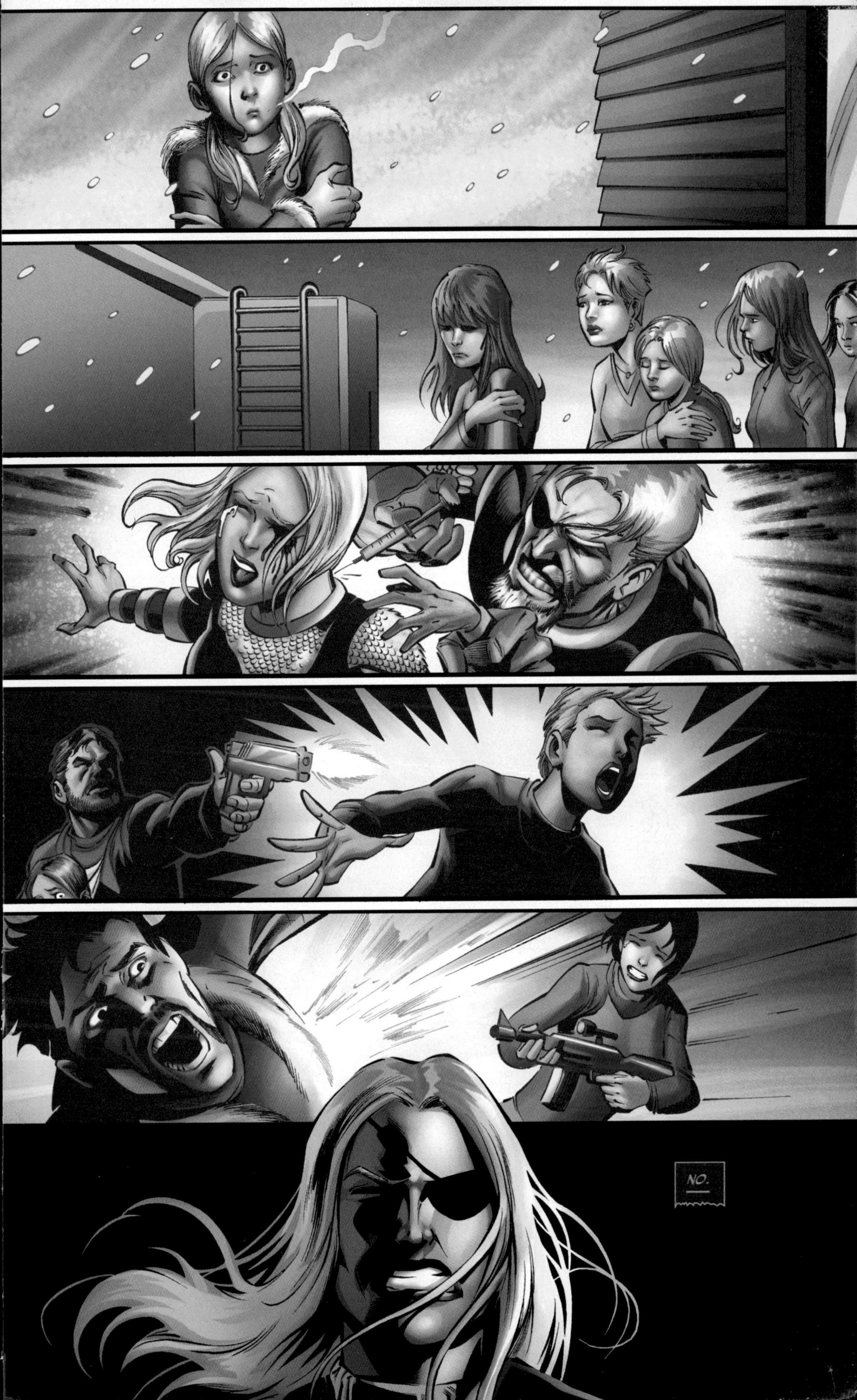
NO.